DATE DUE

D1248820

# THE THEORIES OF TALCOTT PARSONS

# THE THEORIES OF TALCOTT PARSONS

## The Social Relations of Action

Stephen P. Savage

St. Martin's Press        New York

ISBN 0–312–79699–4

---

**Library of Congress Cataloging in Publication Data**

---

Savage, Stephen P.
    The theories of Talcott Parsons.

    Bibliography: p.
    1.  Parsons, Talcott, 1902–    —Criticism and
interpretation.  2.  Sociology—United States.
I.  Title.
HM22.U6P378    1980      301'.01      80–13828
ISBN 0–312–79699–4

---

To my Parents

# Contents

# Acknowledgements

I would like to offer special thanks to Barry Hindess for his help prior to and throughout this work, and to all the others who have given useful comments on the various chapters.

Thanks also to my wife, Carol, for her encouragement and help with typing the manuscripts.

# List of Abbreviations

In the following chapters a number of references to Parsons' work have been abbreviated. They refer to the following texts:

| | |
|---|---|
| *SSA* | *The Structure of Social Action* |
| *Essays* | *Essays in Sociological Theory* |
| *TGTA* | *Toward a General Theory of Action* |
| *SS* | *The Social System* |
| *WPTA* | *Working Papers in the Theory of Action* |
| *ES* | *Economy and Society* |
| *TS* | *Theories of Society* |
| *STMS* | *Sociological Theory and Modern Society* |
| *Societies* | *Societies: Evolutionary and Comparative Perspectives* |
| *SMS* | *The System of Modern Societies* |
| *PSS* | *Politics and Social Structure* |

# Introduction

The chapters that follow constitute an attempt to develop a theoretical reading and critique of the work of Talcott Parsons. For all the acknowledgements regarding Parsons' apparent influence on contemporary (particularly American) sociology, there have been surprisingly few serious attempts to explain the mechanisms of Parsonian analysis. There have been even fewer theoretically-effective critical analyses of Parsons' work, and all too often critical commentaries have resorted to glib dismissal and uninformed polemic. This work aims to go some way to alleviating such a state of affairs.

Three areas of necessary investigation stem from this objective. To begin with, some assessment of the achievements of existing criticisms of Parsonian theory must be made. Does, for example, the label 'consensus theorist' and its attendant accusations find support in the actualities of structural-functionalism? Is the claim that Parsonian theory effectively rules out any consideration of social change, conflict and deviance substantiable? These are questions which must be decisively approached.

The second area of investigation follows on quite closely from the first one. No critical analysis of Parsons' work can ignore the relationship between his work and other major theoretical attempts to conceptualise the respective areas of investigation. Does Parsons, in fact, develop a distinct mode of social analysis or is his theory, as has been implied by some, a mishmash of earlier (incompatible) positions? In the arguments advanced in this volume comparisons between Parsons' theses and both early and subsequent sociological theories are made wherever applicable.

The third, and most important, objective is to present a theoretical reading of the primary concepts of Parsonian theory and to offer a number of criticisms which, it is argued, reflect severe theoretical shortcomings. In order to achieve this I have broken Parsons' work down according to the major areas of his theory – the epistemology of analytical realism, the 'action' frame of reference, the theory of the social system and social relations, and the theory of social change and social evolution. In addition, I have included a separate chapter on the structural-functionalist theory of the economy, both as an illustration of the major distinctive features of Parsonian analysis and as a vehicle for developing a number of critical points.

These three objectives, and particularly the third, constitute, therefore, the primary aim of this work. However, during the course of this study a fourth issue arose which warrants a separate discussion. In addition to questions on the extent to which various criticisms of Parsons (and others) actually find support in his statements, there is a more general issue which concerns critical analysis as a *mode*. A critique is not simply a number of discrete observations about an author's 'point of view' but a relation between a mode of analysis and the text, or texts, in question. It will be seen that it is possible to decipher a number of modes of analysis of theoretical discourse from the literature, and that not only are these quite often conflated and confused, but that each independently can be shown to induce a number of theoretical problems. Chapter 1 of this book is concerned with tackling the problem of modes of critique of discourse in general and is, in effect, a separate investigation altogether.

One point should be made quite clear while discussing this issue. The opening discussion of this book is not intended to be an epistemological outline of the 'method' applied in the chapters that follow. It is not an attempt to define 'my' conception of knowledge as opposed to that maintained by others. In fact, as will be seen, it is not an attempt to define 'knowledge' at all, but is concerned with the (technical) problem of the mode of analysis of theoretical discourse. It aims above all to criticise a number of major modes of investigation of texts which dominate in the area and to present the elements of a mode of analysis which, it is argued, avoids similar traps. It must, therefore, be viewed as an exercise which is, in the final analysis, primarily negative.

In the various discussions that follow, it will become apparent that I have chosen the more 'theoretical' components of Parsons' work as objects of investigation. These have been chosen in the main in favour of the many 'empirical' theses developed by Parsons. This is not to imply that the latter are irrelevant or simply expressions of the former, only to argue that the basic concepts and theories of Parsons' discourse must be the major concern of a work of this kind. The concepts of action, social system, functional prerequisites and so on provide the basis on which the empirical theses are maintained, and are therefore of primary importance. However, an analysis of these concepts is not, in itself, exhaustive of Parsons' work and there is a great deal of investigation still to be done in this respect. This is to say that the bias in the following chapters toward Parsons' most abstract arguments is not accidental.

# 1 Modes of Critique and the Theoretical Analysis of Discourse

## 1.1 Introduction

In an investigation of this kind it is necessary to pose as a separate issue the general question of modes of analysis of texts, theories, discourses and so on, if such an analysis is to be realised on rigorous and systematic grounds. To be more specific, an explicit and determinate formulation of the mode of operation to be utilised in the critique of Parsons is imperative if it is to avoid repetition of the tendencies of previous attempts which, it will be argued, are highly problematic. The object of this chapter, therefore, is to pose the general problem of 'criticism', to outline and discuss various modes of critique dominant in this area and to present the elements of a mode of analysis of discourse which make possible the rigorous theoretical critique of sociological theory.

In order to pose such problems it is necessary to operate with a set of questions distinct from the orthodox means supplied by epistemology, philosophy of science and the sociology of knowledge (for reasons that will become apparent), and to propose such questions as 'what is discourse?', 'what is involved in a reading of a text?', 'what is the object and technique of such a reading?', and so on. Every 'interpretation', 'commentary', 'discussion' or 'critique' involves referents to which such questions are directed.

The difficulties in this area are many – either these problems are not posed at all by the various modes of criticism (and this is clearly the case in many sociological critiques), or they are posed in an unsatisfactory manner, in terms which invoke a number of major theoretical difficulties. An additional problem, and one

1

particularly apparent in sociology, is the inclusion within one 'critique' of a number of points which not only derive from a number of discrete theoretical positions (for example, the sociology of knowledge, history of ideas, and philosophy of science), but which also involve points which are in fact contradictory – Gouldner's critique of Parsons is a good example of this tendency.[1]

In this respect this chapter has two major objectives: first to demarcate various *modes* of critique in terms of their *object* and *technique* (in terms, that is, of their determinant concepts), and secondly, to uncover the fundamental conditions of existence of each mode in relation to the (often implicit) conceptions of knowledge, discourse and reading which govern their analysis. The emphasis will be on variant types of critique of Talcott Parsons, first because this work is itself primarily concerned with such a critique, and secondly because it is probably correct to assume that Parsons has been subject to criticisms deriving from a wider spectrum of theoretical positions than any other sociological theorist. Given this, however, it need not be assumed that the analysis of the modes of critique presented below and the points of criticism made in respect of them should be held applicable to these particular critiques alone. On the contrary, the variant types considered here are, I believe, sufficiently general to apply not only to sociological criticism as a whole but to all major types of criticism, whether they be in philosophy, political theory, economic theory, or whatever. In other words, the chapter is concerned with the problem of critique in general, with the abstract problem of the analysis of discourse.

In relation to these modes of criticism two points should be borne in mind. First, I will not be considering here the validity of the criticisms of Parsons in terms of the accuracy of their interpretations and claims on Parsons' theory – although this is an additional issue and one which is indeed quite severe[2] – for the major concern here is the *mode* of critique, the position it establishes in relation to its object. Secondly, it follows that no particular attention will be given to the nature of the 'alternative' formulations that are presented in conjunction with the critiques – again, despite the fact that such alternatives often aggrevate the issue, such problems are peripheral to the objective of this discussion.

The structure of the chapter is as follows. Four very general areas will be delineated according to the distinct modes of critique of Parsons that are common in the literature. These four areas are categorised as the critique of the 'subject', the 'realist' mode of critique, the 'epistemological' critique, and modes of 'internal' critique. In addition, I will discuss a fifth category, what is termed the 'grid reading' or the 'evolutionist' critique which sums up Parsons' own mode of critique as operative in *The Structure of Social Action* and certain other texts, and which involves a tendency which is very general in critical discourse, particularly in theses within the study of so-called 'history of ideas'.[3]

Each of these areas will be shown to involve, amongst others, concepts and categories operative in classical epistemology – subject, object, abstraction, reflection, consciousness, perception, and so on – concepts which can lead to a number of major theoretical difficulties. To be more specific, the fundamental problem for all these modes will be shown to lie in the conception of discourse that is dominant, and subsequently in the concept of reading and critique which is its effect. Primary in this respect is the conception of the determinant function of an extra-discursive sphere (the non-discursive, pre-discursive etc.) which is assigned a specific relation to discourse in which it is seen to determine or govern what is to appear in terms of its concepts and theories. It will be argued that this sphere leads the various modes of critique to a number of insoluble theoretical problems.

Following this discussion an attempt will be made to present the elements of a mode of analysis of discourse or 'critique' which avoids the problematic tendencies of these other modes. This conception, which will be presented as a non-epistemological (and non-sociological) mode of analysis of discourse, will utilise not the concepts of subject, the 'real world', and so on, but those of the 'logical character of orders of concepts', of 'logical coherence', 'logical compatibility' etc., concepts which require that the problem of reading and of critique be restricted to strictly *internal* level, that no reference be made to the determination of discourse or the determination of a critique of discourse by a realm which is external to it.

Before approaching such issues it will be necessary to comment on a very general point relating to the status of the arguments and demonstrations presented in this chapter. As will become clear, one of the central theses developed below is the criticism of readings and critiques which adopt the status of external judge or guarantee of discourse and its validity, which function on the basis of the privileged nature of a philosophy, an epistemology, or a sociology of knowledge. Now given such an opposition to any such privileged status an immediate question faces the form of this paper: does it not merely establish itself as another privileged reading or, alternatively, constitute some form of infinite regress? In fact such properties are only applicable if discourse is seen to be relative to some extra-discursive process and if the reading adopts the status of external guarantee over discourse. No such presuppositions are maintained in the mode of analysis outlined here.

The discussions presented below, and indeed the critique of Parsons elaborated in later chapters, do not depend upon the opposition between the status of the reading and the status of the discourse which is its object, an opposition which is indeed maintained by the modes of critique discussed below and which induces so many theoretical problems. On the contrary, there is no reason why both levels of analysis may not themselves be subjected to precisely the form of internal critique on which they themselves depend. No privileged character is assigned to the discourse which directs these criticisms and consequently no similar problems of contradiction (in which the critique of the epistemology of guarantee merely requires another, superior, guarantee), or infinite regress (in which the reading is always relative to a determination external to discourse) are presented. In addition, it is maintained here that the mode of analysis of discourse outlined approaches the vexing problem of the relation between philosophy and science without precluding the possibility of *any* theorisation of discourse.[4]

In the modes of critique differentiated below, several authors will appear under more than one category. The criteria of classification will be in terms of the concepts of knowledge and its determination that are operative, implicitly or explicitly, in the readings and criticisms of Parsons' theory – a critique may indeed be seen as the mode of operation of such concepts within a set of objectives and protocols.

I have differentiated five major modes of critical analysis which, it is hoped, sufficiently cover all the major approaches to the criticism of theoretical discourse. First, there is the mode which takes the subject or author of the theory as the primary object of analysis, whether in terms of the social or political context of his work, or the personal experiences which apparently shape his thesis. Secondly, I have labelled as 'realist' the mode which judges discourse according to its more or less adequate reflection of the real world. The third mode of critique is classified as 'epistemological' and is self-explanatory.

The last two differentiated modes require a little more explanation. It might appear strange to devote a whole section to Parsons' own method of analysis of discourse as reflected in his treatise on the development of the voluntaristic theory of action in *The Structure of Social Action*. However, Parsons' critique of the 'classics', although based on a more definite objective, is only an example of a more general approach which views theories as moments in an evolutionary process of discursive development and advance. Parsons' particular attempt should therefore be seen as an example of a wider mode of critique. The final category has a wider significance than the other four in the sense that it is intended to cover a number of quite dissimilar critical techniques in terms of a common tendency to claim to treat discourse 'internally'. These positions quite often explicitly disapprove of other methods of critical analysis and in that sense tend to produce more complex and systematic readings. However, it is argued that in the final analysis most of these proposed modes of critique fail to restrict the investigation to 'internal' questions and as such must be queried.

## 1.2 The Subject of Discourse as the Object of Critique

One relatively common mode of critique in sociology is one which attempts to turn the discipline in on itself: this is to read a discourse or a number of discourses in terms of the sociology of knowledge. Whether the theses of the sociology of knowledge be used as a simple passive commentary or as the basis of an explicit set of criticisms, its major effect is to read knowledge in terms of the social context of its production and to assess the relation between that context and the forms which knowledge takes.

Involved here however is an order of problems of an altogether more fundamental nature. For although it may be the case that in the various positions which utilise the concepts of the sociology of knowledge the problem of the status of the 'subject' of knowledge is not explicitly posed, any attempt to maintain consistently arguments which derive from it must of necessity invoke the general issue of the subject of knowledge. In fact, it is possible to differentiate conceptions of the subject in the sociology of knowledge which correspond to variant formulations of the subject of knowledge in classical epistemology: the conscious subject, the psychological subject, and so on. For this reason there are two levels of problems which present the sociology of knowledge: on the one hand, the internal problems of epistemologies which invoke the concept of the subject of the knowledge process, and on the other, the specific problems of a sociological interiorisation of that concept, one which is effected with little concern for the major issues that arise in this area. The first order of problems will not be approached here as they are dealt with in a later chapter. Suffice it here to refer to the consequences of any formulation which presents the epistemological subject as the constitutive centre of the knowledge process – scepticism in Hume (subjective idealism), the psychologisation of knowledge in Descartes, the essentially mysterious (unknowable) nature of subject of knowledge in Kant, and so on.[5] Such consequences are not only inherited by the sociology of knowledge, they are *aggravated*.

To turn to critiques of Parsons we find that the reference to the functioning of a constitutive subject is quite common. Nowhere is this more explicit than in Alvin Gouldner's attack on Parsonian theory in his *The Coming Crisis of Western Sociology*. I will use his critique as a good example of this critical tendency.

The basis of Gouldner's critique of Parsons and of functionalism in general is a mode of analysis which he calls the 'sociology of sociology'. Its implication is quite clear: 'we will look upon the sociologist just as we would any other occupation, be it the taxi-driver, the nurse, the coal miner or the physician' (Alvin Gouldner, *For Sociology*, p. 6).

In other words, the concepts of sociology are seen to be just as applicable to the analysis of sociological *theory* as they are to the study of social groups, social relations, and so on. Theory may be treated sociologically, sociology being reduced to the status of an occupation. What Gouldner effects in such an objective, however, is the conflation of two distinct spheres, a conflation founded on a play on the word 'sociology' – the two spheres being the instruments with which the sociologist operates, the system of concepts that are the discursive means of the discipline, and the human subjects who operate with them; 'sociology' is reduced to sociolo*gists*. This conflation, which is rather like, to use Gouldner's own example, analysing a lump of coal or a pick-axe in terms of the social and personal experiences of the coal miner, has one very definite effect: discourse is effectively reduced to a set of social relations, it is essentially a *reflex* (hence the programme for a 'reflexive' sociology) of the social. The nature of this reflexive relationship is to be found in Gouldner's definition of a theoretical system, which is seen in terms of the relation between certain 'domain assumptions' on the one hand and 'technical postulations' on the other (primarily empirical or methodological assumptions). The former is dominant and is conceived as embedded in the 'metaphysics' of the author as a human subject (i.e. with a set of meanings) – these metaphysics are fundamentally expressions of the author's social and personal *experiences*. Such an account however suppresses not only the theoretical autonomy of conceptual relations as an independent object of investigation (in so far as they are *necessarily* relative to the experiences of the author) but also the specific effectivity of concepts *as* concepts, for it effectively denies that concepts have any distinctive and irreducible role in the constitution of a theoretical system:

> Starting with the very primitive assumption that theory is made by the praxis of men in their wholeness and is shaped by the lives they lead, and pursuing this into concrete empirical contexts, one is led to a very different conception of what generates social theory and of what it is that many theorists are trying to do. Having pursued this conception, one is better able to see just how complex a communication social theory really is. *It is a complexity that cannot even be glimpsed, let alone grasped, if we fail to see the ways in which theorists are entrenched in their theories.* (*The Coming Crisis of Western Sociology*, p. 483, my emphasis)

This variant of the sociology of knowledge, a particularly humanistic and individualistic form characteristic of many recent ethnomethodological critiques of statistics,[6] clearly reduces the knowledge process to one which is relative to the personal and social experiences of the subject who produces it. This relativist mode of critique of Parsons however is by no means specific to Gouldner – it is implied in many of the attacks which refer to Parsons' 'Conservatism',[7] which interpret his work in terms of his own ideological position or the social situation in which he writes.

It is not possible for such critiques to be seen merely as an attempt to pose the problem of the extra-discursive relations and articulations to which discourse is subjected. There appears to be no reason why such a problem could not be rigorously posed, although to date it would seem unrealised. For, given the mode in which the subject of discourse is conceptualised in these cases (the conscious constitutive subject, the *centre* of the knowledge process), it is inevitable that the knowledge process will be effectively reduced to the exigencies of the subject-as-actor, his intentions, desires, prejudices, etc. (but would, we may ask, these authors view medical knowledge in the same precarious light?).

There are a number of obvious problems with such attempts to direct a critique to the subject of discourse. To begin with, how, within the concepts of a sociology of sociology, is it possible to conceive of theoretical development or even of the continuance of a theoretical position from one generation to another without significantly denying that the social and personal experiences of the author are as decisive as is claimed? To take a concrete example, supposing a sociologist wished to adopt and continue the theses of Gouldner himself. Given the apparent primary dependence of theories on forms of personal and social experience it would seem that this sociologist, in order to achieve his objective, must aspire to reproduce, as exactly as possible, Gouldner's particular life experiences (which include, Gouldner argues, an important role played by wives and mistresses! – *The Coming Crisis of Western Sociology*, p. 57). Conversely, any author, in order to effectively transform his theoretical position, must first of all set out to transform his life experiences and through these his domain assumptions, the infrastructure of theory. This is only another way of pointing out that the sociology of sociology makes the explanation of the continued maintenance of a theoretical position almost impossible. On its own terms (i.e. the sociology of sociology) the conceptualisation of knowledge in any organised sense is effectively precluded. It is clear that such problems are a consequence of the fundamental denial by this area of the autonomy, relative or otherwise, of conceptual relations.

However the problems related to the sociology of sociology can be specified much more definitely. If Gouldner is to maintain consistently his position, to elaborate and demonstrate that form of theory which is the sociology of sociology, then the following questions may be posed: how are we to 'understand' this theory itself?, how are we to judge the sociology of sociology? According to the conception of knowledge and its consequent conception of reading of discourse that is proposed by Gouldner and others, such problems can only be truly resolved by means of another sociology of sociology, which in turn requires a further sociology, and so on into an infinite regression of sociologies; sociological knowledge is always dependent on the next sociological investigation. Either this infinite regress is accepted, which would be an acknowledgement of the relativism endemic to the sociology of sociology (and, it may be added, to the sociology of science), or it is denied – in which case the very pertinence of a study of the way in which personal and social experiences determine types of theory is effectively relegated. It is clear that the former alternative dominates the analyses of Gouldner and others – in this case they are presented with a more general problem.

The paradox inherent in the sociology of sociology is that in directing a *critique* from within its concepts it cuts away the grounds for its own success. Given the proposed intimate relation between concepts and their social context of production it negates the possibility either of demonstrating the validity of its own reading or of demonstrating that another theory is any better than the one under criticism – its effect is to require that *all* forms of knowledge be relative to sets of social conditions. If it is to argue otherwise the sociology of sociology must land itself in contradiction. Gouldner in fact does not deny the relativistic consequences of his conception of critical discourse (although he does inconsistently attempt to propose alternative social theories) – he merely demands in opposition to a conservative social theory a programme for 'reflexive sociology', a relativism governed simply by a different set of life experiences (a thesis developed more extensively by deviance theory by such authors as Becker, Matza etc.). This is a clear acceptance of the irrationalism and scepticism endemic to the sociology of sociology.

Gouldner's case is, however, only an extreme example of

tendencies which are inevitable in any position which relates discourse to the determinations by a constitutive subject. In so far as a mode of critique is directed from within such a position its success as a critique is most definitely severely curtailed: a relativistic conception of knowledge must lead to a relativistic, and hence contradictory, mode of critique. The effect of such a mode is to leave the substance of the discourse which is its object, its theories and concepts, untouched. What it actually achieves is not a critique of a *theory* at all, but a (more or less arbitary) critique of the *theorist*.

## 1.3  The Realist Mode of Critique

Despite the fact that the critique of the subject may be analytically differentiated as a specific mode of critique it is usually accompanied concretely by another mode of critique with a distinct set of referents. The relation between the two is generally presented as the 'ideological' barrier that prevents the author from seeing certain aspects of reality that are more apparent to the less 'conservative' sociologist. The shift is from the author as an actor with certain values to the perceiving subject, to the conception of discourse as a more or less accurate reflection of the real world. This opens up a further area of critique (and one, to repeat, which is in many ways in contradiction to the relativism of the above mode), an area which concerns a reference to the 'real world' and its representation in knowledge. I shall term this mode the 'realist' critique.

The realist mode of critique approaches the discourse in question with a pre-given conception of the essential and true nature of reality – discourse is either praised or opposed on the basis of its apparent degree of correspondence or noncorrespondence with this real state of affairs. In short, the critique is a judgement as to the *realism* of its concepts.

Examples of this mode are easy to find: in Parsons' case they are offered, from a variety of standpoints, with almost startling repetition. There are two major branches (often connected) which predominate; on the one hand the critique levelled from the proponents of so-called 'conflict theory', and on the other hand, the ultra-humanist attack on Parsonian theory which views its concepts in terms of their distortion of the true nature of human existence. Both positions stand diametrically opposed to the Parsonian concept of the social system in particular.

The two most famous polemics from within conflict theory are perhaps the critiques of Parsons directed by Lockwood and Dahrendorf.[8] Lockwood's review of the *Social System* highlights what it claims to be certain fundamental ignorances and omissions concerning what are seen to be crucial and primary features of the social world – in particular the differentiality of interests which generate social change, conflict and deviance. The foundation for Parsons' shortcomings is seen to lie in his failure to elaborate the 'factual substratum' of social life which for Lockwood structure both states of stability and states of social conflict – such substratum (features seen to be empirically demonstrable) are referred to because they are (apparently) *ignored* in Parsonian theory. In this context Dahrendorf's critique is even more explicit: he not only argues that Parsons has 'ignored' certain ubiquitous aspects of the real world (social change, social conflict) but goes on to compare Parsons' theory of the social system to a 'Utopia',[9] a completely fictitious model of society in which the processes of the real social world have no place. This Utopia, in other words, fails to mirror the essential nature of reality.

The humanist form of the realist critique is closely related to this one. In this case, the nature of Parsonian theory is seen to be such that the fundamental character of human existence – generally the capacity of the individual actor to determine his own course of action – is suppressed by the 'positivist' postulation that in certain respects the individual is subject to determination by social processes not reducible to individual manipulation and control. Again, it is Gouldner who provides the clearest example of this humanist polemic

> The human system disappears in Parsons' framework: it escapes through the mesh of his conceptual system. . . . It is as if the obvious existence of people is an embarrassment: as his theoretical system develops, especially as it moves from 'action schema' to 'social system' analysis, the embodied and socialised individual is lost from sight.[10]

The basic similarity between this, the old 'society-or-man' dispute, and the critique stemming from the conflict theory, is that the central question posed against the discourse which is the object of the critique relates to certain *absences* in discourse – it is a question clearly summed up by Lockwood, 'the criticism concerns what has not, rather than what has been done'.[11]

It is this referent to a point outside of discourse which constitutes the specific character of the realist mode of critique, and there are several points which can be made in relation to it. To begin with, in the strict sense as a mode of critique it can only in the last analysis achieve more or less rigorous forms of a *grid-reading*, the simple counterposition of *one discourse to another* and the tabulation of relevant absences and presences between them. This is necessarily the case in so far as what is deemed the 'true' nature of society, man, or whatever, must always be a *concept* of society or man if it is to be talked of in any sense at all. The problem of the grid-reading will be discussed in a later section, but its pertinence here should be borne in mind. However, although the realist mode of critique must effectively invoke the operation of a grid-reading, it is clear that a distinct set of questions and objectives is in operation which require that an additional problem be tackled. As far as such critiques are concerned the reading is seen to be not one of the counterposition of one discourse to another but of discourse to *reality*. This mode is founded upon an apparent comparison between any given discourse and the real world, an assessment as to the *correspondence*[12] between the two orders, the object in thought and the real object. The realist mode of critique, if it is to be maintained, must involve an opposition of this nature.

Now if such a critique is to be successful there are several problems to be posed and a number of points which require demonstration. To begin with, the critique must supply the demonstration that the discourse in question – in this case Parsons' theory – does *not* reproduce the true nature of reality, that the discourse is indeed 'unrealistic', Utopian, or overdeterministic. In the cases cited above, and these represent the major theses in the area, no such demonstration is provided bar an assertive reference to what is apparently already known to be the case. If this demonstration is to be possible then a converse task is required, to show that what is claimed to be the true nature of reality is in fact the case. Again, it is clear that no such proof in any elaborated sense is provided, as in the claim as to the lack of realism of Parsons' theory the claim of the realism of the critique itself is established on assertive, i.e. *dogmatic* grounds.

However these particular points are not sufficient in themselves to dismiss the realist mode of critique *per se*, i.e. as a *mode*. It is necessary to pose the question in the abstract and consider whether such a critique can be maintained in any rigorous sense within the confines of its opposition between concepts and theories on the one hand and the real world or the realm of facts on the other.

In these terms it is in fact possible to refer to one thesis which would, if it could be shown to be sustainable, allow the success of the realist mode of critique. The realist mode can only really be maintained if it can be shown that there is *one* reality, a sphere of irreducible phenomena which may be independant of any theoretical language and which is, therefore, beyond dispute – it could then provide a consistent yardstick against which to judge discourse. The demonstration that one discourse does not reproduce the nature of reality and that another does can only avoid dogmatism if it can be shown that there exists a *sphere of irreducible facts*, an index which may be shown to be distorted or adequately reflected.

Such a thesis is most rigorously maintained in that variant of the philosophy of science which refers to an 'observation language' as distinct from theoretical statements and which is primarily proposed by Carnap's formulation of logical positivism[13] – this being, of course, only one of a number of forms of logical positivism. Such a distinction is necessary to the realist mode in so far as any simple sensualist empiricism in which all the statements of knowledge are reduced to experience would preclude the specific treatment of 'theory' as such.

Carnap's distinction between a theoretical and an observational language represents a clearly systematic attempt to present the case for a theory-neutral realm which can, through certain procedures, constitute the means of demarcation between meaningful and meaningless statements. This distinction was governed by an objective to provide a means of handling the existence of theoretical statements which are non-observable but which nevertheless appear to provide a scientifically admissable interpretation of a number of phenomena – for example, electrons, atoms, electromagnetic and gravitational fields, and so on. It is not the existence of an 'observational' level which is in doubt (i.e. the realm of definable, finite and experiencable phenomena) but the status of this non-observable level.

Carnap's thesis poses the problem of establishing criteria of validity of theoretical statements and proposes the operation of certain 'criteria of significance', the conditions which a theoretical language must fulfil in order to have a positive function for the explanation and prediction of observable events. Primary in this respect is the set of 'correspondence rules', procedures by which to establish that theoretical statements can make a difference for the prediction of the observational level. However, it is not so much the specific means by which the two languages are related which is of pertinence here, but the very possibility of postulating their separation and of advancing arguments as to their correspondence. While no elaborate critique of logical positivism can be given here there are a number of significant questions which can be posed.

To postulate the existence of a realm which is independent of any theory requires some form of demonstration, yet when this is accepted then the status of the form of knowledge which is to advance such a demonstration becomes problematic. In the case of logical positivism two forms of knowledge are maintained, an empirical knowledge or one which consists of theoretical statements which can be made significant for a primitive and irreducible observational language, and knowledge such as logic and pure mathematics which are conceived as purely tautological knowledge forms, and which have no connection with the realm of experience. In order to make the distinction between an observational and a theoretical language, and in order to advance means for demonstrating their relationship, the distinction between these two forms of knowledge is essential – without logic, for example, it would be impossible to define relationships between terms and sentences of the two languages. However, if logic is to be seen as a necessary form of knowledge but one which is independent of experience, logical positivism is presented with a contradiction – it depends upon forms of knowledge which it itself precludes on the grounds of its non-empirical significance. In other words, logical positivism precludes by definition the possibility or validity of a form of knowledge which can make its demonstration and operation attainable.

In this case, it is clearly not possible for positivism consistently to maintain its definition of knowledge – the postulate of a realm which is independent of any theoretical language and the mechanisms for using this realm as a criteria of validity result in a contradiction of that general definition itself. The alternative to such a contradiction while still maintaining the existence of an irreducible level of experience can only be some form of circularity, in which existence of a realm of experience is itself proved by experience, or as in J. S. Mill's case induction is proved by induction.[14] Such circularities have long been dismissed from within the more rigorous branches of positivism.

Given this major problem then it is clear that the realist mode of critique is presented with a definite obstacle. If it is impossible to establish consistently the existence of a realm which is independent of any theory then there is no irreducible yardstick, one which may be used as a criteria of validity of theories, on which it can maintain itself as a general mode of criticism. In this situation the realist mode must find itself presented with the consequence mentioned above – there are as many 'critiques' as there are concepts. If there is no such thing as an irreducible observational level then the realist mode of critique must always be, in the last analysis, *the counterposition of one discourse to another*, the infinite opposition of discourses which are non-equivalent. In the realist critiques considered above even this technique is weak, they fail even to produce a rigorous *grid* reading – the objective is, as Lockwood points out, to consider what has *not* been said. There is, of course, no limit to what has not been said.

Therefore, as a general mode of critique, the realist position involves a number of severe difficulties. Apart from any other tendencies it is characterised by an endemic arbitrariness, for every concept of 'man', 'society', etc. there is a different realist critique. It provides no theoretical knowledge of the discourse which is its apparent object (its logical consistency, etc.) nor does it constitute demonstrations as to the validity, relative or otherwise, of that discourse or its own. It is not a 'critique' in any rigorous sense of the word; it remains, before and after, *exterior* to the discourse in question.

Reference was made above to an often implicit argument offered as supplement to the realist mode which appears to provide some means of demarcating the discourse which is the object of the critique from the proposed alternative set of conceptions. Now although no argument is provided in the above cases to *show* that Parsons does not reproduce the essential nature of reality, it is common to present arguments which intend to show why he *cannot* do so. The referent in such cases is to a notion of the epistemological *form* of discourse, and is to that extent discrete from the realist assumptions. Whereas the realist mode attempts to judge the realism of the discourse in question, this mode attempts to assess the *epistemological structure* of the discourse against what is considered to be an *ideal* of how knowledge must proceed. In the case of the former it is a dogmatic and prior conception of what the 'real' is; in the latter it is a case of a prior conception of what the *means of knowing* what the real is.[15] Its object is not the substantive structure of the world but the structure of knowledge forms. For this reason it will be treated separately as the 'epistemological mode of critique'.

## 1.4  Epistemological Modes of Critique

In this section I will consider those critiques which adopt the starting point of epistemology and the philosophy of science – the notion of an external *gurantee* and judge of the knowlege process. I will not consider the other forms of critique which operate with an epistemological referent – for example Bershady's analysis of Parsons – in so far as the use of that referent in these cases involves a somewhat distinct set of problems. Such critiques will be treated in later section (in so far as they claim to be 'internal' criticisms).

In a similar fashion to the realist mode the epistemological critique, in the sense used here, does not take as its object of analysis what *is* said in the discourse or its relation to some other feature of it (protocols, objectives, etc.), but rather what has *not* been said, or more accurately with a means of knowing which is apparently not utilised in the discourse. In this case the externality of its relation to the discourse which is its object is not simply one of the externality of a set of irreducible facts but the externality of a set of given *epistemological protocols*.

This set of protocols constitutes the conception of an ideal form of discourse, one which is seen alone to allow legitimate knowledge. It creates an opposition not between discourse and the 'real' but between the epistemological form of discourse and a pre-defined ideal form of knowledge. This given ideal is provided by a privileged theory – an epistemological knowledge which legislates both on the possible forms of knowledge and the means which must be utilised if it is to be obtained. Given this, what must be of concern here is not so much the specific issues raised by each particular epistemological standpoint but the critique as a *mode*, the nature of the critique and reading which *judges, legislates*, and can *guarantee* knowledge forms. The epistemological critique is, as it were, epistemology in operation.

In relation to the theories of Parsons, the epistemological critique takes a number of forms according to the particular epistemological theses which are implied, varying in degree both in the level of extremity and in the level of rigour and systematicity. In this respect the most extreme opposition is supplied by the critiques by C. W. Mills and Dahrendorf.[16]

Dahrendorf considers Parsons to be a 'Utopian' in two senses: first, in the sense referred to above in terms of a Utopian model of society, but secondly in a distinct sense in terms of the epistemological form that his theory takes:

> The double emphasis on the articulation *purely formal conceptual frameworks* and on the social system as a point of departure and arrival of sociological analysis involves all the vices and in his case, none of the virtues of a utopian approach. ('Out of Utopia', p. 473, my emphasis)

This involves a clear opposition to the epistemological form that Parsons' theory presents, to its 'formalism', to which Dahrendorf opposes an alternative programme, critical even of Merton's level of theorising, in which 'the prime impulse of all science and scholarship' is over 'the puzzlement over specific, concrete and . . . empirical problems' ('Out of Utopia', p. 474).

In very similar vein Mills' more famous (and very popular[17]) attack on 'Grand Theory' relates directly to the abstract nature of Parsonian theory. Mills' 'translations' of Parsons' concepts into 'straightforward English' – a translation which, incidentally, totally ignores the dominant concepts in that theory, the action frame of reference, levels of organisation, and so on, all of which are not 'common usage' – involve a definite conception of the forms that theory must take if it is to be valid, and hence the proposed protocols on 'how to be a good craftsman' which includes 'Avoid the Byzantine oddity of associated and disassociated Concepts, the mannerism of verbiage' (*The Sociological Imagination*, p. 246).

Such attacks involve more than an impressionistic commentary – they imply a more general epistemological opposition to abstract theory itself, not merely an opposition to Parsons' theory but to abstract theorisation in general, to any theory which involves concepts that cannot be immediately translated into experience – hence the proposed alternative to abstract theory, the 'insightful' craftsman, the indeterminate epistemological subject with fully human capacities of emotion, empathy, and so on. The epistemological critique in this case is a blatant anti-theoretical pragmatism which appears not only to oppose Parsons' distinctively abstract form of sociology but the whole existence of concepts *per se* – a clearly absurd thesis.

A more explicit and systematic example of the epistemological mode is to be found in Merton's critique of Parsons.[18] Merton does not believe that there is something inherently erroneous in concepts as such as instruments of knowledge; he does, however, argue that concepts must take a certain epistemological *form*, a form that is not to be found to an adequate extent in Parsons' theory of the social system. Using a conception of the nature of the evolution of knowledge Merton argues that 'total conceptual structures' of the Parsonian type have continually constituted an obstacle to the development of science (however, note that Merton uses chemistry rather than alchemy, and astronomy rather than astrology in his examples, i.e. *already constituted* sciences, while he provides no justification as to why this should be the case; in other words he avoids explaining the genesis of these sciences and what was necessary for them to break from previous conceptions). On this basis Merton states:

> To concentrate entirely on a master conceptual scheme for deriving subsidiary theories is to risk producing twentieth-century sociological equivalents of the large philosophical systems of the past. (*On Theoretical Sociology*, p. 52)

In opposition to such abstraction in which the determination of concepts is theoretical, Merton advances the notion of theories 'of the middle range', statements which 'consist of limited sets of assumptions from which specific hypotheses are logically derived and confirmed by empirical investigation' (*On Theoretical Sociology*, p. 68). The alternative is for an empirical and not a theoretical determination of concepts. Many other critiques of Parsons in fact operate with a similar epistemological opposition – Merton's own theses on functionalism[19] and the various criticisms from within 'historical sociology'[20] are prime examples. In all these cases the conception that governs the critique is an epistemological one, that all the concepts of a discourse be empirically determined and 'operationalised', again a prior definition of what forms theory must take and against which theory may be judged.

An epistemological critique which is in essence similar but which is more systematic in its actual treatment of its object (for Merton only opposes his own epistemology and he does not attempt to show that Parsons' theory is itself inadequate), is to be found in Homan's analysis of structural–functionalist theory and Turner's assessment of Parsonian theory.[21] Homan's critique subjects structural–functional theory to the acid test of assessing its 'deductive' character, an analysis of its theory in which 'the lowest-order proposition follows as a logical conclusion from the general propositions under the specified given conditions' (p. 106).

Similarly, Turner proposes to assess the logical adequacy of Parsons' system of concepts and in order to do so poses the question of the 'clarity' of the concepts, their systemic nature, and whether or not they have the capacity to generate propositions that can build a scientific theory of society.

It is important, however, to be clear as to exactly what is involved in such readings. The reference to 'deductive nature' and to 'logical adequacy' in these cases is *not* to the *internal* character of the discourse but to the comparison between the discourse and an *ideal* as to what forms theory must take – it represents merely a sophisticated form of epistemological critique in so far as the discourse is subjected to an *external* judgement. What is of concern is not the relations between concepts but the relations between *forms* of concepts, or more accurately the relation between concepts and their empirical potency. This characteristic is clear in Homan's definition of 'theory': 'A theory of a phenomena consists of a series of propositions, each stating a relationship between properties of nature' (op. cit., p. 105).

Although the conclusions of Homans and Turner are distinct – for Homans Parsonian theory can never achieve this objective (for reasons relating to his treatment of the individual) whereas for Turner the capacity of the Parsonian system to generate 'propositions' is limited though potent – the basis of these criticisms and the other critiques which operate with an epistemological referent is the same: discourse is judged by an externally-produced epistemology. The capacity of a theory to generate propositions is an assessment not dissimilar to Popper's critique of Marx and Freud in *The Poverty of Historicism*, one which refers to 'testing' and 'falsification' – it involves a prior (empiricist) epistemological *guarantee*. These readings are therefore only one part of the general mode of critique designated here as the epistemological; the 'deductive method of testing'[22] is only one other epistemological ideal.

However, there are a number of problems with such attempts to found a critique on the status of epistemology, apart from the specific features of each epistemology (the irrationalism of Mills, Merton's empiricism, or the deductive method of testing). To begin with, there is great confusion as to what is the *object* of the reading. In some cases, this is restricted to the explicit epistemological theses that appear in the text (for example, Parsons' analytical realism), whereas in others it is the actual substantive order of concepts of the discourse (the concept of the social system, the concept of action etc.). These two referents are in most cases, however, conflated, which produces a further problem, the postulate of the *realisation* of epistemology in discourse and the dependence in this of the function of a constitutive subject (the author). This issue will be approached in a later section but what I wish to consider here is the more general problem of the epistemological critique which concerns the status that the critical reading establishes *vis-à-vis* its object.

If the epistemological mode of critique is to avoid a simple dogmatism then its status must be shown to be a truly privileged one. *The validity of the epistemological critique depends on the validity of the epistemology of guarantee.*[23] We can here only refer to a few basic points relating to this issue.

Epistemology by definition establishes itself in the space of the 'problem' or 'theory' of knowledge – its object is not the structure of particular theoretical organisations as such but the general sphere of the knowledge process itself. Its concepts and theories are thus concerned to elaborate the essential and necessary structure of all knowledge – not the problem of specific knowledge but the problem of knowledge-in-general.

Posing the problem in this fashion, whatever its variant forms,[24] is to warrant epistemology a privileged status *vis-à-vis* all other forms of knowledge, it is to grant it the capacity for a superior knowledge, *the knowledge of the conditions of existence of knowledge*. These conditions may refer to variant conceptions of Subject and Object, Knowledge and Being, or whatever, but its status in relation to knowledge is the same – it attempts a Master knowledge which is able either to *guarantee* or *legislate* over concrete theoretical organisations. An *a priori* guarantee and an *a posteriori* legislation are thus two forms of the same thesis, the harmony that epistemology is seen to ensure between knowledge and its real object.

Philosophy of science merely inherits this problem and the means of posing it in order to utilise it at a more concrete level – in particular to apply the concepts of epistemology in order to guarantee specific forms of knowledge and judge already-existing knowledges. It is hardly difficult to discover examples of this project in sociology and psychology; consider, for example, the various theses on the 'scientific method' that appear in these areas. It is the second capacity of philosophy of science which is pertinent here – the epistemological mode of critique involves the attempt to provide *de facto* legislations upon existing knowledge forms. Yet in so far as it is of this form then it relies upon the general problem of epistemological guarantee.

While there are excellent examples to show that in particular theoretical developments of the sciences philosophically-produced techniques were of no determinant significance,[25] there is a very general internal and theoretical problem facing all epistemology which operates with the questions referred to above. In fact, all epistemology (in the sense of an external guarantee of knowledge) must in the last analysis force itself into one of two positions, either a circularity – in which the demonstration and conclusion are equivalent – or a thesis which depends upon an element of faith in its demonstration.

In posing the general problem of knowledge (is knowledge possible?, what are the necessary conditions of knowledge? etc.) epistemology ensures its own impossibility, for a peculiar difficulty is presented by the status of its own form of 'knowledge'. If the general question of knowledge is posed, then the validity of its answer must by definition apply to *all* forms of knowledge; if epistemology is to be justified then its theses must be relevant to every area of investigation (or else it becomes superfluous). Therefore, if epistemology involves the formulation of certain guarantees of knowledge, conditions which all knowledge must fulfil, then those guarantees must apply to that particular form of knowledge which is the epistemology, i.e. a universal guarantee, to be truly universal, *must guarantee itself*. In order to draw the full significance of this point, I will consider the case of 'empiricist' philosophies, for it is such positions which are most important to the critiques under review here and to those philosophies of science most operative in sociology (although fundamentally similar issues can be shown to be operative in the various transcendentalist philosophies[26]).

Empiricist epistemology postulates as a general principle that the statements of knowledge be at some level reducible to elements of experience or 'total momentary experiences',[27] a position which may lead to a blatant subjective idealism in which knowledge is seen to be relative to the perceiving subject, or it may be presented in a more elaborate fashion in terms of the 'eventual' comparison or correspondence of concepts with the realm of experience (testing, falsification, an observational language, etc). The point is that in all of these cases a definite contradiction is erected between, on the one hand, the generality and universality of the central thesis and, on the other, the status of the epistemology itself. Again, if epistemology is to be effective, and if it is to be able to pose the 'problem of knowledge', then its thesis must apply universally to all forms of knowledge – if it is an empiricist one then all forms of knowledge must comply to the dictate of experience. Now epistemology is itself a form of knowledge, it may have a distinct object but it is the *means* and not the object which is the specific concern of epistemology – its means must therefore correspond to the general protocols elaborated from within that epistemology. In this case, it is clear that a problem of major proportions faces any attempt to found a consistent epistemology; it can only claim to provide a universal guarantee of knowledge if it can also provide a guarantee of itself. Epistemology is involved in an endemic *circularity*.

Classical philosophy has responded to this inherent circularity in a number of ways – scepticism as in Hume and Berkeley, the infinite regress of the psychologisation of knowledge in Descartes, and in Kant the creation of a unique realm of 'understanding' which is transcendental (i.e. beyond naturalistic explanation), and which therefore requires an ultimate element of *faith*. Epistemology can only attempt to guarantee knowledge if it is to accept a circularity, invoke a contradiction (its universal principles are not in the last analysis universal – an example being the case of logical positivism referred to above) or to exempt itself from rational demonstration and determination.

In fact, it is quite easy to locate such problems concretely in the epistemological critique of Parsons, for the contradictory nature of the epistemological project is clear in the positions of Merton, Mills and Dahrendorf which refer to Parsons' abstract level of theory. The opposition to abstraction and its replacement by a conception of knowledge, in which statements are to be directly related to experience, involves an *abstract* argument, i.e. one which concerns not concrete forms of knowledge but knowledge in general. Any attempt to *demonstrate* this or any general definition of knowledge requires a level of conceptualisation which is independent of experience, or it is to be maintained on purely assertive and circular grounds. These opponents of Parsons preclude forms of argument which could make their positions sustainable.

To conclude this section, we might point out that if discourse cannot be consistently guaranteed scientifically by means of a superior knowledge, in an *a priori* or *a posteriori* sense, then the mode of critique outlined here as 'epistemological' cannot be maintained as a theoretically coherent one. If the operation of an externally produced guarantee of knowledge is not possible in any unproblematic sense then the external judgement of discourse which is the essence of the epistemological mode cannot be sustained.

At this stage it might be useful to consider a somewhat distinct mode of reading from those treated above and which is existent in certain of Parsons' own critical discussions where he himself poses the problems of critique, validity, and so on. In discussing this mode we can, in fact, deal with two issues at once – on the one hand it will allow the consideration of a further mode of critique (the 'grid-reading'), and on the other allow a treatment of an important area of Parsons' work itself, his 'proof' of the validity of the action frame of reference.

1.5   Parsons' Mode of Reading in *The Structure of Social Action*:
      the Proof of the Validity of the Action Frame of Reference

In the Introduction to this book it was stated that the problems of
criticism are intimately related to the conception of discourse or
knowledge and of reading that govern them – a critique as such
always involves some general conception of what is involved in
the reading of a text. Nowhere is this clearer than in Parsons'
own reading of theories of action in his first major text *The
Structure of Social Action* (hereafter referred to as *SSA*).[28]
   This study takes as its object the 'theory of the process by which
scientific thought develops' (*SSA*, p. 697). Within this general
conception three logically-related areas are seen: first, the
overall thesis of the universal *evolutionary* tendency of knowledge; secondly, the conception of the 'end-product' or
'present-state' of that knowledge; and, thirdly, the conception of
the theoretical past or heritage of that knowledge. These three
areas together provide the basis of Parsons' thesis in *SSA* in so far
as they involve a general definition of discourse, a conception of
reading, and their derivative, a concept of *critique*. They constitute Parsons' attempt to establish the validity of the voluntaristic
theory of action, the central objective of the text.
   *SSA* is not simply a commentary on distinct forms of social
theory, nor a simple comparison between them, for its thesis is
far more fundamental; it involves a very definite conception of
the *development* of theory, or, in this case, of the development
of social theory in the direction of the 'voluntaristic theory of
action'. Given this combination, a definite hierarchical status is
assigned to the forms of social theory under consideration; they
are conceived of as the 'past' of that development, formulations
which have been superceded by subsequent theoretical advances. Such theories are phases in an evolutionary process.
   If such an interpretation is to be maintained then it must be
demonstrated that these theories constitute relatively primitive
or erroneous attempts to theorise their objects – in this case, the
means–end relationship. This demonstration is supplied by
precisely the conception of theory which dominates the form of
*SSA*, theory as subject to a natural process of evolutionary
advance. It is thus clear that *SSA* involves a definite conception of
*criticism*: the concept of the evolution of scientific theory establishes both the proof of the validity of the constituted theory (the

voluntaristic theory of action) and the critique of which pre-ceded that theory (utilitarian, positivistic, Durkheimian, etc.). Parsons cannot establish the voluntaristic theory of action in the way he does without correspondingly directing a critique at those theories which pre-date it as phases of the evolutionary process. *SSA* thus involves a definite conception of reading – theories are to be read in terms of an evolutionary pro-gramme – and a definite conception of a mode of critique.

If any one label can be given to Parsons' interpretation of the more 'primitive' theories of action it is 'empiricism'. Thus Parsons ends *SSA* with the statement: 'In particular, it has been necessary to criticise, in terms of their unfortunate empirical implications, a group of views which have been brought together under the term empiricism' (p. 728).

This category includes 'positivistic' empiricism (mechanicism); particularistic empiricism (scepticism); 'intuitionist' empiricism (specifically a tendency of German historicism, i.e. Dilthey and Ranke); the fourth tendency being the 'fictionalism' of Weber's concept of ideal-type. It is necessary first of all to note that the term 'empiricism' is in fact quite misleading, for under its category is included distinct forms of theory. In particular, it conflates (i.e. makes no distinction between) empiricism as an epistemological category and empiricism with reference to substantive concepts. In the case of the former, reference is made to the absence, in the authors considered, of the 'correct' *epistemology* – 'analytical realism'; in the latter, reference is to the absence of one or more *substantive forms of theorisation*, of one or more of the irreducible analytical elements of action – actor, end, situation and norm. It is argued that the former necessarily leads to the latter, or at least this is what is implied in their conflation. This clearly involves some of the issues raised above with reference to the possibility of an epistemological guarantee – Parsons merely inverts the opposition empiricism/ abstraction and advances the principle of analytical realism as a general character of valid knowledge (it also involves certain issues which are raised in the following section, in particular, the postulate of the *realisation* of epistemological presuppositions in discourse). We can therefore dispose of these aspects of his critique of empiricism and turn to an order of problems more specific to Parsons' particular mode of critique.

This refers to an aspect of the critique of which the label

'empiricism' is only an index – here the major reference is not to the correct or incorrect set of epistemological protocols but to the presence/absence of certain theoretical elements. In *SSA*, Parsons claims to demonstrate a 'convergence' in social theory towards the conception of the voluntaristic nature of action, culminating ultimately in the action frame of reference; that in their own ways Marshall, Pareto, Durkheim and Weber were 'supports' of a general process of development within the sphere of 'ideas', each adding significant transformations (analytical elements) to the way in which action is thought and thus contributing to the total construct of social theory. Conversely, each theory in its own right is characterised by certain *absences* – they suppress, in varying degrees, one or more of the elements of action. This is more the case in those forms of social theory which existed prior to Marshall's treatise on economic theory. Rationalistic conceptions of action are seen to erase the distinction between ends, means and conditions of action (action is thus a process of adaptation to given conditions); utilitarian theory leaves the character of ends uninvestigated, and so on – the major absence in these cases being a concept of the determination of forms of action by the operation of value-orientations. Such examples illustrate the locus of the Parsonian critique, what he refers to as 'given-ness', 'erasures', 'supressions' and so on – in short, what is absent in the discourse in relation to what is seen to be the fully constituted form of the theory of action.

The major effect of this referent as a mode of critique is to reproduce a clear case of the *'grid-reading'*.[29] Its technique is to apply an external principle to the text in question as a means of extracting its meaning or essence, but this essence is not defined in terms of the internal forms of the discourse but in terms of an *external* principle. As a critique it operates so as to register certain presences or absences in the discourse according to the forms of the theory of the external discourse which governs and directs it. An absence is always an absence in relation to this external principle, it is to read and criticise a discourse in terms of its correspondence to another.

The first point to make in respect of the grid-reading and the mode of critique that it entails is that it induces a necessary element of *arbitrariness*, for given its dependence on a discourse which is external to that which is the object of the criticism, it is clear that there are as many critiques as there are grids to constitute them – there is no definitive basis on which the critique can operate. A further effect of the grid-reading is to disperse the discourse in question into a series of discrete meanings, elements or postulates, in which the determinant criteria is simply the presence/absence axis; it can tell us nothing about the discourse in terms of its conditions of existence, logical or otherwise (i.e. about the discourse as a *determinate* object), but only what meanings are present or absent. If the arbitrariness dominant here is to remain unqualified then this reading achieves no more than the realist critique discussed above; if there are no demonstrable grounds for preferring one grid to another then any critique directed from within it must of necessity be merely *dogmatic*.

However, in Parsons' case it is clear that some attempt is made to qualify this primary problem; the essentially dogmatic character of the grid-reading is qualified by the additional notion of the imminent *development* of theories, 'The god of science is, indeed, Evolution' (*SSA*, p. 41).

A central thesis in the attempt to establish the validity of the voluntaristic theory of action is the conception that scientific theory is subject to a process of natural development:'The central interest of the study is in the development of a particular coherent theoretical system, as an example of the general process of "immanent" development of science itself' (*SSA*, p. 12).

This evolutionist conception of knowledge – one that is distinct from Merton's notion of 'stepping-blocks in so far as its determination is not an inductive one but is seen to be rooted in the basic categories of the 'understanding' – is the means of demonstrating the validity of the voluntaristic conception of action in relation to the forms of theory which pre-date it. The voluntaristic theory provides the grid through which these other theories are read. This theory is an order of concepts which represent an advanced phase of the general process of development of theoretical systems. What this implies is that the set of concepts which provides the grid (and consequently the critique) is not completely arbitary because it is in these respects *superior* to the forms of theory that precede it.

Yet this qualification has its own price. If the final/present phase of the evolutionary process of knowledge is to be deemed capable of directing a critique of discourses relatively 'primitive' to it, then the discourse that is the object of the critique and the discourse that constitutes the grid must be moments in a *teleology*. Apart from other more general features of an evolutionist conception of knowledge,[30] the mode of critique that is directed from within it assigns certain specific teleological properties to discourse and its theorisation. If the location of presences and absences in a text is not to be totally arbitrary then there must be a specific relationship between the grid and the discourse in question, in which what is absent in the latter is already *immanent* or potent to be realised in the course of the process. In this case, the whole of the evolutionary process is immanent within even the most primitive stage of its development; its advanced forms are simply blocked subject to the natural unfolding of the overall process.

The major problem with this teleological reading concerns the demonstration necessary to its thesis. If there is a concept or category absent in a text (for example, the concept of ends of action as effectively ignored in certain branches of positivistic theories of action), how can it be shown that it is neverthless immanent or potent in it, as this mode requires in order to be effective? In fact, this can only be known by means of a prior conception of the final or present phase of the evolutionary process. What is defined as absent is thus founded upon the concept of its *future anterior*,[31] a concept determined by the conception of what has already been known to exist. The history of the process is a history read backwards, what is defined as immanent is merely what is already known to be the end of the process. For this reason the registration of presences and absences as mode of critique only avoids a dogmatism in so far as it is founded upon a teleology of knowledge.

Such a teleology involves, in fact, yet another example of the privileged reading – in this case, its privileged status exists in that it knows what the end of the process is to be, a knowledge which supplies the conditions of existence of its reading and critique. It can legislate and judge over discourse because it is granted both the knowledge of the process of production of knowledge in general and the knowledge of the final or present phase of development of that process. This form of privilege is, in fact, more severe than in the case of the other modes of critique considered to date, for in this case the object of the critique is reduced to an *expression* of the grid that constitutes it.

Thus, in Parsons' particular case the developments within social theory are developments defined in terms of the already constituted end of the process – the full definition of the action frame of reference in terms of the four analytical elements: actor, end, situation and normative orientation. 'Social theory' is thus effectively reduced to an expressive totality, a unity governed by the levels of representation of its determining purpose, the full development of the theory of action. This expressive totality is one in which the theoretical 'past' becomes a hierarchy of moments of realisation of the essence which dominates it.

Parsons' proof of the validity of the action frame of reference as represented in the voluntaristic theory of action, and conversely his implied critique of other forms of social theory (positivistic, idealistic, etc.), is thus clearly founded upon a teleological conception of discourse and a teleological technique of reading. Its major consequence (one central to all grid-readings and/or evolutionist readings) is systematically to ignore the specificity of particular discourses, to deny the relations between their concepts, objects and conditions of existence. The teleological relation between the discourse which provides the grid and the discourse which is its object merely reproduces in a sophisticated form the *dogmatism* shown to be operative in the realist mode of critique. In *SSA* the dogmatism which is the necessary effect of the form of externality that the reading establishes in relation to its object is simply interiorised within an evolutionist and idealist teleology. Parsons' 'convergence' thesis is a clear illustration of this point – its project is to trace a development in which the end-product is already known, what is defined as an 'immanence' is merely what is pre-given. In this respect the grid-reading and its mode of critique involve an essentially arbitrary and idealist set of mechanisms for the analysis of discourse.

At this juncture it is possible to register one very general tendency in all the modes of critique discussed to date. All of these examples of critical discourse involve the domination of the reading which is its technique by an extra-discursive referent, a referent which is *external* to the discourse in question. Thus, the critique of the 'subject' of the discourse (as exemplified in Gouldner's sociology of sociology) refers to the constitutive subject of knowledge but not to the means with which knowledge can operate (theories, concepts, etc.); the realist mode quite clearly chooses to criticise discourse in terms of what it does not treat, a realm external to its concepts; the epistemological critique involves a referent not to the relations between the concepts of the discourse but to their correspondence/non-correspondence to an externally constituted epistemological ideal form of theory; finally, the critique which stems from the classical and explicit operation of the grid-reading was shown (with specific reference to Parsons' reading of forms of social theory) to depend upon the externality of a conception of the end-product of an evolutionary process of development of knowledge.

In all of these cases the externality of the critique has been shown to produce a number of significant problems which severely curtail their possible success as theoretical critiques. In particular, given an external referent the critique is necessarily arbitrary and there will be as many critiques as there are external conceptions. The discourse itself is left, as it were, untouched, and *its* concepts left essentially uncriticised.

In this situation it is clear that a number of types of criticism explicitly claim to be *internal* analyses of theoretical positions – in this case of Parsonian theory – and therefore to direct a critique at what the discourse in question actually says. At first sight such readings would appear to avoid the difficulties of the modes discussed above in that their object is the internal structure of the discourse and not its treatment by a set of external conceptions. The choice, it seems, is quite simply between internal and external criticisms. The following section will consider several types of 'internal' critique and argue that, in fact, the choice is by no means as straightforward and that the concept of this internality must be strictly problematised.

## 1.6  Internal Modes of Critique

It is of course common to distinguish between 'internal' criticisms and other types of criticism, but as in the modes considered above it is apparent that, given any sort of rigorous analysis, a number of issues are raised which present problems for the possible success of these critiques. In particular, it is apparent that a number of significant questions remain unposed: those concerning the operative concept of discourse, of reading, and of the nature of this supposed 'internality' of the critique. This section will demarcate several forms of 'internal' critique and investigate these issues, and it will argue that in these cases (and implicitly in many other examples of this mode), despite the formal reference to an internal analysis of theories, there is in fact a very different referent: the reading and critique are governed by an *extra-discursive* referent. Although these readings are directed at the unity of a text or an author, they fail to relate adequately to the internal structure of the *discourse*, the concepts and theories which are the conditions of existence of a text or an author's position.

Two broad forms of existing 'internal' critique will be considered; on the one hand, the critiques of Parsons which operate with notions of the relations between Parsons' theory and his 'doctrine', the role of his methodology, epistemology, 'world-view' or whatever; and on the other hand, the forms of analysis of discourse which have stemmed from the work of Althusser and, in particular, the critique of 'empiricism'. Following a discussion of these two very different modes of internal critique certain general points will be made concerning the analysis of discourse and an outline will be given of the mode of critique adopted in the reading of Parsons in the following chapters.

## (i) *Modes of Internal Critique of Parsons*

The forms of internal criticism of Parsons – forms common in critiques throughout the humanities – have been presented as analyses of his 'basic assumptions', as critiques of the relations between his texts (in particular, between *SSA* and the later works) and so on, but in all of these cases, despite different approaches and conclusions, there is one unifying principle which justifies them being included under one general category. This refers to a relation between the substantive theory that Parsons advances (the theory of action, the concept of the social system etc.) and certain basic *notions*. These notions, which I shall refer to here as *presuppositions*, take different forms depending on the conception of discourse in question; they may involve the Weltanschaung of the author, his ultimate beliefs, his 'philosophy'; they may be seen more technically as the methodological protocols of the author or his epistemological beliefs, and so on. In such cases the 'internality' of the reading and critique is concerned with *registering* these presuppositions, or in some cases with locating conflicting sets of presuppositions, and tracing their effects throughout the discourse in terms of their *realisation*. The internality of the critique is in terms of the relation *between discourse and its presuppositions*.

These readings tend to be relatively theoretically progressive in so far as they often systematically attempt to avoid the dogmatism of the external type of critique; Schwanenberg, for example, repels the tendency of Parsons' critics to impose their own position onto Parsons' theory (he cites the logico-empiricist attack), and advocates an analysis which on the contrary assesses Parsons 'on his own terms'.[32] It is thus not surprising that it is under this general category that one should find the most rigorous and extensive criticisms of Parsons. I will cite the major exemplars of this mode of critique as they appear in their variant forms. Three general senses in which the role of presuppositions has been used in readings of Parsons may be delineated, differing in degree of rigour and systematicity: the first is the notion of the role of *'doctrines'* in discourse, the second that of *methodology* and/or *philosophy*, and third that of the place of *epistemological* presuppositions. Each form involves certain specific problems, together with a more general problem concerning the overall consequences of this dependence on the notion of presuppositions.

Perhaps the most explicit example of the reliance upon a concept of presuppositions and their effectivity in discourse is the position which conceives of discourses and theories as essentially a matter of *doctrine*; the reading serves to uncover the essence of the discourse which is its guiding doctrine, the set of ultimate beliefs which constitute the forms taken in discourse. A clear example of this approach is Dawe's distinction between the 'two sociologies'; these are demarcations which involve two diametrically-opposed concerns, those concerned with problems of social 'order' and those concerned with problems of 'control', and they result in two types of social theory – a sociology of social system and a sociology of social action. The basis of this distinction is the concept of the determination of theoretical forms by the doctrine:

the doctrine is the inclusive category. Systems of concepts and general propositions derive their significance, their meaning and their relationships of interdependence from it. In this sense, the problem of order is a label for a doctrine which defines a universe of meaning for sociological concepts and theories. As such, by a logical progression, it penetrates and shapes sociology at both the metatheoretical and substantive levels of analysis.[33]

The doctrine is truly the *essence* of discourse, it determines not only the substantive forms of the theory, but also supplies it with the means of analysing its object, philosophically and empirically. This position, one which has many exponents in sociological commentary and critique in general,[34] has one very definite consequence with regard to its conceptualisation of discourse: discourse is effectively reduced to a 'meaning-complex' in which its theories and concepts are seen as the *expression* of an essential meaning or fundamental postulate. To take Parsons' case, the overriding doctrine is seen to be the 'problem of order' and his theory is viewed simply as an expression of this centre; the doctrine of order penetrates the Parsonian system as its Geist.[35]

Discourse in these cases is presented as a *language*, and discourse is the relation of language and meaning rather than a system of concepts and the relations between them. It is for this reason that it is possible for such readings to present epistemological statements, methodological protocols, 'objectives' and anything else that appears in the text on an equivalent level to the substantive concepts of the discourse. Concepts that have no determinate logical relation may be united because they are merely expressions of the same essence, a constitutive meaning. Thus, Schwanenberg conceives of theories explicitly as 'meaning-systems' and consequently defines reading as 'meaning-analysis'. The notion of the ubiquity of the doctrine constitutes a reading whose task is to discover the essential meaning(s) of the discourse; given this, it can attempt to criticise these central meanings or ultimate beliefs (on moral grounds?), or register the existence of conflicting doctrines either within the one text or between different texts, or it can simply stop at registering the doctrine itself. But whatever use is made of the results of the meaning-analysis, the object and means of the analysis remain roughly the same.

The immediate effect of the conception of discourse-as-doctrine and the forms of critique it entails is to reduce the discourse to an *expressive totality* (in many cases located in the consciousness of the author as subject – hence the links between this position and the sociology of knowledge critique referred to above). In this totality each part (term, statement, concept, theory, protocol, etc.) is to be seen as the expression of the essence of the whole – its doctrine or its meaning. The totality is not one governed by the unity of its concepts (for as we have seen it can include concepts which have no determinate relations), but is governed by the relation between essence and expression.

Now, if it is indeed the case that in this conception discourse is effectively reduced to an expressive totality governed by an essence, then it would seem that there are two possible alternatives open concerning the way in which this conception can view discourse and knowledge in general: either the discourse is to be seen as ever-already coherent, systematic and rationally coordinated, i.e. as necessarily consistent; or the possibility of rational knowledge is denied altogether and discourse is explicitly reduced to the contingencies of one's own doctrine, i.e. discourse is to have no rational conditions of existence. In a way both, clearly contradictory, alternatives are strictly necessary to any consistent form of this position, but we may deal with them separately as both invoke quite serious problems. To take the latter alternative first – that discourse is denied any rational conditions of existence – it is apparent that such a thesis is equivalent to epistemological conventionalism and relativism in so far as all knowledge is to be seen simply as the expression of one's Weltanschuung, a way of 'looking at things' – knowledge is relative to one's doctrine. Yet, if this is the case, then that particular form of knowledge which is the reading itself must be another convention, in this case a conventional way of analysing discourse; the reading is itself an expression of the doctrine which governs it. Therefore not only would it be impossible to demonstrate rationally that particular theory which asserts that 'all theories are ultimately doctrines', but it would be impossible to establish that any one reading of a discourse is valid, for there would be as many readings as there are doctrines. Any position which is to maintain consistently the determination of discourse by the doctrine must accept this infinite regress or attempt to create a distinguished status for its own form of discourse and to offer it as an objective knowledge; in this case it both contradicts its own central thesis and makes any reference to the determining role of the doctrine completely fatuous.

The other alternative to the expressivism of this position is to argue that all discourse is ever-already consistent and rational. If concepts and theories are expressions of the same essence, then discourse can only be rationally perfect (or else it is to involve a determination distinct from the doctrine – on this see later). Yet if this is maintained then the very possibility of theoretical incoherence is denied, inconsistency is ruled out *a priori*, and forms of knowledge such as black magic, alchemy, astrology and theology would have to be seen as necessarily rational positions. In addition, the very operation of a 'critique' would be made superfluous, discourse would have to be necessarily consistent with the protocols, and objectives and concepts would have to be perfectly compatible with each other. However, apart from the absurdities of such a consequence, a more general problem faces this conception of discourse, for if the ubiquity of the doctrine is to be maintained then discourse is clearly subject to a *teleological* process (one somewhat distinct from the evolutionist teleology referred to above), the conception and presentation of theories is to be governed by a Purpose, it can only express its doctrine. The teleological character of this conception of discourse is most apparent in its technique of reading, for the latter is reduced to the 'discovery' or 'uncovering' of what is already known to be the determining doctrine, the clearing away of the dross in the phenomena to disclose the essence that governs it. The reading cannot avoid invoking a teleology – if it does not achieve its pre-given conclusion and discover the essential meaning of the discourse then it denegates its own thesis concerning the determination of theories. The atheoretical character of this mode of reading is clearly evident.

These problematic tendencies are, however, by no means specific to ambiguous and idealist notions of discourse-as-doctrine. More complex conceptions of discourse may be advanced which still depend upon the postulate of the effectivity of presuppositions in discourse. Thus, discourse may be seen as a relatively complex set of differentiations but still be governed by certain notions which determine what is to appear in it; such positions refer not so much to a doctrine but to the role of an author's methodology or his philosophical assumptions in the determination of his theory. In fact, however, the overall theoretical effect of these referents is roughly the same as that of the doctrine.

One example of this more complex use of the concept of discursive presuppositions is Menzies' critique of Parsons.[36] Menzies operates with a conception of discourse as a set of 'programmes' – theories are seen as programmes which are as base linguistic tools for 'coming to grips with the world'. Programmes in turn are dominated by 'core assertions', ultimate conceptions of the structure of the world and the means of comprehending it. Programmes are conceived as particular forms of unities, but a unity not of the logical character of its concepts but of its metaphysical postulates and methodological beliefs. Parsons is seen to operate with two programme-unities: on the one hand, an 'idealist programme' centring around the concept of action and voluntarism, and on the other hand, a 'positivist programme' in which the concept of the social system predominates and in which the emphasis is on 'society seen objectively'. Consequently it is argued that Parsonian theory is torn between two essences which are incompatible, for the metaphysical foundations of the general theory involve conflicting worldviews.[37]

The concept of programme is seen as an answer to all 'empiricist' philosophies of science which seek primarily to establish the validity of statements through the formulation of empirical conditions. On the contrary, it is argued that, although such conditions have a limited pertinence at one level, empirical statements are themselves merely differentiations from the core assertions of a theory; theories are seen in terms of a hierarchy with the basic 'definitions' at the top, through 'ontological claims' to empirical postulates. The important point is that the core assertions themselves *are beyond proof*. This thesis, which in the last analysis is necessary for any attempt to read discourse as doctrine, metaphysics of the author, and so on, is made quite explicit: 'while a scientist can give some justification to whether he continues to accept a particular programme, he cannot prove he is right. In the final analysis there is an element of faith in whatever choice men make. Science is in part an art' (Menzies, *Talcott Parsons and the Social Imagery of Man*, p. 21).

This involves a referent which is common, implicitly or explicitly, to epistemology. Although there may be restricted grounds for the demonstration or proof of a statement, in the last analysis adherence to it requires a degree of faith. At this point rational argument has no place and it is not possible to penetrate any further on strictly theoretical grounds: the decisive element is one of *commitance*, presumably on moral, metaphysical, ethical or aesthetic grounds.

However, the paradox shown to exist in the case of the notion of the doctrine applies equally here: if discourse is ultimately reducible to an act of faith then this must apply equally to that discourse which advances such a thesis and to the readings which it invokes. Consequently, Menzies' own reading of Parsons and the conclusions which it draws must itself be reducible to an act of faith – the reading and critique involve the simple confrontation of one programme to another in which there are no grounds for rational demonstration and argument. Given this decisive status of faith, critical discourse is then bound in an infinite regress in which there is no theoretical backdoor, and reading is condemned to the external counterposition of one programme unity to another. This apparent 'internal' critique in fact cannot maintain a consistent internal referent and technique.

The references to Parsons' 'idealism' and 'positivism' are reminiscent of another more famous critique, that advanced by J. F. Scott.[38] Very briefly, Scott's thesis is that the totality of Parsons' work is almost completely divided, 'conceptually' and temporally, by a fundamental alteration in its project and schema. More specifically, the pre- and post-war foundations are seen to be so distinct that no reconciliation is possible. They are on the one hand the 'philosophico-metaphysical' project of the early works (with an emphasis on the free, self-determining actor), and on the other what Scott refers to as the 'cautious naturalism' of the post-1950 works (a project which attempts to internalise such spheres as behaviourist psychology, rather than dismiss them as simply 'positivisitic').

Scott's critique relies upon the postulation of certain *unities* in discourse; they are unities which are constituted through the effectivity of 'foundations', of 'schemas', i.e. of *presuppositions*. It is as an effect of these notions that a series of controversies have arisen over the Scott thesis, particularly as to whether he oversimplifies both realms of Parsonian theory and ignores significant overlaps between them,[39] for the immediate effect of his position is to simplify the complexities of discourse. It is not my intention to enter into these arguments at this stage, although many of the points made are convincing (these issues and more besides are considered elsewhere in the work), the concern here is with the basic features of his conception of discourse and the consequences of his mode of critique.

Scott's major means of constructing discourse is in terms of methodologies; the essence of discourse is its methodological protocols – in Parsons' case there are two sets, the subjectivist position of the earlier works and the apparent pro-positivist statements of the post-1950 works. Discourse is governed by its methodological protocols and presuppositions, subjectivism leading to idealism, positivism leading to a 'system' emphasis.

There are several points of criticism to be made in this respect. In the first place, and at a purely technical level, this form of reduction of discourse to the methodological or philosophical doctrines which accompany it is riddled with difficulties. It is not as an effect of a simple set of 'errors' that Scott so severely misrepresents Parsons; it is inherent in the very nature of his reading that the complexities of discourse are denied. Once it is appreciated that methodological statements may be more or less arbitrary in relation to discourse (and this is certainly the case for the sciences[40]), or that one set of 'substantive' concepts may be accompanied by a number of distinct methodologies as they are expounded in a text (witness the different forms that are presented under the rubric of 'individualism' in sociological theory), then it is clear that the type of reading that Scott advances may have disastrous consequences for the interpretation and differentiation of theoretical positions. There are, however, problems here of a more fundamental nature.

To begin with, this conception of discourse involves a definite epistemological thesis: discourse can indeed be *guaranteed* by methodology – in this case it is seen as the realisation of methodological protocols. This form of reading merely inverts the epistemological relation. Whereas in the latter methodology determines knowledge, here we find that identification of methodological protocols leads to the identification of the essence of discourse. These protocols take the place of the doctrine or the programme in the positions reviewed above: discourse is seen as the realisation of methodological *presuppositions*. It is this relation between presuppositions and the concepts of discourse which presents the most significant problem for these 'internal' critiques. Before approaching this very general issue, it is necessary to discuss one more position which comes within this general category in order to illustrate its central thesis (discourse as the realisation of presuppositions) with greater clarity: this is Bershady's reading of Parsons in *Ideology and Social Knowledge*.

Although there is some confusion in Bershady's analysis as to exactly which mode of critique he is utilising (for example, he operates in certain places with a form of the realist thesis – see later), there is one very clear order of concepts which he advances as the means of his critique. At one level Bershady proposes the doctrine thesis considered above, in so far as he locates the unity of Parsonian theory in the centrality of its problem, its 'concern', with the problem of social order.[41] He adds, however, that this alone is an insufficient basis for conceiving of Parsons' theory in so far as it could not explain developments within that theory which nobody, not even Parsons, denies. A more inclusive category is necessary to enable one to grasp the theoretical system more efficiently:

> there is a unity in his work that does not come from his
> sustained interest in the problems of social order, social
> integration and equilibrium alone. This unity comes as well
> from another equally pervasive set of interests in problems
> concerning the nature of the theoretical enterprise itself.
> They are epistemological problems and they are of two kinds.
> One is the question of even the possibility of a general science
> of society. The other is the question of the admissability of
> certain kinds of conceptualization in a general science of
> society. (*Ideology and Social Knowledge*, p. 22)

Bershady's reading of Parsons is claimed explicitly to be an 'epistemological analysis'. The object of this critique is the epistemological project that Parsons advances and its objective is to demonstrate that despite the shifts and alterations of his theory throughout its development, and despite 'new bases and structures', the *manner* in which its spheres are related reflect a certain consistency. This manner is fundamentally epistemological and it refers to a strategy or a mode in which theory develops or unfolds – it is this strategy which is the object of Bershady's analysis

The main interest of this study shall be to reveal the logical

nature of the strategy Parsons employs throughout his work
and to inquire into its limits. Not until that strategy or mode of
theorizing is made clear may a critique of it sensibly be made.
Once clear it may be subjected to a number of tests; in
employing this strategy does Parsons fulfill *its* logical requirements; does this strategy accomplish the objectives intended
for it; in such an accomplishment are there new problems
opened which cannot be solved by this strategy alone; in what
senses are the objectives themselves 'defensible'. . . . (*Ideology
and Social Knowledge*, p. 23)

It is essential to draw the full significance of this mode of
reading for it represents a position which constitutes perhaps the
most rigorous example of the internal mode of critique of Parsons. Its object is the strategy of Parsons' theorising and two
questions are posed in relation to it; one is directed at the 'logical
nature' of its functioning, and the other inquires into the validity
of the strategy itself. They may be summed up as follows: first, is
this objective *realised* at the substantive level? Secondly, is this
objective a valid one? Note that what Bershady refers to as the
'logical nature' of Parsonian theory (for this, as will be seen, is a
central issue for this discussion) is the relation that may be
uncovered between (epistemological) *objectives* and the (substantive) *concepts* of the discourse. In Parsons' case the objective is
provided by the epistemology of 'analytic realism', and a central
concern of Bershady's reading is Parsons' exposition and justification of this conception in relation to various forms of 'empiricism'. This analytical 'world-view' is seen to set up explicit
requirements for discourse prior to its formulation; it demands a
knowledge which is objective, a knowledge which is universal
(with concepts applicable to all situations), and a knowledge
which is causal, and so on. For Bershady, Parsons' analytical
realism is the general and abstract *a priori* formulation which
provides the project for a knowledge of the social in opposition
to all relativism, ideal-types, etc.
     This appears to provide the answer to Bershady's second
question, that the epistemological strategy erected by Parsons is a
valid and justifiable one. I will not approach this issue here (this is
dealt with in another chapter) for it is the arguments which relate
to the first question which are significant for this discussion.
     Having identified the epistemological strategy, Bershady pro-

ceeds to discover the extent of its realisation in the substantive concepts of Parsons' theory (hence his argument that Parsons may be seen at a very general level as Kant + Newton: the provider of both the general conditions of knowledge and of concrete forms of knowledge). These substantive concepts are seen as 'solutions to the epistemological problems' and as such may be ranked in order of importance with the means-end framework in the major role. The action schema is viewed as the 'content' of the formal structure of analytical realism (the latter provides the necessity of the analytical elements, the former the elements themselves). This supplies the basis of Bershady's critique, the foundation for the assessment of the 'logical nature' of Parsons' theory. Bershady does not appear to argue that epistemology is necessarily realised in discourse, indeed this would effectively make his form of critique superflous, but he does intend to discover the extent to which it is actually realised or if it is realised at all. 'Consistency' in his analysis refers to the consistency with which the strategy is realised, the relation between epistemological objectives and what is 'achieved' substantively. It is not significant here that Bershady concludes that Parsons has not, in fact, completely succeeded in his project[42] – what he refers to as 'inadequate on internal grounds' – for what is pertinent here is that this criticism involves a specific mode of analysis. Bershady's 'internal' reading in the sense operative in this case is one which *measures the distance and the relation between stated epistemology and substantive concepts*. The epistemology which is the object of this mode of critique is not any epistemology, not even that of the critic (as in the case of the epistemological mode outlined above), but the epistemology of the author, one which creates *his* objectives and *his* strategy. What is referred to as 'logical' is the consistency between that epistemology and the concepts which attempt to realise it.

Bershady's internal reading and critique of Parsonian theory thus depends upon a very definite conception of discourse. Discourse is seen to be the (more or less successful) realisation of *a priori* epistemological *presuppositions*. It is in this sense that his critique establishes a link to the other forms of internal reading discussed above, those which invoke the operation of doctrines, world-views, methodological protocols, etc. The validity of this mode of critique depends upon the success of this relation between epistemology and discourse. However, this mode shares many of the problems endemic to the general thesis of the effectivity of presuppositions in discourse, some of which have already been argued, and many more besides.

To begin with, if the reading is intended to judge the degree to which epistemological objectives are realised in discourse then it is faced with the very elementary problem of just how any such judgement can be made. More specifically, how does one establish whether objectives are achieved, or that the 'solutions' satisfy the 'problems'? It is clear that in this case strictly logical grounds are inapplicable, and there is no sense in which, for example, the substantive concepts of the action frame of reference can be *derived* from the epistemology of analytical realism, from an analytical 'point of view'. The former refers to a specific form of knowledge, the latter to the conditions of all knowledge, and there is no way of establishing a *logical* relation between them – one could just as well attempt to derive logically the space-time framework from the same epistemological protocols. If this is the case, then it is clear that if any such judgement is to be made it must utilise means other than logical ones. In fact it is at this level that Bershady's critique uses certain inadvertent types of criticism which are in no sense 'internal'; thus, although he states approval of Parsons' objective, he refers to what he considered to be a 'dilemma': 'The dilemma lies, I believe, in the fact that all of the characteristics and functions Parsons offers us, no matter how few or many are used, or how they are combined, cannot reproduce the features of any single society' (*Ideology and Social Knowledge*, p. 13).

In the absence of strictly logical criteria for making critical judgements it is clear that Bershady uses certain *realist* arguments – the above thesis requires a prior conception of what a 'single society' really is. Not only does such a recourse reproduce the problems of the realist mode of critique outlined above (in particular its essential dogmatism), but it conflicts with his claim to direct an 'internal' critique in whatever sense that word is used. Bershady's critique is forced to operate with elements which are more or less arbitrary.

At a more general level, the reading of discourse through the notion of its realisation of epistemological objectives impinges certain necessary characteristics on the structure of discourse itself. Given the apparent determinant status of epistemology, one consequence is that transformations, discontinuities, inconsistencies, etc. which exist in the substantive orders of concepts are strictly ruled out or are beyond explanation. The importance of this point is particularly apparent in Parsons' case (it is a more general issue which will be discussed later), for Bershady's mode of reading necessarily involves a distorted conception of that discourse in so far as it requires that *significant* transformations are precluded by definition. Herein lies the ultimate circularity of the Bershady analysis: he chooses to use Parsons' epistemological project because this alone can provide the explanation of the totality of his theory, yet he argues in addition that those who talk of significant discontinuities in Parsonian theory are mistaken! The assumption of the unity of Parsonian theory is both the premise and the conclusion of Bershady's analysis. The postulate of a 'strategy' is characterised in this: theoretical discontinuities or inconsistencies[43] at the substantive level are ruled out *a priori*, and consequently any discussion for or against such discontinuities is made superflous, the epistemological reading rendering its analysis pointless. If any such characteristics are in fact accepted, for example that Parsonian theory contains important transformations at the substantive level, then it is clear that the referent to strategy cannot account for them. If the same strategy can be employed to explain different theoretical unities then it is clear that such a referent is fatuous on theoretical grounds – it may provide a passive description of an author's 'oeuvre' but it cannot *explain* the developments in discourse.

A third issue relating to the attempt to maintain the determinant status of epistemology *vis-à-vis* discourse concerns a point already referred to above. If epistemology can constitute knowledge, even in only a small number of cases, then it is placed in a similar position to the classical notion of *guarantee*. While the theoretical problems involved here have been dealt with above, we might here illustrate the 'practical' difficulties of the thesis that epistemological presuppositions determine the substantive concepts of discourse.

A good example, and a pertinent one here, is the notion of a 'General Systems Theory'. This set of epistemological protocols postulates that there is a mode of analysis which is a general one for the social sciences. This mode may be applied to particular substantive areas and is seen to guarantee that knowledge its scientific status.[44] Crudely, this universal method is seen to involve a 'systemic' reference in which objects and parts are conceived in terms of their articulation to the whole, the totality which is the system; it is an analytical process which 'totalises' the constituent elements to form a unified organisation. This *a priori* 'way of theorising' provides general systems theory with a general epistemological formulation of the mode in which the sciences proceed. However, it is not difficult to show why such a status cannot be rigorously maintained, for it is clear that the *a priori* concept of 'system' cannot *in itself* allow or constitute the concept of, say, the *social* system, or of a *biological* system, or whatever. A simple 'way of looking' cannot produce such concepts, for to talk of such systems requires that the 'something' to which they refer *is already conceived as an object discrete from others*. The *a priori* concept of system in fact can only operate if the sphere which it designates is already a 'totality' in the sense that it is already a *concept*. For this reason a general systems theory is not in any strict sense *a priori* or 'general', for it cannot rigorously determine what is to be seen as a system (society, the body, the cosmos, etc.), nor indeed what systemic existence is involved (its parameters, units, internal relations, etc.), for this is subject to the process of 'substantive' theorising itself and not to the application of external protocols.

This point must apply equally to the epistemology of analytical realism. To demand that an object be conceived through the prior separation of its analytical elements, or crudely, to 'think analytically', requires that its structure is already conceptualised – as stated previously, it is not possible to derive the particular concepts of the action frame of reference from the apparently *a priori* formulations which accompany them textually. The analytical operation can only operate once this conceptual labour has been undertaken, once the elements have, in fact, already been differentiated. Such an epistemology cannot, therefore, function in the way it claims to, and it does not *determine* the theoretical process. At this level, then, the formulation that epistemology determines discourse cannot be consistently maintained and therefore the Bershady mode of reading is strictly arbitrary.

These points against the utilisation of an epistemological referent in a theoretical reading of discourse are, however, less important than a more general order of issues relating to the nature of discourse, reading, critique, and so on. In Bershady's thesis, and in all of the positions so far included under the category of 'internal' readings, there is a very definite conception of discourse in which a crucial role is played by a general form which may be termed *presuppositions*.[45] Whether they be expressed in terms of 'world-views', 'doctrines', 'methodologies', 'programmes' or 'epistemological strategies' it is argued that presuppositions determine what is to appear in discourse – the reading and critique must therefore register such presuppositions and trace their course throughout the substance of the discourse. Whatever form these presuppositions are seen to take, the general conception remains in essentials the same, for they refer to forms which both precede and govern discourse and which exist *external* to its concepts. This is an important point, for it is essential to locate the status of presuppositions exactly in order to draw its full significance; they do not refer to the *logical* conditions of existence of discourse (as shown, it is not possible to demonstrate a logical relation between epistemology and the concepts of discourse, nor is it possible to derive any necessary logical relation between the 'problem of order' as a doctrine and the particular concepts of the social system and action, and so on). That such logical relations cannot be shown is, indeed, often acknowledged, precisely because in all of these cases presuppositions refer not to the logical conditions of discourse but to the nature of the *process of production* of discourse itself.

As such presuppositions refer to *extra-discursive* elements, they are seen to be the mechanisms which constitute the generation of discourse; they are extra-discursive because they determine what is to appear in discourse. To recapitulate, the doctrine is *expressed* in discourse as its essence, the methodology is the *technique* of discourse in the sense of a set of protocols which constitute it, and epistemology is assigned the status of external arbiter of discourse or the provider of a 'strategy' which determines what is to appear. Thus, although presuppositions may be seen to exist in a *text*, and this is clearly the case with Bershady's thesis, they are extra-discursive in the sense that they are *logically* distinct from the substantive concepts of discourse (again, there is no logical relation between epistemological and substantive concepts), and in these cases it is clear that the unity of a text is maintained not logically but via the functioning of the consciousness of an *author*, or some equivalent mechanism. In short, presuppositions in these cases are extra-discursive mechanisms for the determination of discourse.

What is the theoretical effect of such a conception? The major one in this respect is that contradiction or inconsistency in discourse is effectively denegated. If presuppositions (whether epistemological, methodological or doctrinal) are rigorously to determine what is to appear in discourse, then what does exist must be conceived as a *necessary* extension of those presuppositions (or else the thesis is denied). Yet if this is the case then logical incoherence is ruled out *a priori*. Although this point is most clear in the case of the role of the doctrine (whereby discourse is seen as the immanent and necessary 'logical' progression from an essential meaning), it is also a problem for those positions which clearly wish to establish certain incoherences and contradictions in discourse, for example, Bershady's notion of a 'gap' between Parsons' objectives and achievements.

Let us for the moment leave aside the relativist thesis that all discourse, as an expression of a 'meaning', is ever-already consistent (in so far as it is an expressive totality), which induces notions of faith and so on, and consider the specific order of problems raised by these consequences for the more rigorous conceptions of discourse. I will again use Bershady's analysis of Parsons.

In fact it can be shown that Bershady's thesis that Parsonian theory is 'inadequate on internal grounds', given the means of establishing it, is an impossible one. This is necessarily so given the co-existence of two incompatible propositions: (a) that epistemological presuppositions determine the forms of discourse, and (b) that epistemological presuppositions *may not* be realised, and that inconsistency between presuppositions and discourse is possible. Why are these two postulates incompatible? Given the general relation between epistemology and discourse in which the former is determinant, the very possibility of theoretical contradiction or incoherence is effectively precluded. The thesis itself requires that discourse is to be seen as the effect of presuppositions, and therefore what appears in discourse must be a pure realisation of those presuppositions, or a form of determination *distinct* from the presuppositions is to be acknowledged, i.e. the thesis is denied. In other words, for the second of these propositions to be possible the first must be effectively curtailed. Once exceptions to the rule are admitted, then it becomes highly dubious to continue to postulate that presuppositions rigorously determine what is to appear in discourse; if logical incoherence is seen to be possible then that incoherence cannot be the logical effect of its presuppositions, and the *general* definition of discourse is no longer 'general'.

In this situation there would appear to be two choices: either extra-discursive presuppositions do indeed rigorously determine the process of production of discourse, and then logical contradiction etc. is precluded (all discourse is ever-already consistent); or such contradictions are accepted and then the whole proposed effectivity of presuppositions is called to question.

Those 'internal' critiques which do claim to register incoherences and contradictions in discourse, yet maintain the general relation between concepts and presuppositions, are thus faced with a major problem as to how to account consistently for their existence without contradicting the original thesis. While those positions which refer to *one* set of presuppositions cannot solve this central problem, it would seem that it is possible to account for incoherence in discourse if it can be argued that there are contradictions in the presuppositions themselves. This, however, cannot avoid the basic problem for this introduces an additional order of issues of a more general nature.

If it is accepted that there is more than one presupposition involved in the determination of discourse, as would seem to be necessarily the case for almost all of the positions considered here (for example, Bershady's notion of two objectives in Parsonian theory – theory of society, theory in general), then a peculiar problem faces such conceptions. Once the existence of more than one presupposition is accepted, then how is it possible to explain why in certain cases one presupposition rather than another is accepted, and how one presupposition and not another is determinant? Thus, given two presuppositions, $x$ and $y$, and given the proposed determination of discourse by such presuppositions, what determines that $x$ and not $y$ is determinant, or vice versa? If presuppositions do indeed govern discourse then one should preclude the effectivity of the other. It is clear that in such cases it is impossible to maintain in any consistent manner the co-existence of more than one presupposition without in some sense denying the original thesis. For to do so requires the intervention of a mechanism distinct from the presuppositions themselves in order to account for the dominance or effectivity of one over the other(s), one which contradicts the proposed effectivity of presuppositions in discourse.

Two conclusions are necessary with reference to the modes of 'internal' critique considered here: on the one hand, given the notion of the effectivity of presuppositions in discourse (whether doctrinal, methodological or epistemological), it is imposssible to theorise incoherency or contradiction in any consistent fashion; on the other hand, once the existence of more than one presupposition is claimed, then mechanisms distinct from them must be invoked to account for their differential determination.

Given all of these points it will be clear that the problem of 'internal' reading and criticism is a complex one. It is not sufficient simply to assert a preference for an internal mode of critique in order to avoid the pitfalls clearly prevalent in the various external modes; the precise nature of 'internality' must be rigorously specified and problematised. In this respect a somewhat different order of issues is raised by a conception of discourse and reading which is in many ways distinct from the types of critique considered so far, and is reflected in the work of Althusser and his followers. I will consider this important theoretical position not only in terms of the distance between it and more orthodox conceptions of discourse, but also in terms of its limitations and difficulties.

## (ii)  *The Althusserian Project for a Theory of Theoretical Production*

In relation to the various modes of critique discussed so far, the work of Althusser would appear to present a specific order of issues. Althusser launched an explicit and vigorous attack on many conceptions of knowledge, discourse, reading, etc., many of which are particularly pertinent here; these include critiques of the epistemology of guarantee, of empiricism, of the notion of a grid-reading, and of many other areas closely related to the problems registered here as involved in the concept of theoretical criticism. If this is the case, the question which must now be posed concerns the actual degree of the success of these theses and of Althusser's own conception of discourse, reading, and criticism. Does Althusser in fact provide us with the concepts necessary for a rigorous theoretical reading and critique of discourse?

Although an exhaustive account and critique of Althusser is

not possible in this context it is possible to select one or two of his major theses most relevant to this discussion. Apart from his specific arguments on Marxism, Althusser's theoretical position may be roughly divided into two areas: (a) a conception of science and the status of philosophy in relation to it; and (b) a conception of 'theoretical ideologies', their determination, structure and consequences.

The first area is not of prime importance here although we might register two significant points. On the one hand, the sciences are seen to operate independently of any *a priori* protocols provided by philosophy or epistemology; philosophy is not seen as theoretically superior to the sciences. The sciences are to be seen as governed by a determinate mode of production, by a determinate system of concepts and relations between them. Consequently, any reading of the discourse of the sciences must primarily restrict itself to the substantive order of concepts (historical materialsim, the theory of the unconscious, etc.), and must consider the relations within that order, relations of logical consistency, dependence etc. The status of particular concepts or arguments is to be examined in terms of their consistency with the system of concepts and propositions of the discourse. The reading can establish on strictly theoretical grounds whether a concept that is present in a text is consistent with the discourse (i.e. is scientific), or whether it is to be classified as incompatible[46] and hence ideological. Although the Althusserian conception of the sciences is by no means devoid of difficulties,[47] what is distinctive here is the explicit attempt to read at least one group of discourses on strictly *internal* grounds – these discourses are not to be judged according to some correspondence/non-correspondence with a philosophically-advised epistemological structure, nor are they to be judged according to the relative representation in them of a reality external to them. The object of scientific discourse is the object of *its* concepts and the internality of discourse is the internality of its determinate organisation of concepts.[48] Given this conception of discourse, the reading can only attempt to think the forms of orders of concepts on a strictly internal basis and not attempt to judge or determine that order on the basis of its own externally-produced concepts. In short, the reading can only aspire to theorise the logical relations between the concepts present in a discourse.

However, Althusser's conception of ideological discourse and consequently of the reading and criticism of such discourse is altogether different. In order to consider this point it is necessary to distinguish between two sets of 'theoretical ideologies' in Althusser's critique. On the one hand are the variants of the 'empiricist conception of knowledge', epistemological discourses whose object is the problem of knowledge. On the other hand there are what may be referred to as 'substantive' discourses, whose object is not at all knowledge, but specific substantive areas (for example, sociology, history, economics, etc.). The critique in the first case is toward the conception of empiricism as a *concept*; in the second it is altogether different, to the existence of 'empiricism' as a *practice*; in other words, one is concerned with empiricism as an object of knowledge and the other with empiricism as a process.

The critique of empiricist epistemology in the work of Althusser and in various Althusserian theses involves an internal referent; it is argued that the empiricist conception of knowledge is faced with a number of insoluble theoretical problems, predominantly in so far as it must at some stage invoke circular, contradictory or infinite arguments in order that its thesis be maintained,[49] and several of the above discussions of the epistemology of guarantee etc. may indeed be seen as an extension of the elements of a critique supplied by Althusser.

So far so good. Despite certain reservations, the Althusserian reading of both the sciences and of the epistemological sphere of theoretical ideologies (they are criticised not *because* they are ideological because they are logically incoherent), involve an essentially internal referent, and what is of concern is not some putative process in the production of discourse, but the relations between the concepts present in it. However, a distinct issue is raised in the critique of the second area of theoretical ideologies, the substantive sphere. The critique of empiricism in this case invokes a completely separate order of problems.

The decisive conceptual elaboration in this respect is the distinction that Althusser makes between two theoretical realms, science and ideology. Whereas the former, as has been shown, is to be defined in terms of the auto-development of its concepts, ideology is defined in terms of a category more extensive than the purely theoretical sphere – theoretical ideology is conceived in terms of the general category of Ideology. While no elaborate discussion of the concept of Ideology can be given here, two of its assigned characteristics are relevant for our purposes. On the one hand is the centrality of what is termed the 'practico-social function': ideology is seen to be grounded in a specific functional–political relation to the social formation in which it exists (in the theoretical realm, this function predominates over the internal-theoretical considerations). On the other hand, ideology is seen as the 'lived-relation' between men and their conditions of existence; ideology, in similar fashion to the generation of 'myth' and 'image', is constituted by a definite relation between the objective world and the structure of human consciousness.[50]

What is most significant with this general category for the theorisation of discourse is that one realm of discourse is seen to be governed by the intervention of the human subject. Althusser's definition of 'theoretical ideologies' involves the *effectivity of the human subject within the structure of discourse*. Just as ideology is the lived-relation (write 'experienced relation') between human subjects and their social conditions of existence, theoretical ideology is the interiorisation of this (essentially misrecognised) relation within the theoretical forms of discourse. In both cases, the determinant element is the intervention of the operation of a real human consciousness. While a critique of the general definition is out of place here (in particular, its patent sociologism), the subsumption of the conceptualisation of certain realms of discourse under the general category of ideology has a number of very definite consequences which may be specified.

In fact this relation of Ideology/theoretical ideology allows Althusser to effect an ambiguous 'shift' in his theorisation of discourse. This shift is the extention of his critique of the empiricist *conception* of knowledge to the critique of theoretical ideologies as empiricist *practices*, or as Althusser calls them 'empiricist problematics'. Consider, for example, his conception of the 'object' of Political Economy:

> The peculiar theoretical structure of Political Economy depends on immediately and directly relating together a homogeneous space of *given phenomena* and an ideological anthropology which bases the economic character of the phenomena and its space on man as the subject of needs (the *giveness* of homo economicus). (*Reading Capital*, p. 162, my emphasis)

The combination of two spheres is seen to determine the object of Political Economy, a realm of *given* economic facts (e.g. that such facts must, in line with actual economic practice, be measurable), and a philosophical anthropology, itself given by ideology (the 'obviousness' of man's ubiquity). The structure of this particular theoretical ideology is given by Ideology. Such knowledge-unities are merely the form of theoretical representation of Ideology, and they involve essentially the same processes of constitution as Ideology, the processes of misrecognition as an effect of the functioning of a human consciousness, an imaginary relation to the world.

Because of this process of reflection representation of Ideology in theoretical form, Althusser designates the mode of production of theoretical ideology as *parallel to the abstractive relation which constitutes the theoretical postulate central to classical epistemology*. The process of production of theoretical ideology is explicitly conceived in terms of an experiential or 'lived' relation, and although the process is not defined in exactly the same terms as that proposed in epistemology (for the latter the relation is one of mirror-reflection, whereas for ideology it is one of essential misrecognition), the relation is in both cases governed by the intervention of human subjectivity. Theoretical ideologies are thus to be designated as 'empiricist', they are ideological *because* they are the effect of an empiricist process of production.

What Althusser in fact achieves by means of such a thesis is a silent *theoretical slide*. He moves from the concept of the empiricist conception of knowledge to the notion of a 'real' empiricist process of *production* of knowledge. The slide is from the specification of a concept to the concept of a process. Theoretical ideologies are seen to be the effect of a real empiricist process of knowledge, one that interiorises and ensures the dominance of Ideological forms and Ideological considerations in theory. The epistemological relation of abstraction between the subject and the object (or 'real'), finds its counterpart in theoretical ideology in the abstractive relation between the human subject and ideological forms. The given-ness which is the essence of theoretical ideologies refers precisely to this relation between the subject of discourse (if it is given it must be given *to* something), and the obviousness of Ideological representations.

The immediate effect of such a conception is to induce a central contradiction in Althusserian analyses of discourse.[51]

Within the one category of 'discourse' is to be included two radically distinct realms, science and ideology. These two realms are ascribed completely different modes of production: science is seen to be the effect of a determinate system of concepts and their relations, whereas ideology is seen to be the effect of the appropriation of ideological forms via the intervention of the human subject, the interiorisation of those forms in the theoretical realm. Thus the *process of production* of knowledge is seen to constitute the validity or non-validity of discourses; it is enough to locate the empiricist process in a certain discourse to brand it 'ideological' and consider the critique fulfilled. The radical distinction between the two realms is reflected in the means by which Althusser conceptualises the mechanisms by which one tears itself away from the other. A science can only be constituted by what Althusser (following Bachelard) refers to as an 'epistemological break', the transmutation of discourse as an effect of the transformation of the process of production of its knowledge forms from the 'preconceptual' to the conceptual, from the external to the 'internal', etc.

The contradiction of the Althusserian analysis of discourse lies in the differential status and theorisation of these two discursive realms. Whereas in the case of the sciences the organisation of *concepts* defines the process of production of discourse itself, in theoretical ideologies it is the process which defines the concepts (their theoretical status, coherence, etc.). In brief, in the sciences, the process of production of discourse = effectivity of concepts; in ideological discourse the process of production → concepts. In one concepts determine the structure of discourse, in the other concepts are the effect of certain non-discursive exigencies, and the structure, as it were, is *prescribed prior to its concepts*, the structure of the 'empiricist problematic'.

This distinction has a differential effect on the mode of reading and critique' that are adopted in each case. Given that the determination of the discourse of the sciences is located at the level of the atuo-development of its concepts, the object of any reading of those sciences is to be the relations that obtain between its concepts in relation to the internal development or logical order of those concepts. Any decisions that are to be made in respect of any propositions or statements in scientific discourse must be grounded on a consideration of their compatibility with the major system of concepts that dominate its theoretical operation (see note 47, p. 240). The object of a reading of theoretical ideologies is altogether distinct. Given the determinate intervention of an extra-discursive realm into the theoretical level (the dominance of the 'practico-social function'), then the task of the reading of such discourse is oriented primarily to the location of the presence of extra-discursive determinations, to locate and register the presence of *empiricism*. The *mode* of reading and the form of critique in these two cases is thus clearly distinct; both the object and the technique of the reading involve radically different operations.

Now, if this is indeed the case that Althusserian analysis of discourse utilises two distinct modes of reading, then a problem of the first order concerns the means by which a decision is to be made as to exactly which mode is to be used in any particular case. This in itself requires some means of differentiating between 'empiricist' and scientific discourse. Crudely then, how is it possible to demarcate, prior to the actual analysis of its concepts, whether or not a discourse is empiricist?

One method of demarcating between empiricist and scientific discourse would seem to be to refer to the protocols (methodological or epistemological), which appear in a text as an accompaniment to the discourse itself. The task would then be to classify a discourse as 'empiricist' if it is presented under the category of an empiricist project or is claimed to operate on the basis of empiricist objectives. However, such a means of demarcation is faced with two problems, for, on the one hand, it reproduces many of the tendencies of both the epistemological mode of critique and the notion of the determination of discourse by presuppositions referred to above, and, on the other, it is clear that many of the accepted sciences, including physics and chemistry (and of particular significance to Althusser's project, Marxism), offer explicitly empiricist theses in their attempt to describe their procedures of investigation.

In fact Althusser and his followers do not as such *identify* discourses simply with the epistemological protocols which accompany them but rather use such a referent as a form of *demonstration* of the claimed 'empiricist' character of a discourse.[52] This demonstration takes on a peculiar status, for, in fact, the central point is that the demarcation between science and ideology is already beyond doubt: the 'identification' of the character of discourse is not strictly an indentification at all in so far as it is not the reading which establishes the distinction. If, as has been shown, two completely different means of analysis of discourse are to be used depending on the case, that is, two distinct *types* of reading, then it is obvious that the reading itself cannot determine which type to select; such a decision must be made *prior* to the actual reading so that such a selection can be possible. The status of discourse is *already known* independently of any theoretical reading of its concepts.

Two points follow. First, such a mode of categorisation and 'analysis' of discourse is *teleological*. The reading is such that the already determined conclusion constitutes the condition for the mode of analysis; discourses can be classified as 'ideological' because their essential structure (empiricism) is already established. The reading itself is thus reduced to the location of the presence of this structure in the apparent 'given-ness' of its central notions, and it is at this level that the referent to epistemological or methodological statements becomes operative, and they are seen as the tell-tale marks of a process that governs the discourse. In other words, the Althusserian analysis of theoretical ideologies can be seen primarily as the identification of that which is already beyond doubt; the status of a discourse as ideological is not the product of the reading but its precondition (in so far as it determines whether a certain mode of reading is to be adopted or not). The teleological property of this mode lies in the fact that the reading is constituted on the basis of its conclusion.

The second point is an extension of the one above. If the distinction between science and ideology can be established prior to the reading itself, then this requires the existence of a *privileged* form of knowledge. This knowledge is not simply a means of analysis of discourse but one which has the capacity to determine which means of analysis is applicable in any particular case. It can determine which discourse is scientific and which is ideological on the basis of its privileged status in relation to knowledge forms. It is for this reason (amongst others) that Althusser's project for 'Theory' (defined as the theory of the mechanism of production of the knowledge 'effect') reproduces the structure of classical epistemology that he set out explicitly to avoid.[53]

For these reasons it is the science–ideology distinction and not, as is often assumed, the concept of 'problematic', which governs the Althusserian analysis of discourse. According to whether a discourse is to be classified as 'scientific' or 'ideological', the character of the concept of problematic is transformed. The science–ideology distinction, resulting in the conception of two distinct *modes of production* of discourse, displaces the concept of problematic as applicable to the discourse of the sciences (as *equivalent* to its system of concepts), and assigns it the status of an extra-discursive mechanism (one which exists *independently* of its concepts) for the determination of discourse. The empiricist problematic is the pre-discursive structure which governs the process of production of ideological discourse; it is not, as in the case of scientific problematics, the concepts which define the structure but the structure which defines the concepts, which gives them their 'empiricist' character.

While the Althusserian analysis of the sciences is not without its difficulties, it is clear that problems of major proportions face the theorisation of theoretical ideologies. Given the concept of the empiricist problematic as empiricism-in-operation, a definite shift is effected away from the strict analysis of the concepts and relations between concepts of discourse (although, as stated, not exclusively), toward the direction of the conception of the *realisation* in discourse of certain *presuppositions*, which in Althusser's case are supplied by the notion of 'givens'. The effectivity of concepts, hailed in the sciences yet denied in ideologies, is made strictly superfluous from the point of view of the critical reading by the reduction and conflation of two issues: on the one hand the process of production of discourse, and on the other hand the *logical character* of that which is produced. The logical character of ideologies, their theoretical status, is to be known through a conception of the mode in which they are produced.

The object of this discussion is to show that Althusser (despite an explicit attempt to escape the problems of the epistemology of guarantee, and despite his opposition to the teleology of the grid-reading, and the rigorous character of his analyses and of those who have applied his concepts to other spheres of discourse), has returned indirectly to the position that discourse is indeed determined by presuppositions, and that extra-discursive mechanisms do indeed govern the order of discourse.[54] 'Givens' take the place in theoretical ideologies that doctrines, world-views, etc. take in the modes of 'internal' critique discussed above. For Althusser and his followers, empiricist discourses are theorised as the *realisation* if not of epistemological objectives then certainly of ideologically supplied givens, the intervention in knowledge of the 'practico-social'. The major problems of the conception of the realisation of presuppositions have already been outlined above. In Althusser's specific case the problems are only more acute given the systematic attempts to ground the reading of discourse on strictly theoretical conditions; the project for the 'symptomatic reading', for a theory of theoretical production, etc., only serve to highlight more the theoretically dubious character of the Althusserian mode of analysis of discourse.

## 1.7 Conclusion: the Concepts for the Analysis of Discourse

This book has considered many distinct modes by which theories have been criticised and has attempted to show that in all cases the means of analysis of texts, the object of the reading and the technique through which the discourse is subjected to criticism reflect major theoretical difficulties. If any one general feature can be deciphered from these often quite distinct positions, it is the conflation of two orders; the logical nature of the discourse in question on the one hand, and the process of production of that discourse on the other. While there would appear to be no reason why some form of theorisation of the process of production cannot be established, this chapter has argued that in so far as such a referent is combined with an attempt to direct a theoretical *critique* of discourse (concerning its 'validity', coherence, or whatever), then a number of problems will of necessity emerge. The conflation of the two orders has differential effects depending on the conception of discourse which is adopted. With reference to the various types of 'external' critique, and excluding the realist and epistemological modes as designated above (for, as has been shown, these modes do not even attempt to criticise the discourse in question, but merely aspire to counterpose a different position), the conflation produces relativism in the case of the critique of the subject – the production of discourse is reduced to the exigencies of the human subject – and a teleology in the evolutionist mode, as shown in Parsons' own conception of reading. In the case of the forms of 'internal' critique the combination of the logical nature of discourse and its process of production (as the effect of presuppositions) induces an even more acute order of problems. If these internal analyses are to maintain their conceptions of discourse, then they are faced with the problem as to how incoherence or inconsistency in discourse is to be accounted for, as well as being faced with the problem of explaining the process of realisation of presuppositions when more than one presupposition is acknowledged (see pp. 46–8).

Given these problems, it is clear that a rigorous *separation* must be maintained between questions of the logical character of discourse and questions of the process of production of discourse. A rigorous exclusion of any conflation of these two orders precludes the elaboration of all of the modes of critique discussed above, in so far as no referent can be made (if this distinction is consistently maintained) to the constitutive role of the subject, to an immanent 'progress' of theories, to their capacity to produce empirically verifiable propositions, or to their degree of reflection of 'reality' (as held by the critic). Also, given this separation, no attempt can be made to theorise discourse in terms of its methodological assumptions or epistemological presuppositions, in which a critique of methodology is *carried over* to a critique of the 'substantive' concepts of the discourse.

It will now be clear that the position maintained here is that a strictly theoretical mode of critique of discourse must involve an analysis of the *internal* forms of discourse, but also that this 'internality' must be clearly and systematically defined. It is not sufficient simply to assert a preference for an internal mode of analysis to constitute a rigorous critique for, as has been shown, if no distinction is made between the internality of a *text* and the internality of *discourse*, a whole host of difficulties will emerge. It is essentially the unity of a *text* which provides the internality of the object of the various forms of 'internal' critique discussed in section 1.6 above, in that the relation which is the object of the analysis is that between discourse and its methodology, epistemology, etc. *Discourse* however must be specified as a set of concepts and the relations between them in which the relations that can be demonstrated are strictly *logical* ones. A text may be a purely arbitrary unity in which any number of discrete propositions may occur – it may reflect the author's conception of knowledge-in-general, his 'world-view', his 'philosophy', or whatever, in addition to his substantive concepts (e.g. in Parsons' case, the theory of action). To maintain a strict unity of a text in the absence of demonstrable *logical* relations is to induce the effectivity of the consciousness of the author-as-subject, a speculative conception which is merely a sophisticated version of the critique of the sociological subject considered in section 1.2.

This reference to logic by no means implies that discourse is governed by a *logos*, an essence which determines what is to *appear* in discourse. The conception of discourse and the means of analysis of it which are advanced here refer strictly to the *character of what is produced* and not to any putative process of production itself. There is no imputation of an inherent logical spectre in this conception, no appropriational relation of Reason–Being or any other epistemological opposition is presumed. The mode of analysis of discourse adopted here is restricted to the elaboration of logical relation between the concepts present in discourse, and on that basis is concerned to investigate the coherence and consistency of it. It does not, however, attempt to argue that any such relations (whether coherent or not) are *effective* in the constitution of the discourse, merely that they exist and can be demonstrated to exist. It is in this sense that the analysis is an internal one, it makes no reference to an extra-discursive mechanism which governs discourse, only to the logical relations that can be shown to obtain in it.

At this level the outline of the mode of analysis will appear extremely schematic and formal; I will therefore briefly illustrate the nature of its reading and the forms of conclusion it entails via an example of the critique of Parsons elaborated in later chapters.

In the chapter on the Parsonian mode of analysis of the 'social' (chapter 5), it is shown that two levels of theorisation are operative in Parsons' conception of the social system, on the one hand the notion of the functional prerequisites and their derivates, the functional subsystems, and on the other, the famous 'pattern variable' schema. It is clear that both referents are decisive to his theoretical position. The pattern-variables are the means by which Parsons establishes the unique status of the cultural system in relation to the other systems of action and the mode in which the 'subjective' element of action effects itself in the action complex; they refer to culture patterns which constitute actor's conceptions of and orientations to their relation to the action nexus of which they are a part. The functional prerequisites, on the other hand, involve a distinct order of issues. An action system, Parsons emphasises, is much more than a set of orientations and modalities of objects; it is a *structured* system with aspects that the pattern variables themselves cannot exhaust. The primary issue in this respect concerns the functional problems that face a system of action and the structures and subsystems that exist to meet them.

Both orders of concepts are necessary to Parsons' theorisation of the social system, and hence we find repeated attempts to demonstrate their compatibility.[55] However, it is shown below that as Parsons presents it the relation between the two levels – pattern-variables and functional prerequisites – cannot be maintained on logical grounds. Parsons must assert the effectivity of both if he is to avoid a reduction of one or other system (the social to the cultural, or vice versa), but in doing so he produces a theoretically incoherent unity. There is no logical relation between the choices possible to the actor and the requirements of the social system as Parsons theorises it; to say that there is a necessary relation between the two effectively denies the original definition if the social system as a level of *organisation* of action elements, and reduces the organisational component to simple *conceptions* on the part of the actor. This is clearly a position more consistent with social phenomenology than the structural–functionalist theory of the social system.

There are many examples of similar problems in the chapters that follow, but at this stage we might draw an outline of the mode of reading and critique that such a thesis entails. The criticism of the pattern-variable/functional prerequisite relation does not involve a reference to any apparent 'real' state of affairs, for example, that the variable schema is not exhaustive enough (many critiques take this form), nor does it attempt to speculate on any underlying causes of their appearance as concepts (contradictory or otherwise), within Parsons' sphere of concern. The criticism, on the contrary, is restricted to the analysis of concepts in terms of their logical character, logical compatibility and logical coherence.

The mode of critique of discourse adopted here is one which attempts to investigate the properties of discourse in terms of its logical character. This specifically logical mode of interrogation clearly attempts to preclude the reading of discourse as the

realisation of epistemological or methodological protocols, doctrines or programmes and for this reason does not analyse
discourse in terms of some extra-discursive mechanism or
structure. The object of the readings which follow is the logical
character of the orders of concepts of Parsonian discourse. This
does not, however, preclude the analysis of Parsons' epistemological position. On the contrary, a chapter is devoted to a
separate consideration of this issue on exactly the same basis as
the analyses of the 'substantive' orders of concepts, in terms of
the logical character of its propositions *internally*. What the
critique does not do is conflate a critique of epistemology with a
critique of the substantive component of Parsonian theory.

   The chapters that follow attempt to read and criticise Parsonian theory on this specifically internal basis.

# 2 The Epistemology of 'Analytical Realism'

It will have been clear from Chapter 1 that the analysis of Parsons attempted here does not begin with the epistemological theses which Parsons has advanced and treat them as a 'foundation' from which his work flowers. We have seen that Bershady's reading of Parsons operates on precisely such a basis: the analysis attempts to relate and compare epistemological objectives with their realisation or non-realisation in Parsonian social theory. Against this, the analyses of action, the social system, the structural–functional theory of the economy and social change which are developed in the following chapters deny the determinant status of epistemology over discourse-in-general. These areas of theory are treated internal to themselves, not as substantive reflections of epistemological objectives; they are treated as *concepts* and not as products.

This position, however, need not be taken as a blanket opposition to the analysis of Parsons' epistemology. There are, indeed, several reasons why, on the contrary, such an analysis is quite pertinent. To begin with, the epistemology of 'analytical realism' and its definitions of 'theory', 'facts' and their relations constitute a discursive order in itself. Epistemology should be treated as a system of concepts in exactly the same sense as theory of, say, political power. In this sense, epistemology is equally 'substantive'. The opposition between 'epistemological' and 'substantive' maintained here is purely a means of guarding against the conflation of two discursive orders. From the point of view of discursive analysis, they constitute equivalent bodies of concepts and theories. Hence Parsons' epistemology warrants an investigation of this type.

Secondly, while I have maintained that no reduction between epistemological and 'substantive' elements of discourse is to be made, there *is* a sense in which some form of relation exists.

Epistemological arguments and concepts function in a text as forms of proof and demonstration, as expositional forms. A very clear example of this is the account of the 'action frame of reference'.[1] The general concepts of action supplied in *The Structure of Social Action* are preserved as 'analytical elements' – these are the actor, the end or goal of action, the situation of action, and the normative orientation of action. Here, the concepts of action are offered in the form of an epistemological relation between the empirical world and its 'analytical components'. While that epistemology does not actually determine such substantive concepts, it *does* provide the expositional form in which those concepts are problematised. The status of those forms must therefore be interrogated in order to demarcate rigorously concepts from the mode in which they are advanced.[2]

A final justification for an analysis of Parsons' epistemology acts as a supplement to the arguments advanced in chapter 1. There it was argued that to treat discourse as the realisation of epistemology is a mode of analysis that cannot be coherently maintained. In particular, it was argued that 'epistemology' itself must in the last analysis be an inconsistent form of theorisation. If it is incoherent in this sense then clearly it *cannot* be realised in the way in which it is presupposed. The example of Althusser's analysis of discourse demonstrated the paradox contained here. An epistemology which Althusser explicitly believes to be an incoherent and contradictory one – 'empiricism' – is nevertheless held to be responsible for 'ideological' discourse. Yet surely if it cannot be maintained as a theory-in-itself then it cannot be realised in that sense.

It follows that, in the case of the object of this thesis, i.e. Parsons' theories, if it can be shown that his epistemology is theoretically incoherent, then it can also be assumed that it cannot have the effects it is purported to have. If the epistemology of analytical realism involves fundamental contradictions then it cannot be held to be realised in his discourse.

These three above points provide the basis of the objectives of this present chapter. The epistemology of analytical realism will be outlined, compared with a number of prominent epistemologies, and then critically analysed. I will argue that such an epistemology may be more sophisticated and less openly problematic than many other, more popular, theses, but nevertheless still involves significant points of inadequacy.

## 2.1  Analytical Realism: Anti-Empiricism and Anti-Fictionalism

Parsons has not only provided a body of theory which, according to most of his critics, is distinctively 'abstract', but he has also elaborated a conception of knowledge and its evolution which expressly defends such a strategy in general. It is an epistemology which opposes 'empiricism' and the epistemology of the 'ideal-type', and which is, in sociological terms at least, conceptually elaborate.

There are a number of basic principles which are distinctive to Parsons' epistemology, but above all it is his peculiar definition of 'theory' and the relation between theories and concepts on the one hand, and the empirical world or 'facts' on the other, which are the main characteristics of his position.

Theories are not to be seen as 'mirror reflections' of reality, a one-to-one relation between concepts and reality. This thesis is referred to as 'the fallacy of misplaced concreteness', a phrase which Parsons adopted from Whitehead.[3] Nor are theories and concepts 'fictions', simplifications or one-sided accentuations of reality as presupposed in the formulation of the 'ideal-type'. Parsons does not accept the empiricism of the former thesis nor does he accept the inevitable arbitrariness of the epistemology of the ideal-type.

The central component of his epistemology is the conception of the knowledge process as one of abstraction. There are in this case two points of reference in the knowledge process, the 'analytical' and the 'realist', which together form the epistemological thesis labelled as 'analytical realism'. It is a thesis which entails a double critique, that of fictionalism and empiricism. For example, on the former, Parsons says:

> As opposed to the fiction view, it is maintained that at least some of the general concepts of science are not fictional but adequately 'grasp' aspects of the objective external world. This is true of the concepts here called analytical elements. Hence the position here taken is, in an epistemological sense, realistic. (*SSA*, p. 730)

Yet he also avoids an acceptance of realism *per se*. Again, realism or empiricism entail an objectionable restriction on knowledge purely within the grounds of the concrete. Hence the element of realism is qualified by the term 'analytical'. In short, analytical realism is an epistemology which apparently overcomes the shortcomings of both extremes of fictionalism and empiricism while maintaining the advantages of both.

Now in order to advance such a thesis, it is necessary for Parsons to show how the knowledge process involves a 'functional' relation between concepts and reality. In particular, he needs to show that to separate the realms of theory and reality in the traditional sense is itself illegitimate, and that the world of 'facts' so-called is itself dependent on the existence of theoretical systems. Hence his initial definition of a 'fact' already spaces itself from the orthodox empiricist notion.

Facts, according to analytical realism, are not in themselves concrete phenomena. Against the classical formulation, he proposes that facts are not entities of experience but are themselves determined by, and dependent upon, a 'conceptual' scheme

> It is fundamental that there is no empirical knowledge which is not in some sense and to some degree conceptually formed. All talk of 'pure sense data', 'raw experience' or the unformed stream of consciousness is not descriptive of actual experience, but is a matter of methodological abstration. . . . In other words . . . all empirical observation is in terms of a conceptual scheme. (*SSA*, p. 28)

A fact is not the phenomenon itself but a statement about a phenomenon; hence the distinction between 'a fact, which is a *proposition about* phenomena, and the phenomena themselves, which are concrete, really existent entities' (*SSA*, p. 41, Parsons' emphasis). This definition clearly states: (a) that phenomena are, as opposed to the fictionalist conception, the basic source of knowledge, but that (b) the mode in which phenomena enter into science, as opposed to the empiricist view point, is not one of mirror reflection (reality/concepts) but of a process of abstraction according to a conceptual scheme. Bershady has cogently and accurately summarised the basic principles of the epistemology of analytical realism as follows:

(1) Phenomena are the data of science, but
(2) phenomena are themselves governed and grounded in a

set of universal categories and elements which analysis
must produce;

(3)  that these universal categories do not consequently become ficticious – they may not be observed but they are no
less real and are actually constitutive of the phenomena,
they are its parts and relations;

(4)  that these parts and relations which constitute the
phenomena together form a system of elements or that
system is at least the objective of scientific work.

(Bershady, op. cit., p. 40)

This is precisely the epistemological reasoning behind Parsons' exposition of the 'action frame of reference' (hereafter
referred to as AFR). Independent of the particular concepts of
this frame of reference (actor, end, situation and normative
orientation), the fact that it is advanced explicitly as a frame of
reference reflects Parsons' own peculiar formulation of the
mode in which theoretical systems operate and progress. The
AFR is precisely the form of conceptual scheme which constitutes the 'facts' of action; it is a system of elements seen to be
abstracted from concrete action and of which action is made up.
The system makes possible the very analysis of action from which
it is abstracted. This is the mode of operation referred to as the
'functional' relation between concepts and reality.

Note that Parsons refers to the conceptual scheme in certain
cases as a *system*. The AFR, for example, is a system of theoretical
elements in the sense that its components bear mutual logical
relations to each other. In other words, the propositions which
constitute a body of theory should be such that any substantive
change in an important proposition will have logical consequences for the statement of other propositions. A system of theory
has a *logically determinate structure*. This is the basis of Parsons'
reference to 'logically closed' and 'empirically closed' bodies of
theory. All theory tends, according to the principle of scientific
evolution, to form logically closed systems of propositions. This
means that they will increasingly involve propositions which are
mutually and logically connected, and decreasingly rely on
'unstated assumptions' which bear no logical connection to other
propositions of the theory.

For this reason, the development toward logically closed
systems of theory (of which the AFR is seen to be an example), is

regarded as an approvable if not inevitable state of affairs. This is a very different thing from an empirically closed system. This is precisely a case of 'empiricism' and its shortcomings. Here one, and only one, theoretical system is held to provide the explanation of a given object or event, i.e. a one-to-one relation between concepts and the empirical world. Such a system, reflecting 'the fallacy of misplaced concreteness', allows only those concepts which are observable or experiencable, thus restricting the growth of scientific knowledge.

These arguments show clearly that for Parsons scientific 'theory' and general concepts constitute an *independent* variable in the development of science. He explicitly opposes the view (so common in sociology), that the process of discovery of scientific facts is one essentially independent of theory. Facts are governed by conceptual schemes and in that sense cannot be seen to be constitutive of scientific knowledge. While he is not hostile to empirical verification of theory, he does not allow this to become a case of empiricism

> It goes without saying that a theory to be sound must fit the facts, but it does not follow that the facts alone, discovered independent of theory, determine what the theory is to be, nor that theory is not a factor determining what facts will be discovered, what is to be the direction of interest of scientific investigation. (*SSA*, p. 6)

Facts are situated in relation to theory in two ways. First, the very process of factual knowledge is itself governed by the theoretical systems which are its 'searchlight'.[4] Secondly, in so far as facts may be discovered which are not consonant with the theoretical system, it is only those facts which make important *theoretical* changes (i.e. which change a theoretical proposition) which become significant events in the development of a science.

It is clear then that the theoretical components of knowledge, in Parsons' epistemology, are assigned a dominant role in scientific development. While these components are not the exclusive sources of knowledge, they do at least permeate *every* level of the process. However, assuming this to be the case, then how does Parsons actually conceptualise the dominance of theory?

One thing is clear from all of Parsons' writings on the issue: the relation between theoretical systems and the empirical components of science is a hierarchical one. It has already been pointed out that he makes a distinction between the concrete realm of phenomena and the conceptual scheme or frame of reference. The latter are constitutive of the fact and are the core of knowledge systems. It should also be noted that he proposes a distinction *within* the frame of reference between 'descriptive frames of reference' and 'analytical elements'.

Descriptive frames of reference are defined as 'modes of general relations of the facts implicit in the descriptive terms employed' (*SSA*, p. 28). The prime example of such a schema is seen to be the space–time framework of classical mechanics, a frame of reference which defines the objects which are pertinent to its sphere, the facts relevant to the theory itself. A further example is the supply and demand framework of orthodox economic theory. For a phenomenon to become a fact for economic theory, it must be possible to locate it in terms of supply and demand. It must be capable of interpretation according to the notion of qualifying as either a good or service for which there is demand and which is also scarce relative to the demand for it. The descriptive frame of reference is, as such, the 'indispensable preliminary to explanation'.

Descriptive frames of reference are thus presupposed in the second form of conceptual scheme: the 'analytical elements'. Once the phenomena relevant to the theory have been delineated, it is then possible to assign 'values' to these general properties, to break down the concrete phenomenon into its attributes and to form combinations of those attributes. Once again physics provides a good example. The concepts of mass, velocity and so on, are held to be the analytical elements of physical science which operate on the phenomena originally demarcated by the space–time framework.

The analytical elements do not themselves necessarily correspond to concrete phenomena, nor even do they have to constitute hypothetical phenomena. Yet this does not reduce their status to 'ideal-type' elements or mere fictions. They represent an indispensable step in scientific theorisation and, ultimately, explanation. They are abstractions but, as Parsons insists, are no less 'real' for it.

It is in terms of the exposition of the action frame of reference that, of course, these definitions and distinctions are most extensively spelt out. Parsons' argument is as follows.

From the multiplicity of events (both physical and human) which characterise human behaviour, it is possible to decipher one realm of phenomena which are relevant to the theory of action. In other words, it is possible to identify, on the basis of the descriptive frame of reference of the theory of action, certain events which constitute relevant phenomena for action analysis (and, conversely, phenomena not pertinent to other frames of reference). These are the 'concrete' phenomena of action and primarily take the form of 'unit acts'.[5] Now, while the unit act is the ultimate level of concrete analysis – it cannot be further reduced without losing its identification as a subsystem of action – it is still, as it were, only an elementary definition from an explanatory point of view. Concretely-described phenomena from a theoretical point of view are still complex objects. The unit act can itself be broken down into a number of concrete *analytical* elements which together form the concrete unit act. These are the well-known elements of actor, end situation and normative orientation. These become the analytically (as opposed to concretely) separate elements which are the condition for the theoretical (as opposed to the purely descriptive) investigation of action. They are the abstracted elements of a concretely existing realm of phenomena.

It is on the basis of the descriptive frame of reference and the analytical elements and their combinations that the substantive theorisation of science can emerge. Considerations of explanation and the construction of causal relations and laws are held to be possible only within the bounds of the frame of reference. While the frame of reference is not in itself equivalent to the substantive theory of a science, it does contain all of the elements and descriptions necessary for the specifications of the object of such theory.

Theory is situated in terms of a relation between the analytical and empirical. Theory is defined as 'a body of logically interrelated "general concepts" of empirical reference' (*SSA*, p. 6). Substantive theory is seen to exist as a set of related propositions referring to concrete phenomena defined in the conceptual scheme. As such, it is a product of empirical investigation on the one hand, and the generalised frame of reference on the other. The latter is, of course, the precondition of *both* levels.

It is in this sense that Parsons refers to the primacy of the 'theoretical system' over empirical generalisation. It is, above all, the frame of reference of a body of knowledge, the general conceptual scheme, which is pertinent in this respect. It is a naive reading of Parsons that labels his work 'abstract' and devoid of empirical content. Ignoring the wide range of quite 'substantive' material that he has presented,[6] it is his formulation of the *relation* between the two realms which does most damage to such categorisation. Parsons does not deny the empirical realm – he merely situates that realm within an overall conception of knowledge and, in particular, the role of the frame of reference.

This point is formulated more explicitly in his later epistemological writings, especially in the paper 'Introduction to Culture and Social Systems'.[7] Parsons here presents the notion of the 'cybernetic hierarchy' of knowledge.[8] Cognitive systems are seen to be organised according to hierarchical relations of 'information' and 'energy'. The informational component of the knowledge process is the primary and dominant sphere of cognition.

The lowest order elements of the hierarchy (components which are high-energy but low-information subsystems) are simple empirical statements or facts. Second order components consist of 'solutions' to empirical problems, organised statements of fact which have been subjected to some form of processing and which are related to theory itself. The third level in the cybernetic hierarchy of cognitive systems is the structure of theory itself, the 'substantive' theory which involves the integration of empirical knowledge according to logical criteria.

The highest order of the hierarchy is the realm of theory involving the general frame of reference. The frame of reference supplies the fundamentals of meaning and information to the cognitive system as a whole. It dominates not only the empirical process but the general structure of theory

> theory itself is relative to the level of the frame of reference that is not empirically provable, but is necessary in order to give meaning to problems and to theory itself ... the frame of reference controls the significance of the system of theory. (*TS*, p. 965)

Parsons adds, interestingly, that it is the first two levels of the hierarchy (low-information, high-energy) to which the 'empiricists' pay too exclusive attention. Against this he situates the frame of reference and not the empirical world as dominant in the cognitive process. Analytical realism in this sense is quite clearly distinct from what is generally accepted as 'empiricism' and indeed from other major epistemologies defended from within sociology.

Perhaps at this stage it might be beneficial to spell out more clearly the extent to which analytical realism is actually distinct from most other sociological epistemologies and methodologies. I do not intend at this point to provide a universal outline of methodology, but to discuss a number of positions which are very influential in this area. In any case, to a certain extent other important epistemologies and methodologies have already been discussed.[9]

I will take up three conceptions of knowledge which have been circulating amongst sociological attempts to define the cognitive process. These may be referred to as (a) the 'irrationalist' or anti-logical conception, (b) the inductivist notion of the fact–theory relation, and (c) the conception of models or ideal-types. The first two, in particular, are opposed to Parsonian theory.

What has been referred to as the 'irrationalist' conception of knowledge has been put forward in certain theses presented by C. W. Mills and Dahrendorf. It is above all against the level of abstraction of Parsonian theory that such theses are directed, but this is by no means the only conception of theory which they oppose. Dahrendorf, for example, not only directs violent attacks on abstract forms of theorisation – as 'Utopian', in the methodological and substantive sense – but also takes a stand against more moderate conceptual systems such as Merton's 'theories of the middle range'.

Above all, the irrationalist argument asserts the ubiquity and essentiality of experience as opposed to theoretical processes. It is not only systems such as Parsons' theory of the social system which are castigated, but *any* position which postulates some form of separation between theory and 'research'. Dahrendorf accuses Merton of a 'diagnostic error' in his programme for sociological activity in maintaining some specific realm of existence for theory. He argues 'There is no theory that can be divorced from empirical research.'[10] Theory cannot be separate from the concrete and particular puzzlement over experience.

According to Dahrendorf, the order of science is purely experiential, and theoretical abstraction (forms of conceptualisation independent of empirical events) is viewed as more consistent with metaphysics and speculation.

A fundamentally-similar approach has already been introduced: C. W. Mills' 'translations' of Parsonian theory into 'English'. For Mills it is possible to exclude all forms of theoretical abstraction from any given position without forfeiting anything that is 'meaningful'. Any attempt to maintain a body of concepts on logical or systematic grounds, or in a form which does not retain a bond to specific empirical problems, can only end up in 'Fetishism of the Concept'.[11]

Thus, it is apparently possible to distinguish in Parsons' text *The Social System* between 'statements about something' on the one hand, and 'definitions of words and of their wordy relations' on the other.[12] In other words, the only meaningful statements are those which directly refer to an empirical phenomenon. The implication is clear: non-empirical statements *cannot* be considered meaningful.

But like Dahrendorf, Mills is not content with denying only the pertinence of abstract systems of concepts. Just as the former opposes both Utopias and middle-range theories, Mills attacks both 'grand theory' and what he calls 'abstracted empiricism'. Whereas grand theory is characterised by fetishism of the concept, abstracted empiricism is guilty of 'methodological inhibition'.

Abstracted empiricism is the polar opposite of grand theory. It is a process of sociological knowledge dominated by a concern for methodological rigour, statistical analysis and, consequently, by a 'cautious' approach to the understanding of social problems. Whereas grand theory involves the isolation of theory from the realities of social life, abstracted empiricism isolates method from real concerns. Yet there is an apparent parallel between them: both are obstacles to a true sociological knowledge.

> Were there nothing else but these two, standing supreme and alongside each other, our condition would indeed be a sad one: as practices, they may be understood as insuring that we do not learn too much about man and society – the first by formal and cloudy obscurantics, the second by formal and empty ingenuity. (ibid., p. 86)

This is clearly the most vulgar form of empiricism. Any form of cognitive rigour (theoretical or methodological) is discounted in favour of the free-play of inspiration and 'scholarship'. The shortcomings here are obvious.

To begin with, let us take the notion that the only meaningful statements of a discourse are those which are directly translatable into empirically grounded objects, i.e. statements about a particular phenomena. This argument goes back to the subjective idealism of Hume and Berkeley, and which ultimately leads to epistemological scepticism.[13]

More specifically, the notion that statements which do not comply with, in Kolokowski's terms, 'the rule of phenomenalism',[14] cannot be considered scientifically meaningful, entails rather disastrous consequences for the sciences in general. This limiting of meaningful statements would immediately preclude from knowledge such concepts as electrons, atoms, gravitational fields, electromagnetic fields, etc. Even positivists have recognised this as a real problem and have attempted to overcome the obvious shortcomings of such a classification.[15]

It would, however, credit the arguments of Mills *et al.* with more rigour than they deserve to push this connection with sensationalist philosophy too far. In fact, they have not seriously elaborated the problems of meaningful–meaningless statements on anything approaching the scale of philosophy, nor even openly attempted to explain the origins or conditions of knowledge. They choose, rather, to rely upon a spurious and arbitrary notion of the agent of the knowledge process as a moral, sensitive and intuitive human *actor*. Indeed, what both Mills and Dahrendorf postulate as the basis of a true knowledge of society is little removed from the ethnomethodological programme for the social–psychological determinants of knowledge.[16] In both cases we find the dual opposition to theoretical abstraction and to the limits imposed by methodological protocols.

Once both forms of control of the knowledge process (theoretical, methodological) are denied, a free run is given to the 'moral' responsibilities of the investigator. For Mills this is the 'intellectual craftsman', an actor committed to moral correctness and political responsibility. This clearly opens the door to a relativist conception of science. Forms of social knowledge are to be dependent on the social characteristics of the investigator. In short, sociology is the playground for intellectual anarchy.

One final point. For Mills and Dahrendorf to propose such a thesis, they need to be able to distinguish *between* 'Utopias' and 'verbiage' on the one hand, and actual meaningful knowledge on the other. Now at this point a peculiar problem emerges. The paradox is that the content of their epistemology backfires on its objective. The notion that abstract conceptualisation must be excluded in all cases precludes the possibility of ever *demonstrating* such a thesis. They pose the question of 'knowledge' yet rule out conceptualisation which can define it. The conceptual conditions required to distinguish between knowledge and mere abstraction are actually precluded by the definitions of what are meaningful and meaningless statements. Are we then to accept this conception of knowledge on purely dogmatic grounds?

Merton's outline of the conditions of sociological knowledge are altogether more serious. While he emphasises the decisive importance of empirical verifiability and concrete conceptualisation, he does not deny the pertinence of theoretical concepts *per se*. He also lays great stress on methodological considerations.

It is in terms of the relation between theory and empirical data derived from methodologically disciplined research, that Merton proposes the famous notion of 'theories of the middle-range'. These lie mid-way between the 'total conceptual schemes' of the Parsonian type and the particularistic compilation of empirical facts. Consequently, they avoid the problems of the exclusive reliance on one or the other.

> Middle-range theory is principally used in sociology to guide empirical enquiry. It is intermediate to general theories of social systems which are too remote from particular classes of social behaviour, organization and change to account for what is observed, and to those detailed orderly descriptions of particulars that are not generalized at all. Middle-range theory involves abstractions of course, but they are close enough to observed data to be incorporated in propositions that permit empirical testing.[17]

Merton sees empirical generalisation, isolated propositions summarising observed uniformities of relations between two or more variables, as only the 'raw material' of science. As yet they only constitute *ad hoc* unrelated observations. For them to be scientifically significant they must have a place within a set of interrelated propositions. This is only attained when empirical inquiry is organised such that when empirical uniformities have been located, they can be shown to have direct consequences for a 'theoretical system'.

It is important not to be misled by this term 'theoretical system', however. Merton defines 'theory' in a very different way from, for example, Parsons. The 'systemic' character of a body of theory does *not* refer to logical connections as such, but to a relation between concepts and the empirical world. Herein lies the opposition to 'master conceptual schemes' and the subsequent denial of Parsons' conception of the pertinent and necessary steps of scientific knowledge

> To concentrate solely on the master conceptual scheme for deriving all sociological theory is to run the risk of producing twentieth-century equivalents of the large philosophical systems of the past, with all their suggestiveness, all their architectonic splendour and all their scientific sterility.[18]

These characteristics are the consequence of the separation of theory from specific empirical phenomena. General theory and general concepts (forms which are not mirror reflections of empirically existing phenomena) can only lead to speculation. If, for Merton, the concepts and theories of knowledge are not empirical statements in themselves, they most certainly are propositions/hypotheses *about* empirical phenomena. Merton thus advocates the organisation of theory according to specific types of phenomena. This is defended by an interpretation of the histories of a number of sciences which apparently show that scientific progress follows from theories of the middle-range. Sociology should model itself on this course: 'Sociology will advance in the degree that the major concern is with developing theories adequate to limited ranges of phenomena and it will be hampered if attention is centred on theory in the large' (ibid., p. 166).

Scientific theory is defined as a system of 'clear verifiable statements of relationships between specified variables' (ibid., p. 166). *All* theories must be verifiable and be subject to empirical confirmation. Merton provides the philosophical support of Francis Bacon and J. S. Mill amongst others to emphasise the strategic importance of 'a general series of empirically confirmed intermediate theories'.[19]

It is interesting that such a position coincides almost exactly with Parsons' definition of empiricism, i.e. 'the identification of the meanings of the concrete specific propositions of a given science, theoretical or empirical, with the scientifically knowable totality of the external reality to which they refer' (*SSA*, p. 23).

Parsons follows this definition with the statement that 'In other words, they deny the legitimacy of theoretical abstraction'. On this point Merton would appear to agree with Parsons. Theory, or rather scientifically legitimate theory, refers not to a level of abstraction from empirical phenomena but, according to Merton, to a set of symbolic expressions of relationships *between* empirically verifiable variables: 'Middle-range theories consist of limited sets of assumptions from which scientific hypotheses are logically derived and confirmed by investigation' (op. cit., p. 68). While the concepts of a theory need not be directly induced from empirical phenomena, they must at least at all times refer specifically to them.

It would, however, be stretching it too far to assume that what Merton provides is an elaborate epistemological or philosophical position. For example, he fails to define precisely the status of 'assumptions', hypotheses or verifiability – all of which are central to theories of the middle-range. Nor does he develop the problem of the distinction between meaningful and meaningless statements which he intimates and which for many positivists is a crucial question. Merton's thesis is more pragmatic than epistemologically informed and defended.

There are at least two points at which his argument is problematic, the first concerning his conception of the 'history of theory', the second the issue of causal explanation.

The defence of theories of the middle-range relies heavily on an additional thesis on the history of theory in scientific progress. It has already been noted that Merton equates 'general conceptual schemes', which are abstract and not subject to direct translation into empirical statements, with the philosophical systems of classical philosophy. This level is doomed to scientific sterility despite its wordy splendour. The implication is clear: forms of theory which do not refer to specific empirical phenomena are *philosophical*. The history of the sciences is summoned as evidence that such forms belong to the pre-scientific stage. For example, Merton cites physics and chemistry to show that they are modelled on empirical and theoretical lines: 'Note how seldom they deal with "physical theory" or with "chemical theory" and how typically they deal with the theory of *specific types* of phenomena'.[20]

It is argued that *progress* in the sciences consists of the formulation of theories of the middle-range specific to certain types of phenomena, and not to theoretical issues in themselves. Scientific advance is characterised by the replacement of 'total systems' of theory by more adequate sets of limited theories.

However, Merton's use of the history of science is, to say the least, opportune. Note that we are referred to physics and not metaphysics, chemistry not alchemy, medical science and not black magic – that is *already constituted* bodies of knowledge. The problem of that constitution itself is not posed. Of course, there is a great deal of controversy surrounding the definition of the scientific procedure, from Popper's notion of the 'logic of scientific discovery' to Kuhn's conception of 'paradigm shifts',[21] and this is not the place to enter into the discussion. However, Merton merely suppresses the problem of the *constitution* of the sciences and refers us immediately to the advanced stages of physics and chemistry, holding these as models for progress in sociology. Thus, experimentation is seen as the central activity of scientific investigation. Yet, as Koyré has shown, experimentation and reference to 'specific phenomena' were also characteristic of the pre-scientific disciplines.[22] The questions remains: what distinguishes physics from metaphysics, chemistry from alchemy etc.? What are the conditions which allowed the break between these types of 'knowledge'? On these issues Merton is conveniently quiet.

The second epistemological problem in Merton's programme concerns the question of causal explanation. This is contained in his definition of 'theory' as symbolic expressions of relationships between empirically verifiable variables. Abstract systems of theory are seen to fall down on precisely this issue – they speculate rather than inform us of cause–effect relationships.

Merton's outline of 'functional analysis' makes this most apparent. His proposals for functionalist investigation situate empirically observable relations at the very centre of the scheme: 'the concept of function involves the standpoint of the observer', and functions are defined as 'observable objective consequences'.[23] Functionalism, in this sense, is simply reduced to the analysis of the observed effects of event or object A on event or object B. A cause is a relationship derived as a result of repeated empirical examination of one event followed by another.

This stems from the classical empiricist conception of cause and effect summed up in Hume's definition. Hume defined a cause 'to be an object followed by another, and where all the objects similar to the first are followed by objects similar to the second.[24] In this sense 'functional analysis' is not really distinct from the majority of other forms of empirical investigation, cause apparently being established in terms of empirical observation. For Merton, explanatory sociology cannot establish cause–effect relationships on conceptual grounds alone or even primarily; such relationships must be based on empirically derived and empirically verifiable relations.

In assessing such proposals we are again faced with the overall pragmatism of Merton's arguments and defences. Nevertheless we can push his thesis on causality to its logical extreme and see if the empirical criteria of causality can be maintained. It is perhaps J. S. Mill who has most extensively presented the logic of causal explanation in this sense in his formulation of the 'method of science'.

Mill attempts to provide an outline of the scientific method in terms of 'synthetic propositions' – strictly empirically determined statements. For Mill, concepts are simply empirical categories, and causal relationships cannot be determined outside of experience. This clearly requires certain assumptions concerning the nature of the empirical world, and Mill proposed the notion of the 'Universal law of Nature' to support his epistemology. It is possible to determine causal relationships from purely empirical techniques precisely because these relationships are already present and apparent in nature itself.

> The course of nature in general is constant, because the course
> of each of the various phenomena that compose it is so. A
> certain fact invariably occurs whenever certain circumstances
> are present, and does not occur when they are absent; the like
> is true of another fact; and so on. From these separated
> threads of connection between parts of the great whole which

we term nature a general tissue of connection unavoidably weaves itself, by which the whole is held together. (*A System of Logic*, p. 206)

Mill also provided a number of 'methods of empirical inquiry' as a means by which this conception of nature can effect itself, via observation, into causal propositions.

It is on the basis of the general conception of nature as 'regular' that his claims to supply strictly empiricist grounds for causal explanation rest. However, it is at precisely this point that his thesis, as the Willers have shown,[25] most clearly breaks down. Apart from the technical problems of Mill's canons of inquiry, the Willers have shown that the universal law of nature itself can only be 'demonstrated' in circular fashion. In other words, the basis of the inductive process is maintained by reference to induction itself. Induction is proved by induction.

The Willers have also pointed out that if nature is indeed to be seen as a 'web of interconnected causes' – if there are regular and recurrent sequential relations between phenomena – then Mill's own canons of empirical inquiry cannot establish them as laws. If any effect has multiple causes, it is not possible to be certain in any particular situation that the cause isolated was the only significant one. In other words, there is a contradiction between the empirical referent – the world as a web of inter-related causes – and the attempt to establish rigorous causal relationships.

It is not clear where Merton stands in relation to these issues. Isajiw, for example, argues that Merton's conception of causality is similar to the classical empiricist conception (which he terms 'productive causality'[26]), i.e. the linear effect of one event or object on another. If this is indeed the case (as Merton's functional paradigm, albeit in an arbitrary fashion, intimates), then Merton must adopt some notion of nature as a regular and ordered field of existence. If not, then he must abandon the very possibility of a rigorous specification of causal relations, as seems to be the case in the notion of 'probability' relationships proposed by certain methodologists. Merton's programme for a 'codified' method of functional analysis, far from clarifying the problems of explanatory sociology, merely makes explanation in any rigorous sense impossible.

Before moving on to a more extensive analysis of Parsons'
epistemology there remains one other methodological thesis
which has attracted a good deal of attention with which we must
deal. While the proposals of Mills, Dahrendorf and Merton are
concerned with differing ways in which to reflect empirical
reality, this last position *does* admit the significance of abstraction. It is to be found in Max Weber's concept of the 'ideal-type'.

Weber does indeed accept the possibility of an abstract
sociological knowledge in the sense that ideal-type constructions
are seen not as one-to-one reflections of objective reality, but
'one-sided accentuations' or abstractions from it. While this may
not necessarily stem from an epistemological anti-empiricism[27]
(it is imposed more because of the subjective 'direction of
interest' of the investigator), it at least avoids the obvious traps of
simple empiricism.

However, Parsons has himself provided a good critique of the
ideal-type. The central critique of Weber's methodology concerns the type of abstraction seen to be involved in the knowledge
process and the particular mode in which Weber presents the
relation between the concepts and categories of scientific theory
and the reality from which it abstracts its concepts. If ideal-type
formulation is to be the ultimate objective of analysis then
Parsons concludes it will result only in a 'fictional' conception of
theory.

The ideal-type is explicitly presented as a 'Utopia', not a
hypothesis about concrete reality, not a description of reality,
nor an average, but a 'useful fiction'. Types are fictions,
one-sided accentuations of reality, and if this is all that concepts
aspire to, then, Parsons argues, we can never achieve an objective
knowledge. Empirically, such a mode of analysis is seen to lead to
or allow bias and distortion; analytically, it requires a separate
general concept for every possible combination of relations
between the values of the relevant elements present in any
particular case.

As a result, the ideal-type is seen to prevent the construction of
general concepts and theories and to lead to a 'mosaic' theory of
history.[28] The knowledge of history and society is reduced to the
processs of shuffling the ideal-types. A strictly *causal* knowledge
is precluded from within ideal-type conceptualisation. Parsons
locates the barrier to causal explanation (in his sense) precisely in
the fictional character of the ideal-types. They are not descrip-

tions of what actually happens, nor are they causal explanations – they are conceptual utopias.

What Parsons refers to, although he did not logically develop the point, is the total *arbitrariness* of the epistemology of ideal-types. As useful fictions there is essentially little control of the apparent relation between concepts and reality. This relation is not to be governed by questions of validity but only by the (pragmatic) extent to which reality deviates from the type. They are types and as such cannot be theoretically evaluated. In this respect the ideal-type reproduces the pragmatism of the epistemology of models.[29] In both cases conceptual work is reduced the assessment of similarity/dissimilarity between the model (or type) and reality. In both cases, the conditions on which one model or type is to be replaced by another lie in arbitrary decisions of the investigator (as observer or actor).

Parsons argues that, in order to overcome the dead-end arbitrariness of the ideal-type, it is necessary to admit the existence of forms of conceptualisation of a greater level of generality than type formulation. In other words, he *does* accept this process has validity as a first step in the knowledge process. We will not question this point at the moment. What he has provided is a critique of the ideal-type, classifying it as a more or less elaborate fiction, and hence an arbitrary epistemological thesis. Analytical realism is both disticnct from, and critical of, the epistemology of ideal-types.

Having outlined Parsons' epistemology and discussed several other major methodological positions, we can now take the investigation a step further. From what has been established so far it is clear that analytical realism goes a great deal further than the more widespread methodologies in asserting and defending the significance of theory to scientific development. It is now necessary to approach seriously this thesis and question the mode in which it conceptualises the relation between concepts and reality. I will argue that Parsons does not in the final analysis provide a theoretically-coherent epistemology, and that analytical realism contains a number of major flaws.

The abstractive relation proposed by Parsons clearly involves two reference points. On the one hand are the concepts and theories which abstract from reality, on the other hand that reality itself. I shall treat both sides of the process in turn.

## 2.2  The Theoretical Component of Analytical Realism

That Parsons refers to the theoretical framework as primary in the knowledge process is a thesis that must be taken in the strict sense. This level dominates the process by means of a hierarchy of control, for it both theorises and makes possible the objects of knowledge. However, contained in the definition and apparent operation of 'theory' is a *double* process. Theory refers not only to logically interrelated concepts but to an *activity*: that activity is a *human* process.

The hierarchy of control stipulates that the theoretical framework is not merely a component of knowledge but is the *subject* of the cognitive process. The theoretical framework is conceived as both a 'human' element *and* a level which is 'logical'. It is comprised not merely of concepts but also of *categories*. In order for these categories actually to determine the objects of knowledge, it is necessary for Parsons to turn to the operation of human subjectivity.

Herein lies the explanation for the alleged parallel between the role of the cultural system *vis-à-vis* the social and personality systems, and the role of the theoretical framework in relation to the empirical levels of knowledge. The analytical framework provides the 'information' component of knowledge in the classical *action* sense as the functioning of human subjectivity, a constitutive human subject. Parsons, indeed, has never denied this point, and Bershady has quite emphatically spelt out this humanist element in his epistemology.[30]

Theory as such becomes both a logical and a human operation, and when Parsons opposes the empiricists we can now see that it is not simply a preference for theory over experience, but one for a certain conception of the human subject and his functioning as an epistemological subject. It is a thesis of the 'thinking' human actor as opposed to the experiencing subject. In other words, the critique of empiricism is also a debate about *types of subjectivity* and how they determine knowledge.

Parsons thus establishes a direct link between knowledge and *action*. This is apparent in his *Structure of Social Action*, where he equates the debate about epistemological empiricism with that on 'positivistic' theories of action. In both cases similar errors are seen to appear.

This leads to a very different conclusion from that drawn by

Bershady. It will be recalled that the basic assumption of Bershady's reading of Parsons is that the theories of action etc. can be viewed in terms of an epistemological project, with the obvious interpretation being that the former are governed by epistemological protocols. I would argue almost the reverse – that in fact the epistemology of analytical realism is itself greatly determined by the theory of action. Thus, Parsons analyses knowledge processes in terms of information–energy relationships in the same way in which action processes are conceived. It is not a mere metaphor: human subjectivity plays an essential role in the operation of cognition in his epistemology.

So, the 'analytical' function in knowledge involves problems of human subjectivity and action. Theoretical work is, to a great extent, a similar operation to the subjective components of human action. This raises two issues. First, the extent to which analytical realism is, as is claimed, similar in significant respects to Kantian epistemology; and secondly, the problems that it raises with respect to epistemological relativism.

Bershady, and indeed Parsons himself,[31] have argued that analytical realism, in its repudiation of empiricism, is parallel with Kantian epistemology in its attack on subjective idealism. It is argued that the analytical process of Parsonian epistemology can be equated with Kant's conception of the transcendental conditions of all knowledge. In particular, an equivalence is maintained between Parsons' 'analytical elements' and the 'universal categories' of Kantian transcendentalism.[32] Both formulations are held to conceptualise knowledge according to an *a priori* determination.

However, there is a very great difference between the *a priorism* of Kant and the notion of analytical abstraction. Against all intuitionist or experientalist theories of knowledge Kant argues for the ultimate subjectivisation of knowledge. Recognising the inevitable scepticism of the epistemologies of Hume and Berkeley, Kant proposes that knowledge is the determination of a *transcendental* system. For objective validity to be possible, it must be the product of *a priori* cognition. This is posed in terms of the '*a priori* categories of Understanding', concepts which determine all possible forms of knowledge.

The concept of 'cause' is an example. The statement 'when the Sun shines on the stone, it grows warm' is a judgement of perception, and only subjectively valid. But if one says 'the Sun warms the stone', one adds to the perception a pure concept of the understanding, the cause: 'which connects with the concept of sunshine that of heat as a necessary consequence, and the synthetical judgement becomes of necessity universally valid, viz. objective' (*Prolegomena*, p. 59)

What is decisive of such concepts is their transcendental character: 'The concepts . . . which contain *a priori* conditions of all synthetical and necessary judgements, accordingly constitute a transcendental system' (ibid., p. 64). The transcendental system ascribes to subjective intuition its objective validity. The highest legislation in nature is seen to lie in ourselves, i.e. in our understanding. But for this knowledge to be objective, i.e. autonomous of intuition, it must be defined as the determination of a realm which is itself transcendental, being itself *beyond determination*.

The categories of the understanding ascribe laws *to* nature – they do not derive laws *from* nature. Objectivity is the determination of a universal consciousness, a transcendental intersubjectivity. It is truly constitutive of all knowledge but is itself beyond naturalistic determination and hence beyond naturalistic explanation, i.e. it is indeterminate in principle. The cornerstone of Kantian epistemology is precisely the *irreducibility of consciousness*.

However, Parsons' account of the analytical elements and their role in the knowledge process cannot possibly be said to maintain similarly the postulate of the transcendental character of human consciousness. As has already been shown, a central assumption of his *Structure of Social Action* is the immanent tendency for theoretical systems to develop, or more precisely to evolve. The functional relation between the categories of the frame of reference and phenomena is seen to produce a natural tendency toward scientific progression. In this progression not only the substantive theories and data *but the categories themselves* are transformed. For example, various authors and schools of thought are deemed to contribute new categories (analytical elements) essential to the theory of action.

Thus, the categories of the action frame of reference are seen to be the products of an evolutionary process, and the various attempts at a theory of action only phases of an overall tendency which determines the course of theoretical elements. Therefore, the elements are *products*, subject to determination by a process external to them (scientific evolution).

It is this conception that is most at variance with Kantian epistemology. While Kant does not preclude some conception of scientific development this cannot be seen to take the form of a process of development of the categories themselves. This follows from Kant's definition of the epistemological subject.

In order to save knowledge from the ravages of psychological or physiological relativism, Kant distinguishes between the natural human body (man as appearance) on the one hand, and the realm of consciousness on the other. The former is subject to natural determination and hence explanation, whereas the latter, on the contrary, is a realm beyond naturalistic explanation, one excluded from the realm of objects of scientific knowledge. Consciousness or 'Reason' provides the conditions of existence of all possible knowledge but is itself a realm of 'freedom'. While the sphere of consciousness may be studied by means of an ethics (one governed not by reason but by 'faith'), it is not subject to any process of determination. Consciousness is irreducible.

Parsons clearly does not consistently support such a definition. In fact, the analytical elements are subject to a *number* of forms of determination. As well as the effect of Scientific Evolution, the elements are also determined by, on the one hand, culture in general (e.g. by the 'process of rationalisation') and, on the other, by the empirical world itself. We shall return to the role of culture shortly, but this second form of determination clearly conflicts with a rigorous *a priorism*.

As part of the functional relation of knowledge the analytical elements are not only conditions of phenomena but are also to some extent *effects* of phenomena. While Parsons talks of the primacy of the frame of reference, we must also make it clear that this takes the form of a hierarchy, and not a relation of simple determination. Accordingly, the empirical world or 'energy' component does have an effect on the information side. For Kant, on the other hand, while knowledge is conceived in terms of a connection between categories of the understanding and sense impressions, the realm of understanding is not itself subject to determination by sense impression or intuition. It is transcendental. The notion of a 'functional' relationship between categories and the empirical world as in Parsons' thesis would effectively destroy the strictly *a priori* nature of the categories in Kantian epistemology, and open it to the problems of scepticism.

Emphasising this point is not to be pedantic. The basis of this distinction from Kantian transcendentalism lies in a very important flaw in analytical realism. Mention has already been made of the role of culture in the determination of the theoretical framework of knowledge. The analytical elements are not transcendental but subject to the effects of the cultural system. Herein lies the second major problem with Parsons' epistemology.

Of what does this conception of the epistemological subject consist? It has already been pointed out that Parsons operates with several conceptions of the subject of knowledge: the thinking human actor, the perceiving or experiencing subject, together with conceptual frames of reference. These together operate according to the cybernetic hierarchy. Yet for all his insistence on the primacy of the conceptual frame of reference, it is the notion of the theorist-as-actor which really unites the elements of hierarchy. Analytical realism is a genuine epistemological attempt to account for the process of production of knowledge with reference to a socio-cultural process, introducing a definite element of *sociological relativism.*

The subject of knowledge is not transcendental but socioculturally determined. The process of production of knowledge is theorised in similar terms to the processes of action themselves, they both operate in terms of the information–energy relations of the cybernetic hierarchy. In both, the cultural system is primary in supplying the fundamentals of 'meaning'. If the subject of knowledge is to be conceived as an actor, then knowledge must itself be subject to the determinations of action.

In defining the epistemological subject as a human actor, Parsons must eventually ascribe to that subject the determinations of action in general. There is always, therefore, a clear element of socio-cultural relativism in his epistemology. In the next chapter it will be shown that Parsons' proposals for a methodology of the *social* science involve a necessary element of cultural relativity. The relation between sociologist and object in the social sciences becomes, in the final analysis, a communication between values. The point being made here is that such relativism applies not only to his outline of the social sciences but to his epistemology in general. If it is not necessarily a communication *between* values, the knowledge process in general is at least *governed* by values. Concepts and theories are not *a priori* but merely part of a hierarchy in which the cultural system is primary. The process of development of knowledge is governed (cybernetically) by the process of development of culture. As long as the element of human subjectivity is seen to be crucial to the process of knowledge, then the charge of socio-cultural relativism is inescapable.

However, the 'theoretical' or 'analytical' component of knowledge is only one side of the abstractive relation of analytical realism. If we have shown that there is a definite element of sociologism in Parsons' theory of knowledge, this is not to argue that this is the only problem. There is, as it were, a genuinely epistemological character to his theory of knowledge and this exists around the 'other side' of the abstractive process, i.e. 'reality'.

## 2.3 The 'Reality' Component of Analytical Realism

From what has already been said, it is clear that in many ways the so-called 'theory *vs* empiricism' debate launched by Parsons is little removed from his wider attacks on positivistic conceptions of action. His conception of knowledge bears close relations to his theory of action (whether that be the early or later positions). However, the conception of reality so important to his epistemology is not so much dominated by action theory and involves a distinct thesis.

Parsons claims to maintain a position which is neither empiricist nor fictionalist. While the theoretical component of knowledge is not to be seen as a one-to-one reflection of the empirical world, it is also not held to be devoid of 'realism'. This position at once involves a definite conception of the nature of reality itself.

If the systems of scientific theory are not immediately and directly congruent with external reality, they nevertheless 'grasp' that reality. In short, at some point in the process, reality must be adequately reflected in theory, and concepts correspond with reality. This clearly implies that there must at some stage be a correspondence between the *logical order* (the theory of action, the theory of the solar system etc.) and the *real order*. What makes a theory 'scientific' is a relation whereby the logical order of the theory adequately reproduces the natural order of the real world. Therefore, a definite conception of *nature* is essential to Parsons' epistemology. Consider the following comment:

the applicability to it [of external reality] of scientific theory implies that empirical reality . . . is a factual order. Furthermore its order must be of a character which is, in some sense, congruent with the order of human logic. Events in it cannot occur simply at random in the sense which is the negation of logical order. For a common feature of all scientific theory is the logicality of the relations between its propositions. (*SSA*, pp. 753–4)

This may not be a classic rationalist conception of the world – there is always, Parsons argues, a discrepancy between logically closed systems and empirically open systems – but it does involve at least a partial rationalism. In the case of fully developed or evolved systems of scientific theory, the order of the real world corresponds to a logical or rational order. Science actually reproduces the natural order in its logical propositions. Indeed, the basic condition of the 'evolution' of scientific knowledge is the ubiquity of order in the real world, an order eventually grasped by the various sciences.

The abstractive relation of knowledge is the reproduction of the factual order in the system of analytical elements. This is the condition on which Parsons can maintain both the realist element and the abstractive relation between concepts and reality. It is the factual order which, in the last analysis, makes possible logically ordered scientific theory.

It must now be clear that what is involved here is a definite *ontology*. The epistemology of analytical realism depends not only on a conception of the epistemological subject, but also on a conception of the nature of the object world. It relies upon the proposition that reality is an ordered and regular system which makes possible its adequate representation in theory. The evolution of knowledge consists in the eventual congruence between the logical order and the natural order.

Now we come upon a peculiar problem. The epistemology of analytical realism itself requires and depends upon, amongst other things, an ontology of the essential nature of the real world. It rests upon the fundamental presupposition of the (possible) congruence between the conceptual order and the natural order of reality, between reality and the rational order.

Epistemology is, by definition, a theory of knowledge-in-general, a conception of the nature of *all* knowledge. Yet most

epistemologies themselves rely upon various ontological conceptions, and in Parsons' case, as we have seen, this takes the form of
the 'factual order'. The problem lies in this: *the ontological conception cannot be justified by the epistemology*. It has been shown that the
ontology is the logical condition of the epistemological thesis; it
cannot, therefore, be in turn demonstrated by means of that
thesis. This would clearly be a circular argument, the ontological
conception being, in the last analysis, its own justification.

The paradox is apparent. The epistemology of analytical
realism is only a theory of knowledge 'in general' on the assumption that a certain form of knowledge is independent, because
logically prior to it. This form of knowledge cannot be situated
within the general definition of knowledge, being the logical
condition of that definition. Analytical realism is not, therefore,
a theory of *all* knowledge. It is subject to yet another Master
knowledge.[33]

What then of the ontology itself? The notion of an essentially
ordered real world can only, in the final analysis, lead to an
infinite regress. It cannot be demonstrated on theoretical
grounds. This follows directly from rationalistic epistemologies.
The rationalist conception of reality involves concepts which in
turn presuppose the nature of reality, and so on into infinity. Any
attempt to demonstrate theoretically an ontological thesis of this
kind must eventually come to terms with the problem that theory
or knowledge is itself seen to be possible because of the nature of
reality – in Parsons' case, its systemic character.

If we take the case of the theory of action this problem becomes very apparent. Parsons argues that a theory of systems of
action is the product of an evolutionary process of knowledge
whereby the reality of action is effectively grasped in theory. It is
not simply reflected in theory, but parts of reality are abstracted
from the concrete world according to their significance to the
action frame of reference. As a highly developed theory, it
adequately reproduces the systemic character of action processes, the factual order being precisely these systems. Therefore
the fact of systems of action becomes both the *condition* of a
sociology and its *product*. How do we know that action takes the
form of systems? – because sociology informs us that that is the
case. But then we are also told that the factual order (systems of
action) is the condition of that knowledge.

The problems here are quite clear. An ontology which is the

condition of all knowledge cannot, in turn, be demonstrated by any knowledge without returning us once again back on itself. The thesis of a factual order as the condition of all knowledge must remain, in a sense, pre-theoretical, if not fatuous. If a conception of the essential nature of reality is truly the *condition* of knowledge, then such a conception remains dogmatic, i.e. devoid of demonstration. If a conception of the nature of reality is the *product* of knowledge, then to talk of such a reality as existent prior to a theoretical knowledge is meaningless. Analytical realism maintains elements of both alternatives.

## 2.4 Conclusion

As a polemical attack on the predominant epistemological conception of sociology, and indeed on certain theses in the philosophy of science, Parsons' presentation of the epistemology of analytical realism contains many acceptable and theoretically valid points. As a critique of anti-theoretical empiricism and of the fictionalist presuppositions of the ideal-type it achieves a number of justifiable conclusions and highlights several major internal contradictions and problems.

That is as far as it goes. As a theory in itself, as a positive attempt to provide a general conception of knowledge, it is unacceptable. Both levels of analytical realism have been shown to be problematic, the analytical component being based on several (often contradictory) processes, the realism element involving unjustifiable reliance on an ontological conception of the essential nature of the real world.

Having gone this far, we can return to one of the objectives stated at the outset of this chapter. I have already provided general arguments against the mode of reading which views theoretical discourse as the realisation of epistemological conceptions/presuppositions. This discussion has shown more specifically that the epistemology of analytical realism is itself internally problematic. As such, it is difficult to see how it could possibly 'produce' a knowledge according to the procedures claimed. Once we attempt to go beyond the polemic we find in analytical realism an inconsistent and logically incoherent body of concepts.

# 3 The Structure of Action: Parsons' Formulation of the Action Frame of Reference

## 3.1 Introduction

The object of this chapter is to discuss the theoretical character of Parsons' theory of action, or more specifically what Parsons himself chooses to call the 'action frame of reference'. While it is certainly true to argue that the substance of the general theory of action has been subject to a number of major transformations, this does not preclude the isolation of certain essential concepts that may be considered general throughout Parsons' elaborations. These do not refer to any ubiquitous 'doctrines' to which Parsons adheres, or to any apparent metaphysical concerns which linger behind his theses, but to definite theoretical conditions which the theorisation of action (whether Weberian, structural-functionalist, or whatever) must invoke. It is to precisely these conceptual conditions that the following analysis is directed.

The discussion will operate with a definition of action sufficient to incorporate the different forms which Parsons' theory of action has taken throughout its development. The following minimal definition may be taken as a starting point:

> Action consists of the structures and processes by which
> human beings form meaningful intentions and, more or less
> successfully, implement them in concrete situations. The word
> 'meaningful' implies the symbolic or cultural level of represen-
> tation and reference. Intentions and implementation taken
> together imply a disposition of the action system – individual

or collective – to modify its relation to its situation or environment in an intended direction. (*Societies*, p.5)

It is clear that two major spheres are invoked in this definition: on the one hand a level of 'culture' (values, meanings, ideas, rules, etc.), and on the other a level of what may be generally referred to as 'nature', a non-ideational realm which can incorporate anything from biological organisms to social systems. This distinction is not simply commensurable with Parsons' demarcation between the 'natural' and the 'cultural' sciences, in which sociology is classified categorically in the latter, but is a more fundamental distinction between the ideational realm and the sphere in which that realm is realised, represented, and so on. The object of sociology in this sense involves both levels. As will be seen, it incorporates both a level of ideas and a level distinct from the ideational which concerns processes subject to a different form of determination.

It will also be seen that for Parsons action is defined by a specific *relation* between the two basic levels. Indeed, the notion of both a distinction and a determinate relation between the two realms is inherent in the elementary definition of the action frame of reference itself. In *The Structure of Social Action*, Parsons differentiates between the elementary and *irreducible* components of the 'unit act' – the actor, the goal or end of action, the situation of action (conditions and means), and finally, the normative orientation of action. The elements of the unit act provide the minimal components of any specifically action process, and none of them can therefore be ignored in any attempt to analyse such processes. While the cultural or meaningful elements intervene at every point in the unit act, there is, nevertheless, one very general relation which is seen to structure the whole action complex and which concerns the distinction within the unit act between what is referred to as the 'normative' and the 'conditional' spheres. Action may indeed be seen as the articulation of the two levels:

Action must always be thought of as involving a state of tension between two different orders of elements, the normative and the conditional. As process, action is, in fact, the process of alteration of the conditional elements in the direction of conformity with norms. (*SSA*, p. 732)

The normative component of action is, of course, of primary significance to Parsons' formulation, for it is both one element of the unit act and an element whose intervention is decisive in any situation in which there is an absence of 'objective' determination of action, i.e. where there exists *choice*. Normative orientation is of unique status in the theory of action and it signals the point at which the 'meaningful' component of action decisively begins to take effect. It would seem then that there are two levels of issues which any discussion of Parsons' conception of action must consider. On the one hand, there is the problem of the conception of normative orientation itself, which involves the fundamental concepts of 'values', 'meanings', and of culture in general; on the other hand, there is the issue of the proposed *relation* that Parsons erects between this general sphere and the conditional or natural level, which in turn introduces the problem of the mode in which the unity which this relation invokes is theorised, how the apparent determinate relation between the two realms is to be posed. It is these two general concerns which comprise the primary object of this chapter.

The first section of the chapter is devoted to the concept of 'voluntarism' and its status in the Parsonian theory of action. It considers the problem of the function of such notions as 'free-will' and 'subjectivity' in the action frame of reference, and compares its formulation with the mode in which what may be referred to as the 'ultra-humanisms' in contemporary sociology (ethnomethodology, phenomenology, and so on) handle such issues. It is argued that even in its earliest and most explicitly 'humanist' presentations, the Parsonian conception of action distinguishes itself from such tendencies. Action is never, for Parsons, the totally unstructured and indeterminate process it becomes for the ultra-humanisms. The idea of a free and indeterminate human individual is foreign to the action frame of reference in so far as a crucial role is played by 'complexes of meaning' on the one hand and the conditional exigencies of action on the other. The voluntaristic issue can only be approached in this light.

On this basis the discussion moves on to consider critically the action frame of reference itself. Two areas are demarcated; on the one hand the concept of 'values' and, in particular, 'ultimate values', and on the other the more general issue of the relation between the value level as an ideational realm and its effectivity in action complexes, or more specifically, the relation between the normative and conditional elements of action.

The first of these sections argues that, as an effect of his concept of 'ultimate reality', Parsons is forced to accept a definite component of theoretical arbitrariness. On the one hand, in his attempt to formulate a means of avoiding the assumption of the inherent rationality of action (in trying to establish the importance of 'non-logical' determinations of action), Parsons is forced to maintain a realm of action (the crucial realm) which is beyond determinate explanation. On the other hand, and as a result of this consequence when it comes to the theorisation of the *effectivity* of such elements, the action frame of reference is ensured a theoretical level which it is unable to unambiguously specify; the theoretical arbitrariness of the one realm of action ensures that the effectivity of that realm cannot be adequately explained. Both the value-component of action and the analysis of the relation between that component and the other analytical elements of action are characterised by significant theoretical incoherence.

The final section takes up the more general problem of the central relation between the two basic realms of the theory of action, what has been referred to as the ideational and natural levels, the latter being the level at which the former is realised. It argues that, in order to maintain the co-existence of both levels, Parsons is forced to accept one of two consequences – both of them disastrous to his theory. He must either face the existence of contradictory or 'double' determination of action, or he must accept that both forms of determination of action, the ideal and the natural, are themselves governed by some form of overall idealist teleology, one which subsumes them both within a universal *purpose*.

## 3.2 The 'Voluntaristic' Nature of Action: the Role of Free-will and Subjectivity

It is, of course, a commonplace interpretation of Parsons which sees his work as an essentially two-stage affair, the division being between the 'voluntaristic' phase of *SSA* and the 'macro-theoretical' or 'positivistic' position of the post-war writings. Two well-known examples of such an interpretation are Alvin Gouldner's demarcation between the early 'anti-deterministic' stance and the later form of 'systems-analysis'[1] (Gouldner's preference is, of course, for the former) and J. F. Scott's division between the philosophico-metaphysical idealism of the early essays and *SSA*, and Parsons' later 'naturalistic-scientistic' foundations[2] – in Scott's case the preference clearly lies in the latter.

Irrespective of which of Gouldner's or Scott's preferences is least problematic, there exists a more fundamental issue which relates to the very possibility of such claims. Without denying theoretical transformations in Parsonian theory (although not, it must be noted, of this order[3]), there are major problems with the construction of a demarcation line between these two phases of Parsons' work in terms of, on the one hand, a simple idealism dominated by the notion of an indeterminate human level of existence, and, on the other, of some apparent 'overdetermined' conception of social life. The implication in such interpretations is that the basic definition of *action* is severed in the later works, and that the basic orientation of action analysis is abandoned. However, there are two basic errors in this thesis. First, these interpretations severely distort the status of action in the early works, and they misplace the concepts of 'voluntarism' and 'subjectivity' as they stand in the action frame of reference. Secondly, such interpretations obscure the extent to which the basic concepts of action *persist* throughout the theory of the social system, social evolution, and so on. To deny that the basic concepts of action in the sense of the action frame of reference continue to exist in Parsons' later formulations is to deny that *culture* has any effectivity in the theory of social systems, which is clearly an absurd position. As the truth of this second point will become more apparent in later discussions, this section concerns itself specifically with the first issue, i.e. the extent to which Parsons' early position on action may be classified as 'anti-deterministic' or 'idealistic' as Gouldner, Scott, and many others have argued.

It is argued here that Parsons' early 'voluntaristic' conception of action can in no sense by classified as a simple idealist metaphysics or as a programme for the freedom of the human individual as the constitutive agent of action processes. While the concepts of 'subjectivity', 'free-will' and 'voluntarism' are clearly of importance to the action frame of reference, the latter cannot be equated with the manifest irrationalism which many forms of contemporary sociology advocate. Parsons' theory of action is incompatible with the notion of the indeterminate and freely constituting human individual which comprises the main object of the various forms of ultra-humanism (phenomenology, ethnomethodology, symbolic interactionism).

It is Scott's thesis that in his early formulations Parsons postulates the essence of action as the 'metaphysical autonomy' of the subjective sphere. This sphere is, apparently for Parsons, beyond any natural determination and cannot therefore be subjected to a 'naturalistic' form of explanation. Its project is a pre-eminently philosophical one; the pre-war writings are classed as an assertive attempt to emphasise the unique character of human subjectivity – human existence is characterised by *creativity*, and it is at this point that, for Scott, the notion of 'voluntarism' takes effect. 'Voluntarism' is equated with the Kantian principle of free-will and the essentially indeterminate nature of human involvement; 'voluntarism' is seen to be equivalent to the *autonomy* of the human subject.

Such a classification obscures the extent to which Parsons qualified his conception of action as necessarily a *relation* between two spheres, the normative and the conditional, or more generally what has been termed here the ideational and the natural. Failure to register this point and to understand fully its significance inevitably presents problems both in the consideration of the relation between the early and late Parsons (and this would seem to be realised in Scott's thesis amongst others), and even of the distance between Parsons' early concept of action and the various forms of what are now known as 'action theories' – phenomenology, interactionism, etc. Without a clear appreciation of the relational character of the action frame of reference it is impossible to situate adequately the concepts of 'subjectivity' and voluntarism as they function in Parsons' formulation.

Voluntarism in the sense invoked in the action frame of reference refers not to a freely constituting human subject but to a mechanism which for Parsons exists in between the normative and the conditional realms. Given the primacy of values in the action frame of reference, a specific mechanism is required by means of which the ideal stipulations of the value-sphere can be realised at the level of action – the human actor is precisely this mechanism. The actor is the means by which the normative component of action is represented. Note that a distinction must be made between the actor and the normative element of action, for this is precisely the point at which Scott's exposition falters – Scott confuses the indeterminacy of *values* with the indeterminacy of *action*, whereas values are only an element of action. The proposed parallel with Kantian dualism is instrumental in this conflation. For Kant, Man is a *noumenon* and cannot be subjected to any form of naturalistic determination or explanation – man is essentially a creature of free-will and is therefore indeterminate. Scott applies this category to the pre-war Parsons and argues that in the latter free-will becomes in similar fashion a realm which is unknowable.

While there is undoubtedly an element of indeterminacy in the action frame of reference (see later), it is illegitimate to classify the Parsonian notion of *voluntarism* in this fashion. Voluntarism refers to a relation between a realm of values and a conditional level of action, but it is the values and not the action in general which supply the indeterminate character of action. The simple category of an 'idealist-metaphysics' cannot account for the essentially relational character of action in the Parsonian sense.

In order to establish this point (that it is the value-level and not the action level which is free and indeterminate), we might consider the concept of action as it appears in the various forms of 'action theory'. In contemporary versions of subjectivist sociology a dominant tendency is to postulate the human realm as *indeterminate in principle*. According to this thesis, any form of determination of human behaviour, whether it be biological, social or cultural, is discounted as some form of 'positivism' – a position which denies the essentially free character of human processes.[4] In this conception, the human *actor* is himself free to constitute his own situation, he not only decides which action is to take place but actually produces through his subjectivity his social world. The meanings which govern action are essentially objects of his own construction and he is seen as the fully constitutive centre of the action complex. While there may be variant extensions of this point, it remains central to the sociological presentations of Alfred Schutz, Harod Garfinkel, G. H. Mead, and others.[5] As an example, we might consider Blumer's argument in his attempt to define the distinctive character of 'symbolic interactionism'.

Blumer's basic thesis is that sociological theory rarely recognises or treats human societies as being composed of individuals who have 'selves'. The preference, he argues, is to treat human beings as passive media through which factors such as 'social structure', 'social systems', 'culture', 'values', etc., operate. Against this view, which denies that individuals have selves by means of which they determine their own involvement in society, Blumer counterposes the view that the actor's behaviour is self-constituting:

> The process of self-indication by means of which human action is formed cannot be accounted for by factors which precede the act. The process of self-indication exists in its own right and must be accepted and studied as such. It is through this process that the human being constructs his own conscious action. (*Symbolic Interactionism*, p. 82)

An explicit opposition is thus erected to any attempt to conceptualise human action in terms of determinations external to or prior to the act itself. The significant point is that such a position is not only at variance with Parsons' post-war stance with its concept of the social system, but is also at variance with the account of the action frame of reference as presented in Parsons' early writings. The central concept is that of the freely constituting human individual who constructs his own process of action and who cannot be reduced in any sense to a determinate object of analysis. It is this mode of conceptualisation of action which is more consistent with Scott's category; it is here that the *actor* and his *action* are essentially indeterminate. The form of 'free-will' that Scott assigns to the early Parsons is far more applicable to the theories of interactionism, phenomenology and ethnomethodology, than to the action frame of reference.[6]

Where the main distinction exists between Parsons' conception of action and these forms of subjectivist sociology is precisely over the role of values and other determinations of action. The paradox is, and on this point Parsons is quite explicit, that the voluntaristic nature of action is never really 'voluntary' and that the subjective element of action is never a self-constituting subjectivity. This point will become increasingly clear as the discussion proceeds, but it is worthwhile at this point to consider the status of Max Weber's conception of action as it appears to be a bone of contention between the ultra-humanistic forms of sociology and the conception of action maintained by Parsons.

Weber, as is well known, provided no really elaborate outline of the concept of action in general, and certainly nothing approaching the degree of explicitness of Parsons' exposition of the action frame of reference. Although Weber develops the concepts of the different types of action, the concept of action itself is not elaborated systematically. Consequently, the status of such notions of 'free-will' and the 'subjective' element of action has been open to much debate.[7]

We can begin by considering Weber's abstract definition of action: 'In "action" is included all human behaviour when and in so far as the acting individual attaches a subjective meaning to it' (*The Theory of Social and Economic Organisation*, p. 88). It is the concept of 'subjectivity' which is of uncertain status in Weber's definition of action and, in fact, it is possible to extract at least two conflicting interpretations concerning the theoretical character of this concept for the Weberian theory of action. The origin of this conflict lies in what seems to be two contradictory qualifications to the definition of action. On the one hand Weber stipulates that action processes must always be in a sense reducible to the action of individuals: 'Action in the sense of a subjectively understandable orientation of behaviour exists only as the behaviour of one or more *individual* human beings' (ibid., p. 10, Weber's emphasis).

The centrality of individual human beings is justified on the basis that they alone can be treated as agents in the course of subjectively understandable action. However, Weber also insists on a further point as a qualification to this proposal which relates to a limitation to the individual referent: 'It is a monstrous misunderstanding to think that an "individualistic" *method* should involve what is in any conceivable sense an individualistic system of *values*' (ibid., p. 107, Weber's emphasis).

Such a qualification is clearly in order if one considers Weber's thesis in *The Protestant Ethic and the Spirit of Capitalism* (1930) concerning the apparent decisive role of certain systems of religious values for the appearance of particular forms of action.[8] If Weber is to assert only the individual role in the constitution of action processes, his arguments on *systems* of values cannot be maintained – arguments clearly important to his sociology. In other words, Weber postulates the existence of a *supra-individual* realm of culture, of 'complexes of meanings' to which the individual must in some sense comply – certain individual forms of action are *effects* of this realm; for example, economically rational action is itself seen to presuppose the existence of adequate complexes of meaning before it can 'break out'.

'Subjectivity' for Weber cannot be read, therefore, as the freely-constituting human subjectivity in the sense claimed by the ultra-humanisms. That is, the individual cannot *constitute* his meanings, or at least cannot constitute the primary meanings, which determine his actions. The individual is in this respect the *agent* of values, the means by which the supra-individual realm of meanings is represented. Subjectivity, if such a thesis as that of *The Protestant Ethic* is to be upheld, it must refer to the individual's *conception* of his ends and situations and not the individual's *construction* of his world as is the case for the ultra-humanisms.

It is clear, however, that both extensions of Weber's conception of action are possible in so far as he emphasises two apparently irreconcilable postulates (individual actions, supra-individual complexes of meaning). Contemporary sociological theory bears witness to the possibilities of extending Weber's conception of action in one of at least two directions. Social phenomenology, ethnomethodology and symbolic interactionism attempt to resolve the contradiction in Weber's position by means of an explicit programme for an individualist and indeterminate conception of social life in which any form of 'external' determination is opposed, whether it be complexes of meaning,[9] social structures, etc. Parsons, on the other hand, particularly in his early writings, chooses the opposite direction and selects Weber's reference to the value sphere as his most important contribution to the 'voluntaristic schema'. Subjectivity has a contradictory existence in Weber and contemporary sociology has taken distinct roads on that basis.

It can, in fact, be shown that the extension of Weber's definition of action in the direction of an essentially indeterminate conception of social existence is rigorously precluded in Parsons' outline of the action frame of reference. Even at its most formal level, the action frame of reference specifies that action processes always involve a minimum set of elements, all of which must be included in the analysis of action. These are the actor, an end or goal of action, a situation of action (including conditions and means), and a normative orientation to action. Any analysis which fails to include one or more of the analytical elements must be classified as incomplete in the direction of a positivism, idealism, utilitarianism, etc.[10] If we take the elements independently, however, the distance between Parsons' theory of action and the forms of action theory will become even more apparent.

To begin with, Parsons' concept of the situation of action places the concepts of 'free-will' and 'subjectivity' clearly into context – it is a concept which, incidentally, is nowhere systematically elaborated in Weber's sociology. All action for Parsons occurs in situations. They are defined as states of affairs which, in one or more respects, are distinct from that to which the actor is oriented, i.e. from the actor's own goals and ends to which he aspires. A situation contains two levels of components, the conditions of action and the means which are available in the action complexes. The conditions of action are defined, significantly, as objects which are out of the control of the actor; they are comprised of physical, social and symbolic objects with which the agent of action must come to terms. Thus, although the situation of action must be subjectively organised in the actor's orientation, in so far as it is a realm beyond his manipulation and control, it is a level which imposes definite limits, constraints and determinations on the actor. The actor cannot alter the conditions of action nor prevent them from being altered, in conformity with his own particular ends.[11] The subjective organisation of the situation is not one which is the actor's own constitution; the actor does not construct his situation but rather *conceives* it.

The existence of 'ends' of action in Parsons' sense also provides a set of limitations to the 'voluntary' character of action. Admittedly, the definition of the end/goal of action specifies the role of the actor's orientation to a future state of affairs regarded as desirable by the actor himself (in the short or long term), but Parsons also argues that the means–end relationship is never reducible to an 'atomism' in which the ends are simply relative to the human individual. The major critique of the utilitarian social theory is directed at the notion that the ends are random, and relative only to the positivistically determinate elements of action. In terms of such a conception, the theorisation of the relation of the ends of action to each other (within and between

actors) is precluded, the effect being to: '... inhibit the elaboration of certain of the most important possibilities of the theory of
action, those having to do with the integration of ends in systems,
especially those involving a plurality of actors' (*SSA*, p. 56).

The ends of action according to the action frame of reference
always exist within forms of systems of action, a feature which
the notion of a randomness of ends would preclude – hence no
concept of social action or social system given the atomism of
utilitarianism. Parsons provides two aspects of the concept of
'system' of action in *SSA*, both of which rigorously preclude any
constitutive individualism. On the one hand, the concept of the
ends of action requires the further notion of levels of 'complexity' designated as 'emergent properties', determinate levels of
organisation of action elements – again the concept of situation
is instrumental. The ends of action are always articulated onto
determinate situational components, as they are always subject
to certain levels of complexity and the forms of determination
which they necessitate. The concept of ends of action, however,
involves a more decisive sphere – this introduces the third
analytical element of action closely related to the ends which the
actor desires, the normative orientation of action – this concept,
and its articulation to that of the cultural system, provides the
second aspect of systems of action in *SSA*, and it is also the most
important one for the analysis of that text.

In *SSA* the primary definition of 'systems' of action is clearly
according to the systemic character of *value-patterns*, organisations of a cultural or ideal character. Action on an organised
basis is made possible by means of certain values which constrain
the actor's orientations and direct him motivationally in specific
directions. One major example of this is 'social action' – this
action is dependent upon the existence of certain social values
without which social order is not possible. The primary element
of values lies in the religious sphere of orientation, the realm of
'ultimate values' which constitute the actor's fundamental conceptions of good and evil, right and wrong, etc. It is by means of
the ultimate reference of values that normative orientation may
be said to govern or organise action – the cultural specification
of values provides the directions that the actor 'ought' to take.
Social action is possible because there exist values which in their
ideal form contain orientations toward other actors which then
become shared. Thus, in *SSA* we find the following explanation

of the existence of a 'collectivity': ' . . . the collectivity . . . [is] a unity, a unity in the sense that society can be thought of as pursuing a single common end (or system of ends) and not merely discrete individual ends' (p. 247). The whole pertinence of the famous 'pattern-variable' scheme stems from the decisive importance of sets of value-components in determining the orientations of individuals and of directing their actions in specific forms.

It is clear, therefore, that to classify the Parsonian conception of the action frame of reference as a metaphysical polemic for the assertion of the free-will of the human individual distorts the issue. Even in his earliest essays it is clear that action is always to be thought of in terms of the relation between the acting agent and the normative exigencies on the one hand (atemporal complexes of meaning), and conditional elements (obstacles to the realisation of ends) on the other. The voluntary character of action must always be viewed in this light, for human will is a mechanism in between the normative and the conditional, it does not itself constitute the norms and conditions of action.

We are now in a position to specify more adequately the status of the voluntary nature of action and the role of subjectivity in the determination of action processes. Given that all action involves a number of elements in addition to the actor, and given that it always is to be seen as some form of tension between the normative and the conditional, then it is obvious that 'will' or the voluntary nature of action are intervening mechanisms and not self-constituting essences. Parsons makes it quite clear in his discussion of Durkheim that although voluntary capacities are essential to the theory of action, this by no means implies that the human individual is autonomous and independent of any conditional exigencies:

> . . . the usual distinction between voluntary adherence and constraint carries the connotation of the utilitarian dilemma. Yet this is just what Durkheim has transcended. He has precisely distinguished, as the utilitarians did not, between voluntariness and arbitrariness. While, on the one hand, adherence is voluntary, on the other, *that adherence is binding* on the individual. But it is binding not from physical necessity but from moral obligation. (*SSA*, p. 384, my emphasis)

The voluntaristic schema does not invoke the indeterminate existence of free human agents – such a conception would be closer to what Parsons refers to as 'irrational' or 'erroneous' action, action which is individually contingent. The primary element of human existence, on the contrary, is moral *obligation*, and it is for this reason that Parsons qualifies his notion of will with the statement that 'the actor is not free to do as he likes, he is "bound" ' (*SSA*, p. 385). Where the issue of 'will' arises is in respect of the *effort* or *energy* required on the part of the actor in order to realise existent value-standards in the context of the inevitable obstacles to their automatic·expression. The normative elements of action exist only in the form of atemporal meaning complexes – for them to be *effective* in action there must be mechanisms which can act on the basis of values while also representing the inevitable conditional requirements to which action is subjected. Such a mechanism is the human subject endowed with the capacity of effort or energy – will is the means by which action treads mid-way between idealist emanationism (action as the simple expression of meaning-contents) and 'positivism' (action as the mechanical reflection of heredity and/or environment).

This is equally the case for the confusing concept of 'subjectivity' in the action frame of reference. For Parsons, to argue that there is a subjective element of action is not equivalent to subjectivism. If he is to maintain the double determination of action, normative and conditional, it is also necessary to include a mechanism by which the conditional elements can be represented at the level of values which can register the discrepancies between the specifications of the ideal totality and the situation in which the action is to take place. This concept is supplied by the notion of the human subject and his system of orientations, wants and needs, his capacity for cognition and for evaluation – in short, the 'ego'. This may explain why Parsons often prefers the term 'states of mind' to that of 'subjectivity' – it refers more to a capacity for *recognition* than to a self-constituting activity.

I do not, by any means, wish to imply that the human subject is 'peripheral' to the action frame of reference, that will and subjectivity are in some sense residual categories brought into the theory of action to help Parsons to get over certain problems. On the contrary, the concept of the human subject is *central* to the Parsonian thesis, and this point will be elaborated later. The point I have attempted to make here is that 'action' is no simple essence for the action frame of reference and that it is distinct from contemporary versions of 'action theory'. The genesis of the ends of action and the decision as to the appropriate means for their attainment unites, through the various orientational processes, the requirements of the actor as a biological organism and as a unit of a system of action to the given system of value-patterns. Will, effort, energy and subjectivity relate to the fact that the means–end relationship is never automatically determined in any direction, ideal/normative or conditional, but requires the actor's *intervention*. The very fact that they are defined as forms of intervention shows quite clearly that the voluntaristic *element* is never really 'voluntary'.

## 3.3 Action as Meaningful Behaviour: the Role of Values

The discussion so far has attempted to clarify certain points relating to Parsons' formulation of the action frame of reference. Three of Parsons' projected critiques of social theory, as presented in *SSA*, show quite clearly that the action frame of reference can in no sense be equated with the notion of the free and indeterminate actor, with simple idealism, or with any form of 'positivism'. Thus, the critique of utilitarian theory attacks the notion of individualistic explanations of social relations, the critique of 'anti-intellectualistic positivism' clearly distinguishes the voluntaristic conception of action from any 'mechanical determinism', and finally Parsons' opposition to 'idealist emanationism' emphasises that action in Parsons' sense has an invariable double referent, cultural *and* conditional. This leaves one further general critique that is decisive to *SSA*, the position Parsons designates as the 'radical rationalist pole' of positivistic theories of action. The discussion will now shift its emphasis and develop a critique of the action frame of reference itself – Parson's own critique of rationalist theories of action will be shown to be of crucial significance to such a critique.

Parsons is emphatic that the role of the human subject cannot be reduced to a cognitive orientation alone, nor indeed in any crucially significant sense. The primary component of action cannot be one in which the choice of ends and the means of achieving them is governed by the 'norms of science'. It is

Parsons' justification for such an insistence and the theoretical consequences it entails that will comprise the major concern of the following sections. Sub-section (i) will approach the problem of 'values' and its repercussions on the concept of 'culture'; sub-section (ii) will trace the theoretical effects of the concept of values for the theorisation of their mode of realisation in action itself. Some very general points will be made in Section 3.4 of the chapter by way of an overall conclusion.

### (i) *The Concept of Values: Indeterminacy at the Level of Culture*

It is clear that in the theory of action a great deal hinges on the problem of the determination of the ends of action. Social action, for example, is seen to be impossible without the integration of ends in 'systems'; therefore the systemic character of ends is an issue of crucial importance. In *SSA* Parsons argues that it is on the problem of ends alone that many existing forms of social theory fall down. Indeed, it is possible to use the different ways in which the ends of action are proposed as a criteria of demarcation between the various forms of social theory. Thus, utilitarianism is characterised by a random conception of ends, anti-intellectualistic positivism obliterates the existence of ends altogether, the metaphysical theories of action postulate unacceptable notions of the 'natural identity of interests', and so on. Parsons also takes opposition to another attempt to conceptualise the ends of action: this form of social theory is termed the 'rationalistic' conception of action, and the basis of this opposition is made clear in the argument in the early paper 'The Place of Ultimate Values in Sociological Theory':[12] 'The ultimate reason ... for the causal independence of ends in action ... is the fact that man stands in significant relations to aspects of reality *other than those revealed by science*' (ibid., p. 290 my emphasis).

It is to this 'other reality' and its effects on action that sociology must pay special attention; it is the sphere of values *per se*, the level of human orientation at which neither form of 'positivism' can apply. More specifically, it is argued that a definite demarcation must be made between forms of action that can be subjected to rationalistic explanation (i.e. in which the analysis is concerned with the rational relation between means and ends), and those forms of action in which a qualitatively distinct referent is to be employed. It is essentially on these terms that a division can be made within the social sciences between the object, say, of economic theory and the specific object of sociology. Of pertinence here is the importance Parsons assigns to the Paretian distinction between 'logical' and 'non-logical' action.

Logical action is defined as that action which is characterised by logically united operations and decisions. These operations are grounded in a scientifically valid interpretation on the actor's part of his goals or ends, and the means which he must utilise to attain them. In Parsons' terms, logical action is action in which the subjective end coincides with the objective end. In such cases, the subjective end is the state of affairs 'which can be *scientifically demonstrated* actually to come about as a result of the actor's proposed action' (*SSA*, p. 191, my emphasis). The best example of this form of action is economic action and its basis, economic rationality. In this form of action the assumption is one in which the allocation of scarce resources is governed by the most rational organisation of means in terms of their marginal utility.[13]

Sociology proper, however, must distinguish itself from the positivist inclinations of such conceptions. While it is argued that economic theory is valid in itself, i.e. within its own limits, it is also emphasised that to extend the model of economic rationality to include all action would be to obliterate a distinct and indeed crucial sphere of action. Sociology as distinct from economic theory must carve for itself a specific object; the germs of this object are to be found, Parsons claims, in what Pareto refers to as the 'residual' aspects of action which centre on what is referred to as 'non-logical' action.

The non-logical sphere is a distinct realm of action. While it cannot be reduced to the rational elements of action (it cannot be judged in terms of the logical nature of its reasoning), it is also distinct from action which is 'illogical' or erroneous – the latter, indeed, is not 'action' in the strict sense. Non-logical action is not 'unscientific' but 'non-scientific', for it is based not on mistake but quite simply on criteria not reducible to rational or scientific judgement. Non-logical actions are thus not to be assessed or understood in terms of the rational character of the relation between ends of action and appropriate means to their realisation, but as 'states of mind', and it is at this point that the role of values in action is introduced. Pareto provides the elements of the voluntaristic theory of action with his conception of 'residual' actions and Parsons elaborates this referent into more than a negative category by means of what is referred to as the 'ultimate' component of action-orientation, the value-element of action. A very definite connection is made between the value component of action and *non-logicality*.

The action frame of reference erects a very clear distinction between, on the other hand, action that is guided by a scientifically verifiable theory and, on the other, action that is governed by 'ultimate ends' – man's ultimate conceptions of his universe, the very basic notions that provide the foundations of his meaningful relation to the world. The primary components of ultimate values are those aspects of the Cosmos which are essentially *unknowable*, those whose referent is to a 'reality' which is non-empirical by definition. The ultimate ends of action *do not have a place in scientific theory*.[14] It is this sphere of action which, argues Parsons, the rationalistic branches of positivism deny or denegate, and a major consequence of this denial is the erasure of the apparent analytical distinction between the ends, means and conditions of action. If the only relation between men and their world is a scientific one then action is reduced to a process of adaptation to given conditions and to predictions as to their future state. From the point of view of a sociology this would have drastic effects. If ends are to be based on purely rational considerations then the specific object of sociology, social action, cannot exist. Social action in the sense of action which is oriented toward others, it is argued, depends on the *integration* of ends in systems, whereas rational action is concerned purely with the immediate problem of the most efficient means of accomplishing given, individual ends. This integration is only possible if there is some higher form of existence of ends toward which the separate ends of action can be directed. This is provided for Parsons by man's ultimate orientations. It is above all the existence of ultimate ends of action, a level beyond the criteria of science, that makes the common-orientedness of ends prerequisite to social action possible.

In order to achieve this thesis, Parsons assigns a definite status to ultimate values – they are *unknowable*. This is made most clear in his argument on the character of ends of action. It is not the ends themselves which constitute the value-element of action, but rather they are

... a rationalized expression of something else, something vague, less defined. This 'something' of which an end is a logically formulated specification, I call a 'value-attitude'. This conception is, it is evident, arrived at negatively – it is the name for an unknown. ('The Place of Ultimate Values in Sociological Theory', pp. 306–7)

In statements such as this, and in many other statements in *SSA*, it is apparent that two realms are involved in the constitution of the ends of action. At its most general level the duality may be referred to as one sphere which is susceptible to scientific explanation and another which is itself beyond scientific investigation in so far as it does not operate according to determinate laws. Yet it is an opposition which Parsons also expresses as the distinction between the 'empirical' and 'non-empirical' worlds or between 'factual' and 'normative' orders.

The significant point of this conception is that the value-element of action is seen to be *unique* in relation to the other determinants of human behaviour. The irreducibility of the value sphere of action to any empirical or factual elements is made quite clear in Parsons' critique of Durkheim's 'sociologistic' account of the ethical and religious components of man's existence:

If the reality underlying religion is an empirical reality, why should religious ideas take the symbolic form in a way which scientific ideas do not? Why could that reality not be represented directly by the theories of sociological science? (*SSA*, p. 429)

If we take religious ideas, as indeed Parsons does, as the central and decisive focal point of ultimate value-attitudes, it is clear from the critique of Durkheim that the reduction of such beliefs to the status of mere empirical objects is antithetical to the theory of action. Ultimate reality, as it later came to be called, is never, and can never be, subject to scientific investigation and explanation in the way that the object world can be. On the contrary, the ultimate element of man's orientation to the world must be seen as one which is essentially non-logical or non-scientific; it involves entities 'which fall altogether outside the range of scientific competence' (ibid., p. 202). There is no sense in which religious ideas can be equated with scientific ideas, for they obey different rules and designate radically distinct 'realities', one 'normative' and the other 'factual'. Whereas a factual order connotes a sphere which is accessible to explanation in terms of a logical theory, normative orders must always be defined relative to sets of given norms themselves (ends, rules, etc.) – it is only if the normative order, as it were, 'breaks down', and is transformed from a purely symbolic to a factual order, that it may be subjected to scientific analysis.[15]

Given Parsons' insistence that a whole sphere of action cannot be subject to logical criteria, that it is in essence non-logical, the theoretical consequence is that this sphere itself *cannot be determinately conceived.* If religious ideas can in no sense be equated or replaced with 'sociological science', for example, then, conversely, it is clear that they cannot be subjected to an analysis by such a science – while they may be 'understood' in a subjective sense, they cannot be determinately conceptualised because this would be to reduce them to precisely the sociological ideas that Parsons claims they can never be. In this sense they could not provide the foundation of meaning that the action frame of reference requires.

This agnosticism of the value element of action lands Parsons in a number of insoluble difficulties. To begin with, it renders the basic project of *SSA* an impossible and contradictory one. This text is concerned with affirming and reaffirming the voluntaristic theory of action against the various distorted conceptions of human behaviour that have existed in the history of social thought. Instrumental in this project is precisely the reference to values which has been discussed – the pre-voluntaristic theories of human behaviour are brought to task for denying or misconceiving the value element of action which, above all, most characterises the distinctively human form of intervention in the world. In *SSA* Parsons, thus, sets out to establish the voluntaristic nature of human behaviour as the only valid form of conceiving a social theory. However, as we have seen, the value component of action involves in certain respects an entity which cannot be determinately conceived; Parsons precludes the possibility of *theoretically* investigating this area. Herein lies the contradiction: *SSA* sets out to *prove theoretically that which cannot be theoretically conceptualised*! Parsons, in other words, attempts to demonstrate that which cannot itself be demonstrated on 'rational' grounds.

It is the character of this 'unknowable' component of action which creates such a paradox. It is theoretically absurd to argue that it is possible to demonstrate or prove that something is 'unknowable in principle', that there is an object which cannot be rationally conceived, for to refer to the object itself means that it is already a concept. Either Parsons is to accept the contradiction or his claim as to the nature of human action is to take on the character of a dogmatic agnosticism, an assertive philosophical anthropology. Thus, while we may disagree with Scott's attempt to reduce action as a whole to the status of a Kantian noumenon, it is not unreasonable to make a parallel between Parsons' presentation of the *value component* of action and Kant's ethical stance on human action:

> Now where determination according to laws ceases, there all explanation ceases also, and nothing remains but defence, i.e. the removal of the objections of those who pretend to have seen deeper into the nature of things, and thereupon boldly declare freedom impossible.[16]

If Parsons is indeed to maintain his conception of the value-sphere in its essentialist form then some similar plea for *faith* as opposed to *demonstration* would appear to be necessary. But then the argument that the value component of action need not necessitate an 'unscientific' approach becomes pointless. Despite Parsons' attempt to distinguish between unscientific and 'non-scientific', it is clear that, in so far as an element of action is to be held independent of scientific analysis, there is no sense in which it is of a better status than simply 'unscientific'. Why Parsons appears to consider it preferable to adhere to a judgement of faith without demonstration rather than to indulge in 'irrationality' we are not told, but from the point of view of a theoretical reading of a discourse the effect is the same: if values cannot be determinately conceived, then they cannot be a part of a scientific theory.

### (ii) The Symbolic Level of Culture and its Realisation in Action: Indeterminacy of Effectivity

We have as yet only considered the specific problems in Parsons' agnostic conception of values for the attempt to demonstrate that conception itself. A further order of issues arises, not surprisingly, when it comes to the theorisation of the mode of *effectivity* of values in action itself. To be more precise, there are two areas in which the mode in which values are conceived appear to produce significant theoretical difficulties: the first concerns the problems surrounding 'interpretative understanding', the second the theorisation of the relation between the different spheres of action. Both relate to the inevitably *speculative* character of the analysis of action processes once they are to include the value-component of human orientation.

With reference to the 'interpretative understanding' of the values involved in action, it is significant that Parsons accepts, albeit in modified form, Weber's thesis that the social investigator *as an actor* is an integral and necessary part of the analysis of action. As is well known, Weber's 'methodology' proposes two levels which a correct causal interpretation of action must take into account; on the one hand, it must be 'causally adequate' as an empirical generalisation, and on the other, it must be 'adequate at the level of meaning'. It is clear that the latter contains a unique set of methodological difficulties in so far as it relates to the task of creating a subjective understanding of the action as opposed to its mere statistical regularity. An adequate account of the meaning element of action requires the understanding of the meaning of the act to the actor who carried the act out, the value or values which govern the action. This additional component of a causal explanation in the cultural sciences is possible, according to Weber, because of the privileged character of the relation between subject and object in the latter. Whereas the natural sciences are restricted to causally adequate explanation, the cultural sciences are distinguished by the fact that the investigator shares with the object of his investigation a similar human essence, subjectivity.

However, it has already been shown that 'subjectivity' for Weber is not without its qualifications – what is important is not merely the fact of subjectivity but the character of what is subjectively conceived. Primary in this context are, of course, values and complexes of values. The fact that the investigator can 'empathise' with his object is always dependent on the fact that this relation is one between the values of the investigator and the values of the object of his investigation, and thus for Weber, between *cultures*.[17] Parsons appears to accept a similar thesis:

Not only are the nonscientific values of the investigator himself and his culture involved, but also those of the persons and collectivities which are the object of his investigation. At the level of Verstehen, scientific investigation is basically a process of meaningful communication.[18]

Investigation in the social sciences is a process of communication between one set of values and another, and without such a relation the realm of meaning would be impenetratable. However, if such a relation need not necessarily induce a personal or individual relativism, it cannot avoid the character at some level of a *cultural* relativism. The value sphere of action cannot, as has been seen, be determinately conceived, it can only be known *by means of* values; for this reason it is always to this extent relative to the values from which the investigation proceeds.

Thus, although both Weber and Parsons propose means of overcoming this methodological obstacle – Weber appears to rest on a speculative philosophy of history in which Western culture is an accumulation of all values past, the past being phases in the realisation of a teleological process of culture,[19] whereas Parsons argues that relativism can be avoided by the conscious intervention on the part of the investigator in obeyance of the 'norms of objectivity' of the scientific value-system (again a completely speculative argument and a primitive one in a methodological sense) – it is clear that some form of cultural relativism is inevitable. This is particularly the case when there is a considerable 'difference' between the culture which is the object of investigation and that from which the investigation is directed. In such cases, the non-scientific values of the investigator cannot easily 'communicate' with those of his object, and the possibility of a correct 'understanding' is curtailed. The greater the separation between the two, the greater the degree of ambiguity and speculation. This is a consequence realised, yet accepted, by Weber:

> many ultimate ends or values toward which experience shows that human action may be oriented, often cannot be understood completely, though sometimes we are able to grasp them intellectually. The more radically they differ from our own ultimate values, however, the more difficult it is for us to make them understandable by imaginatively participating in them.[20]

The problem, however, is of a more fundamental nature. More important than this explicit methodological obstacle which, after all, depends on the acceptance of the possibility of 'meaningful communication' itself (a possibility which, in the light of what has already been said, is at least dubious), is the *theoretical* issue of whether it is possible to relate in any coherent sense the value element of action with action itself. This issue applies not only between cultures but also within a culture.

If the value sphere of action is not to be determinately conceptualised and is to remain as a transcendental and symbolic realm then any investigation into its *effectivity* must of necessity contain an element of ambiguity and a degree of speculation. The contradictory co-existence of an indeterminate realm of values and a determinate sphere of action requires that the theoretical specification of the effectivity of any given set of values can never be rigorously achieved. It is impossible to relate coherently a level that cannot be known and a level that can be, and any attempt to do so will inevitably be characterised by speculation. That is, it is not possible to determine in any particular case that some particular value has determined the action. This is the case in either direction. On the one hand, given any value in the way that Parsons presents them, there is no way that the investigator can deduce a concrete action from it. Concrete action cannot be derived from the symbolic objects that are seen to govern it, because there is always a discrepancy between the two: 'the discrepancy between norm and actual course of action is one main aspect of the non-logicality of action' (*SSA*, p. 213). To attempt such a derivation would be to fall into an 'idealist emanationism'. On the other hand, it is equally not possible to deduce the value involved unambiguously from the concrete action itself – this would imply that the value is purely solipsist, whereas Parsons insists that the most important feature of values is their relation to symbolic *systems*.

The speculative character of the analysis of the relation between action and the values it is seen to realise is apparently acknowledged by Parsons, as can be seen in certain of his arguments on non-logical action:

The nonscientific theories associated with action depart from the scientific standard in general not only in that their major

premises are manifestations of sentiments rather than statements of fact, but also in that the reasoning involved is to a
greater or less degree sophistic, and that the premises themselves are ambiguous. In so far as its premises are not logically
determinate it is not possible for a theory to deduce unam-
biguous courses of action from them. On this fact Pareto
rightly lays great stress. (*SSA*, p. 216)

In attempting to ensure the specificity of ends and norms of
action, Parsons is forced to accept an endemic component of
theoretical ambiguity. It is little wonder that when he actually
confronts the problem of an analysis of values (which is less and
less the case in his later works), Parsons is hardly ambitious.
Thus, when referring to the value-element of action, he admits
to 'the extreme difficulty of finding adequate formulations for
any scientific analysis of this view'.[21]
So we have it: the mode of achieving the autonomy and
effectivity of normative orientation in relation to the other
elements of action involves the apparent intervention of a reality
which is inaccessible to science. The consequences of this project
have been drawn out – the attempt to demonstrate the existence
of that which cannot itself be demonstrated, the agnosticism of a
philosophical anthropology, the inevitable cultural relativism
which any attempt to base social analysis on an 'interpretative
understanding' of the meanings involved, and the speculativism
of any attempt to theorise the mode in which values are thought
to be realised in action. These consequences show the impossibility of uniting an essentialist conception of the specifically 'human' form of existence as inherently religious in orientation with a coherent and consistent determinate theoretical
system.

The points made so far relate specifically to the mode in which
Parsons conceptualises values and their relation to action. There
is a more general order of issues which is independent of the
specific notion of 'ultimate reality' and which concerns the basic
problem of the definition of action as the realisation of 'ideas' in
nature (whether these be defined as unknowable or not). The
final part of this discussion approaches this proposition of the
theory of action.

## 3.4 Action as the Relation between the Ideational and Natural: Idealism and Contradiction

As has been emphasised throughout, action in the sense proposed by Parsons is never to be seen merely as the objectification or expression of values and ideas, nor, conversely as the mechanical responses of heredity and/or environment. Action is in all cases the *relation* between values and the conditional elements of action. For our purposes here we shall refer to the relation as that between a realm of ideas and a realm of nature, and it may be seen as a relation which exists in all of Parsons' analyses of action. It is this relation as a general form which is the object of this section.

It is above all in Parsons' post-1950 writings that this relation is most rigorously and explicitly elaborated (and these will therefore be the major concern of this section). Whereas in *SSA* the primary relation of action is between the 'normative' and 'conditional' realms, in later developments we find the relation between, on the one hand, the cultural system and, on the other, the personality and social systems – the 'three systems of action' constitute the new form of conceptualising the relational character of action.[22]

Whereas the personality and social systems are defined as 'empirical' systems of action, the cultural system (as is normative orientation in the action frame of reference) is conceived as unique in relation to the other elements of action. The cultural system is defined as an *ideal totality*, a realm of ideas and their relations as ideas. In *SSA* this takes the form of a set of 'eternal elements', and in the later works the ideal totality is elaborated as a 'system' with systemic internal relations. The level of culture includes three primary categories of ideas – cognitive, expressive and evaluative – which exist as symbols for the empirical systems of action. As symbols these ideas are non-spatial and non-temporal, and they fulfil the primary function of the provision of pattern-configurations for the action complex – it is a function that Parsons later presents in terms of a 'cybernetic hierarchy', in which culture takes the place of the 'pattern-maintenance' subsystem of the General Action System.[23]

As a system the cultural realm is constituted neither by the interaction of a plurality of actors,[24] nor by the actions of a single actor, but by the atemporal and symbolic organisation of ideas, values and norms necessary for the empirical systems of action to operate. In other words, the cultural system is organised on a completely different basis from the empirical systems of action – it is organised on the basis of ideal relations and the symbolic content of its elements.

The empirical systems of action, the personality and social systems, are conceived as modes of organisation of 'motivated' action – social systems are modes of action organised about the relations of actors to each other, personality systems modes of action organised about the living organism, but both concern action which is *motivated* around certain exigencies, the 'effort' or 'energy' side of action. There is, therefore, a definite opposition between the forms of exigencies according to which the 'empirical' and ideational systems are organised. The empirical systems are organised on the basis of the natural requirements of the biological organism and the forms of social interaction, the cultural systems by the relations between ideal elements. The mode in which the two forms of systems relate to each other is presented as follows:

> systems of value standards (criteria of selection) and other patterns of culture, when *institutionalised* in social systems and *internalised* in personality systems, guide the actor with respect to both the *orientation to ends* and the *normative regulation* of means and of expressive activities, whenever the need-dispositions of the actor allow choices in these matters. (Parsons, *Toward a General Theory of Action*, p. 56, emphasis as in original)

The cultural level is qualitatively distinct from the 'natural' systems of action but is decisive as a mechanism of their functioning. For example, communication through a set of common symbols is the precondition for reciprocity and complementarity of expectations prerequisite for the social system to operate.

Human action itself may be seen therefore as mid-way between two realms – it may be defined as the *mechanism of realisation of the ideal totality in the realm of nature*. Just as the voluntaristic element of action is the mechanism of realisation of the normative component of action at the level of the conditions of action, so the personality and social systems are the mechanisms of realisation of the cultural totality at the level of the natural exigencies of the individual as a biological organism and of groups of actors as part of a social organism – these exigencies being either the impetus of action itself, or obstacles to the automatic realisation of the value component of action.

It is this general relation between a cultural and a natural or extra-cultural realm which constitutes the basic structure of all forms of action theory – although the realms may be differently conceptualised and the mechanisms of realisation variable, the basic opposition is ubiquitous in all forms of sociology.[25] I shall attempt, by means of a discussion of one particular case in which this relation is operative, to show the consequences of such a mode of theorisation.

The case which I shall use as an example of the general form is the distinction and relation which Parsons proposes between 'motivational orientation' and 'value orientation' (referred to hereafter as 'MO' and 'VO', respectively). Given that the personality and social systems are defined as systems of motivated action, and the cultural system is defined as a set of symbols in which value-standards are primary and constitutive, the distinction and the relation between MO and VO is central.

The central axis of action is the relation between the actor and his situation – motivational and value orientation refer to the different modes in which the actor orients himself to his situation. MO concerns the appearances, wants and plans that the actor has *vis-a-vis* his situation. These are categorised into three 'modes of motivational orientation': cognitive (the process of recognition of an object in relation to a set of need-dispositions), cathectic (gratificational–deprivational significance in relation to the actor's drives), and evaluative (allocation of energy into intelligible plans). In short, these modes are aspects of the actor's orientation which are pertinent to gratification and deprivation of his need dispositions. VO on the other hand concerns the symbolic specifications or 'standards' which commit the incumbent to observance of some organised set of rules – the three corresponding modes of VO are the cognitive (for example, knowledge), appreciative (standards pertaining to cathexis, e.g. expression in art), and moral (standards specifying the actor's responsibility to the effects of his action upon the systems of action within which he is operating).

The mode in which the two forms of orientation articulate is as follows: MO supplies the 'interest' side of action, the organised, energetic and cathectic impulses to action which are referred to as the 'gratificational directionality' of the actor, whether individual or collective. If the modes of MO provide the active or motor force of action, the modes of VO provide the 'primacy' or controlling aspects, by means of the relation between these modes and the symbolic order of action – they involve the actor in a form of commitment to sets of ideas of a cognitive, expressive or moral nature. It is the role of symbolic specifications provided by the VO element of action that constitutes the mode in which action may be said to be 'governed' by values and norms:

> Value-orientation refers to those aspects of the actor's orientation which commit him to the observance of certain norms, standards, criteria of selection whenever he is in a contingent situation which allows (and requires) him to make a choice. (*Toward a General Theory of Action*, p. 59)

Parsons, however, claims to make, and indeed must of necessity make, two stipulations regarding the concepts of MO and VO. On the one hand, as discrete components of action they must at all times be kept analytically *distinct*; there is no sense in which the two forms of orientation can be reduced in either direction to its opposite; the 'interest' side is not to be confused with the 'controlling' side of action. On the other hand, there must be some form of determinate *relation* between the two forms of orientation such that VO can really be said to govern action in the absence of an immediate or automatic determination of action (i.e. in a situation of choice). In other words, the VO side of action must be at some level *effective* at the level of motivation in the sense of providing the primacies under which motivation can operate. It is this double proposition, of the distinction and relation between MO and VO, that I shall question.

The basic problem is as follows: given the distinction between MO and VO, how can the mode of effectivity of the latter over the former be conceived? This question, in so far as the concepts of MO and VO are only forms of a more general relation between the cultural and extra-cultural realms of action, may be seen as a particular case of the general question 'how are we to theorise the mode in which action can be said to be governed by ideas (rules, meanings, standards, etc.)?'.

Parsons' position is quite clearly that ideas govern action either positively by providing definite criteria of selection, or negatively by excluding actions which might conflict with those ideas – for example, the cognitive forms of ideas negatively exclude actions founded on an erroneous conception of the situation. A great deal hinges on the way in which the two realms articulate therefore. There would appear to be three ways in which this articulation could be theorised. First, it might be argued that the motivational or interest side of action may be said to be governed by values in so far as it is an expression/objectification of those values. Secondly, it might simply be maintained that the analytical distinction between the two levels is all that is required, and that their relationship be thought of in terms of double determination, two distinct forms of effectivity. Thirdly, and more complexly, the distinction between MO and VO may be proposed with an additional specification that the two realms are not simply distinct but reflect certain pre-given capacities to relate to each other in a determinate fashion – capacities which make their articulation possible. I will argue that each alternative is highly problematic, and that Parsons is faced with a choice between idealism, contradiction and teleology, and that he maintains elements of each of them at some level. The overall implication of this is that the action frame of reference is incapable of avoiding certain quite crucial theoretical problems.

The first alternative posed related to the possible proposition that the articulation between MO and VO can be seen in terms of an expressive relation such that the motivational side of action is subject to the effectivity of values because it is an *expression* of them. The motivational elements of action would, in this case, be automatic realisations or objectifications of the cultural realm. In itself this thesis is foreign to Parsonian theory. If action is to be explained and conceived simply by the idea that is realised in it then we are on the terrain of what Parsons himself refers to as 'idealist emanationism'. All we have are ideas and their objectification and not processes of action in situations – this is precisely the tendency that Parsons finds objectionable in German historicist social theory.[26] With reference to MO and VO, in particular, he is quite emphatic that even at the level of their closest tangent, in the relation between the evaluative mode of MO and the moral standards contained in VO, no conflation of the two levels is to be made:

> let us distinguish clearly between the evaluative mode of motivational orientation and the value standards of value orientation. The evaluative mode 'involves the cognitive act of balancing out the gratification – deprivation significances of various alternative courses of action with a view to maximizing *gratification* in the long run. The value standards are various recipes or *rules* . . . which may be observed by the actor in the course of this balancing-out procedure. (*Toward a General Theory of Action*, p. 71, my emphasis)

It is clear that a dual referent lies in the relation between MO and VO, one towards the gratificational elements of action, the other towards the symbolic or ideal prescriptions within which the gratificational processes unfold. The motivational and value orientational realms of action have different origins and involve a set of different consequences, and they reflect what for Parsons are distinct *directions* in action. Thus, the 'act of choosing' in any particular case is subject to determination both from the motivational prerequisites of the biological organism and the social actor, and from the rules and standards of choice as supplied by the cultural system. The notion that the relation between MO and VO may be seen in terms of the objectification or expression of values themselves is unacceptable and incompatible with Parsons' reference to ideas *and* nature.

If the reduction of one level of orientation to the other is not strictly possible within Parsons' concepts then what of the second alternative? In this case, the relation between MO and VO is simply one of *double determination*. The two realms of action are to be held distinct, and action itself is to be seen as the 'compromise' between them, the motivational and value orientational elements of action are simply 'factors' in the aetiology of concrete courses of action. Again, *in itself*, this thesis is not capable of providing an adequate mode of theorisation of the relation between MO and VO, and this is the case for at least three reasons. In the first place, this thesis requires an account of the *mechanisms* by which the two forms of determination articulate to produce determinate forms of action. Without such an explanation the analysis of action is prey to all forms of eclecticism – a coherent theory must therefore supply at least this qualification to the notion of a simple double determination, and Parsons, as will be shown later, fails to provide one. The second and more general problem in maintaining the unqualified notion of double determination of action is that it is potentially contradictory. If both realms are to be determinant then there must be some form of *conflicting* relationship between them, in the sense that the effectivity of one must preclude the effectivity of the other. There are two senses in which this contradictory relationship is problematic. In the first place, if the two realms really are distinct as forms of determination yet action is to be held as a product of *both*, then there must be some explanation as to why, in any particular case, one form of determination and not another is dominant and excludes the other. In order to achieve this explanation, a form of determination not only distinct but also superior to the other two must be invoked – in other words, double determination must be qualified by a more extensive thesis. In the second place, the simple double determination mode of explanation, although at times operative, is clearly inconsistent with Parsons' theory of action. The notion of two *conflicting* forms of determination, motivational and value orientational, is precluded in the action frame of reference in so far as, and despite the fact that Parsons never assumes perfect harmony between the two (again, they are analytically distinct), it is Parsons' contention that action as such is only possible given some significant degree of complementarity between them. Both of these points show the necessity of a distinct mode of explanation of the relation between MO and VO. It is the third general reason against the double determination notion which, however, makes this most apparent.

It is clear that, although Parsons insists on the existence of two basic forms of determination of action – cultural and natural, normative and conditional, value orientational and motivational orientational, and so on – it is never simply a case of a *double* relation; one of them is *dominant*. In each of these oppositions it is the first category which is of a unique status. In the theory of action the cultural–ideational realm is not just *a* form of determination but is the *primary* one. This realm is primary in two senses. On the one hand ideas and values, at least in their

most important aspect (the 'ultimate' element), are not themselves subject to natural determination in the sense of other
objects, as was shown above in Parsons' critique of 'ethical
relativism' reflected in Durkheim's theory of religion. On the
other hand, the value component of action is not just a factor in
the determination of action but is the *controlling* element – this
was shown to be clear in the status assigned to normative
orientation as both an analytical element of action in the sense of
the 'unit act', and an element whose intervention is decisive in
situations of choice.

All of these points show a clear necessity for a number of
qualifications on the issue of the relation between MO and VO.
Neither an idealism nor a simple double determination is
sufficient as an explanation of the articulation of the cultural and
extra-cultural realms of action, and this is the case.whether we
assess each thesis on internal grounds or consider their consistency with Parsons' major arguments. This brings us to the third
alternative as outlined above – that the distinction between the
motivational and ideational realms is maintained, while in
addition providing the concepts of certain pre-given capacities
on behalf of both levels to relate in a determinate fashion.
Central in this respect is Parsons' attempt to present the concepts
of the *mechanisms* by which the realms of action intervene in each
other.

The complex formulation of these mechanisms in the post-
war writings is to be found in the concepts of the personality and
social systems. These systems are involved in the realisation of
value orientations at the level of concrete action processes – the
personality system internalises such values and the social system
institutionalises them in the context of social processes.[27] The
personality system and the social system are the mechanisms by
which the 'natural' exigencies of biological and social existence
(i.e. the 'functional prerequisites') are represented at the cultural
level, and the means by which the ideal specifications of the
cultural system are utilised in the direction of the fulfilment of
these exigencies.

Now, despite the rigorous fashion in which these mechanisms
are presented, there still exists the problem referred to above –
there is still a difference between, on the one hand, the cultural
system, and on the other, the personality and social systems,
which I have referred to as the problem of double determina-

tion. Yet it is at this point that Parsons introduces the qualification shown to be necessary for a coherent theorisation of the relation between the two levels, for he invokes the notion of definite *pre-given capacities* on the part of the biological organism and the various social units to respond adequately to the cultural realm. According to this notion, it is possible for the MO realm to relate to the VO realm because it has an innate capacity to do so. It is structured so as to allow the intervention of values and for this reason may be said both to be distinct from values themselves and yet to involve no contradiction or conflict with those values. Given such capacities, entities such as the personality and social system are seen to be possible in so far as there is no significant inconsistency between the natural impulses which generate action and the forms of ideas which guide, control or govern action.

This is made most clear in the case of the personality system and its relation to, on the one hand, the biological organism, and on the other, the cultural system.[28] Central to the maintenance of Parsons' thesis is the notion of the 'plasticity' of the human organism in allowing the determinate intervention of the value-sphere of action: 'the way is cleared for value standards to be effective whenever the plasticity of the organism leaves a realm of freedom in the relation between the situation and the organism' (*Toward a General Theory of Action*, p. 72).

The human organism is provided with a pre-given capacity to respond to value orientations. The basic motivational elements of the personality, 'drives' and 'need-dispositions', are in very significant respects already compatible with the existence of value standards. Although the organism has its own prerequisites and is by no means born a well-adjusted citizen, there is already in its constitution an endemic capacity to respond to the culture in which it appears. It is for this reason that Parsons prefers the term 'motivation' to that of 'instinct', for there is apparently a point at which human organism and human *subject* merge.

Now while Parsons advances several attempts to explain the mechanisms by which the personality and cultural system articulate, it is interesting that the mechanisms by which the biological system articulates with the personality system proper are not only not posed but are in fact denied an important status in the theory of action altogether:

the important question of how this energy expenditure will take place, what behaviour will result, what will be accomplished, requires analysis of drive and need-dispositions in the categories of action, *rather than the analysis of where the energy comes from.* (ibid., p. 112, my emphasis)

It is of course clear that there are certain areas which a theory can legitimately exclude without rendering that theory incomplete, but in Parsons' case the situation is significantly different. The theory of action quite definitely *relies* upon various propositions concerning the human organism in order for it to attempt to theorise the genesis of action processes – this has been shown above with reference to the necessity of introducing notions of certain pre-given capacities on behalf of the natural realm to respond to values. In so far as Parsons fails to pose seriously the problem of the mechanisms by which the human organism exhibits the natural tendency to act on the basis of values, his theory is presented with a paradox: *the action frame of reference denegates the theoretical pertinence of that on which it theoretically depends.*

Parsons can, by means of this strategic ambiguity, maintain the distinction between MO and VO while avoiding the immediate contradiction. He achieves this through the notion of an immanent 'design' on the part of the organism – the production of socialised individuals and institutionalised social actors is possible because the capacity to respond to values is written into the human constitution; these processes are thus the *realisation of that which is already immanent* in the human individual. This is most clearly seen in his account of socialisation, the process by which the organism becomes a human subject who can act on the basis of value orientations – it is the process of socialisation which provides, for Parsons, the fundamental mechanism of the constitution of the personality.[29]

Parsons attempts to provide a theory of the personality which is consistent with Freud's theory of the formation of the psyche. He proposes a 'convergence' between psychoanalysis and sociology with respect to the constitution of the human subject.[30] While we cannot enter into the issue of whether it is possible to 'sociologise' Freud in this fashion, it is apparent that Parsons' own account of the constitution of the personality is totally inadequate as a theoretical explanation. The central process of socialisation is that of the 'learning of value orientations'. It is not until the human individual is taught or has learnt to respond to values that he may be said to be truly 'human' – only then can he become an organised individual (fulfilling the requirements of the personality as a *system*) and a social actor (becoming integrated into the social system). However, as has been shown, this capacity is already presupposed, the organism is designed so as to allow the development of the value orientational components of action. In other words, the organism *is already a subject*, and what is considered to be the process by which the 'ego' is constituted is, in fact, merely the realisation of that which is already in every significant respect present in the organism. Parsons does not provide a theory of the mechanism by which the ego is formed but operates with an ambiguous circularity – the process of learning is not a mechanism by which the personality is formed but is a process of *realisation* of an immanent capacity.[31]

This is the point of paradox, for Parsons appears to have returned inadvertently to the idealism which the theory of action explicitly attempted to avoid. MO and VO are kept distinct but only in so far as there is some form of immanent relationship of consistency between them. The motivational level of action can be governed by the value sphere because nature is already capable of responding to values and ideas that exist in culture. The significance of this point is that nature must be assigned a *purpose* to realise values – the human organism, for example, is characterised by a 'plasticity' *because* such a capacity allows the determinate intervention of values. Nature has a purpose to realise ideas, and while this may not be the simple idealist emanationism as criticised in *SSA*, it certainly does involve the subordination of natural processes to the exigencies of the ideational realm. This subordination takes the form of an apparent teleological relation in which the natural organism is already a human subject in compliance with the requirements of action. Parsons does not provide a theory of the constitution of the subject or ego but rather relies upon an arbitrary assumption that the organism already has immanent capacities which must merely be realised. Socialisation is not the process of formation of the ego as such, rather the process of fruition of that which is potent but dormant. Values are to be the primary determinants of action and for this reason the organism is assigned a capacity to respond to and realise them. The theory of socialisation simply presupposes that which it seeks to explain.

The mode in which the theory of action presents the relation between the motivational and value orientational aspects of action (or more generally the natural and cultural realms) has been shown to involve a number of problematic theoretical tendencies. Whereas action, certainly in the post-war formulations but also in the earliest definitions of the action frame of reference, is not for Parsons a purely idealist concept in which all processes are expressions of values, nor a simple eclecticism in which values, motives, conditions, etc., are all factors, it is clear that the basic concepts of action induce elements of both tendencies. In the insistence on the unique and primary character of values in relation to the action complex, Parsons in forced to rely upon a sophisticated yet arbitrary idealism. Whereas the Parsonian theory of action avoids the immediate traps of certain other formulations of 'action' in sociology, it does so only in so far as it eventually leads into problems of it own.

# 4 Action and the 'Three Systems of Action': the Concept of Social Relations

## 4.1 Introduction

An analysis and critique of Parsons' theory of action, while clearly essential to any investigation into Parsonian sociology, is not in itself sufficient. The 'action frame of reference' is only, as it were, the primary set of concepts for sociological analysis. This analysis in itself presupposes a number of distinct concepts which prescribe the object of 'sociology' and make it a region theoretically discrete from other discourses. This chapter presents an outline of the basic concepts of Parsons' sociology, relates such concepts to more generalised conceptions of the 'social' and 'social relations', and through that judges the major criticisms made from within sociology of Parsons' theory of society. On this basis the chapter offers its own critical investigation of that theory and draws a number of conclusions concerning the status of sociological theory.

The chapter begins with an exposition of the notion of 'systems of action' as discrete from 'action-in-general', proceeds with an outline of several conceptions of social relations which figure prominently in non-Parsonian sociology, and, finally, develops a critique of Parsons' concept of society and social relations. The basic question concerns the modes in which the mechanisms of constitution, conditions of existence and mechanisms of reproduction of the social spheres are theorised.

## 4.2 Action and 'Systems of Action'

Parsons' writings in the late 1940s and early 1950s are distinguished by the concern with a body of concepts which were to become above all the hallmark of the Parsonian theory of action, and which consequently took the brunt of criticism from within sociology. The primary concepts here are those of 'social system', 'structure', 'function', 'subsystem' and so on. Yet the basis of these concepts lies above all in a vital distinction between 'action-in-general' and what Parsons refers to as 'systems of action'.

A major feature of the general theory of action is the positive attempt within it to distinguish between levels and realms of action and to avoid conflation and collapse, which are seen as characteristic of the various forms of reductionism in the social and cultural sciences. There may be 'action' in the sense of a set of processes which may be conceived in terms of a general frame of reference, but analysis of a more substantial nature presupposes the distinction between *systems* of action. The earliest formulation of the systems of action specifies three – the personality, social and cultural systems – and later developments added a fourth, the behavioural organism. Parsons is emphatic that failure to register the analytical and empirical distinctions between these systems can only induce reductionism in one or more directions

> On the one hand, the treatment of social systems only as 'resultants' of the functioning of personalities in the sense common to writers of a 'psychological' point of view, is clearly inadequate most fundamentally because it ignores the organisation of action about the exigencies of social systems as systems. On the other hand, to break social systems as only 'embodiments' of patterns of culture as a certain trend of thought common among anthropologists has tended to do, is equally unacceptable to the theory of the social system. (*SS*, p.539)

Just as in *SSA*, Parsons vigorously opposes theories which minimise or eliminate one or more of the analytical elements of the action frame of reference; at the level of systems of action he insists on the theoretical and empirical autonomy of differentiated organisations of action. This is emphasised not only from the point of view of the social system – Parsons is equally opposed to theories which 'sociologise' the personality[1] or which conceive the cultural realm as a simple reflection or idealisation of the social world.[2]

The irreducibility of levels and realms of action is persistently acknowledged. For a general theory of action to be possible it is necessary for there to be determinate relationships between different zonal organisations,

> But this interdependence and interpenetration is a very different matter from reducibility, which would mean that the important properties and processes of one class of system could be theoretically derived from our theoretical knowledge of one or both of the other two. (*SS*, p. 6)

The action frame of reference stipulates that the concrete act may be broken down analytically into its elements: actor, end, situation and norm. Actions themselves, however, are not empirically discrete in the sense of a multiplicity of independent concrete acts, for action in Parsons' sense is *organised*. The elements of action exist within levels or constellations which are defined as empirically differential modes of organisation. In other words, action exists in the form of *systems*.

Three such systems have been predominant in Parsons' work: the personality, social and cultural systems, or in other words organisation of 'need-dispositions', 'role-expectations' and 'value-orientations', respectively. The personality and social systems are defined as modes of 'motivated' action – the personality constituting a system organised around the individual living organism, the social system constituting a system organised around the relations of actors to each other. The cultural system, in contradistinction, is a system of symbolic or ideal patterns which are internalised within the personality system and institutionalised within the social system.[3]

The systems of action do not correspond to 'concrete' individuals or societies. An individual action, for example, will most likely involve all three systems. For this reason, any action will involve relations between the systems:

> action systems are structured about three integrative foci, the individual actor, the interactive system, and a system of cultural patterning. Each implies the others and therefore the

variability of any one is limited by its compatibility with the minimum conditions of functioning of each of the other two. (*SS*, p. 27)

The concept of systems of action is crucial to the analysis of the total action complex and, even more importantly, to the distinct levels of action themselves. Yet if the systems do not correspond to 'concrete' objects, what relation do they bear to action itself? Parsons offers us this relation in terms of levels of *differentiation* of action, and it is the notion of 'differentiation' which above all defines the character given to the Parsonian concept of 'system' in the sense of the three (or four) systems of action. A system here hinges on the relationship between action elements and differentiated levels of organisation of elements. This relationship can be illustrated *vis-à-vis* the concept of the social system, the system of most pertinence to this discussion.

The concepts of action as presented in *SSA* cannot alone permit the elaboration of the concept of social system: Theoretically, they can only allow some concept of 'social action' as merely one form of orientation of action,[4] and not that of a mode of organisation of action elements in which subjective orientation is only a facility.[5] The concept of the social system is just such a concept, and it carries the theorisation of the social realm to a qualitatively distinct level of abstraction.

Parsons is emphatic that the concept of social system must avoid both psychological reductionism and culturalist idealism. The social system is a system of action in which actions are organised around the relations of actors to each other, i.e. interaction. The elementary conceptual unit of the social system is the 'role'. Roles involve individual personalities, but what distinguishes role-action from merely individual action is the *differentiation* of the action elements involved. Interaction is governed by a distinct mode or organisation, by problems of a different functional character than those experienced by the personality system. The central problem at this level is the complementarity of role-conceptions, which allows for stability in the ego–alter relationship. Of decisive importance for such complementarity are the sanction-patterns supplied by the cultural system – symbols which provide consistent guides to action. Yet again the social system is *differentiated* from the other systems of action. The cultural system may be functionally significant to the social system but it is not equivalent to it. It involves a different level of differentiation.

There is also a differentiation of action elements within the concept of the social system. While the role is the 'elementary form' of the social system, 'concrete' social systems are characterised by a further differentiation. We now find the notion of the 'collectivity' which signifies the appearance of a new empirical level of action elements. Collectivities, or 'collective actors', involve more than mere role relationships:

> A social system having the three properties of collective goals, shared goals, and of being a single system of interaction with boundaries defined by incumbency in the roles constituting the system, will be called a *collectivity*. The action of the collectivity may be viewed as the *action in concert* of a plurality of individual actors. (*TGTA*, p. 192)

We shall return to the question of the notion of 'differentiation' later in the discussion. It is sufficient at this stage to signal the importance of the notion of levels of organisation of action elements in Parsons' sociology and the strategic significance of the notion of the three systems of action: the personality, social and cultural systems. Having gone this far, we can now reinforce the point by considering some of the other major approaches to the problem of conceiving social relations that exist in sociological theory and by comparing them with Parsons' position.

## 4.3  Psychologism and 'Methodological Individualism'

It is perhaps fitting to begin the comparison between Parsons' attempt to construct a theory of the social system and other major approaches with an extreme. Whereas Parsons' social theory has sought repeatedly to avoid reductionism, certain positions in sociology have, on the contrary, upheld reductionism as a positive virtue.

By far the most explicit and famous exponent of reductionist sociology is Homans.[6] Homans has persistently launched attacks on the concept of 'social' and 'social relations' as it functions in sociological theory. He holds that it fulfils no significant theoretical or 'explanatory' purpose either in the analysis of small group behaviour or even in that of global societies and historical movements. It is hardly surprising that Parsons' theory has received the brunt of Homans' criticism, and it is indeed Parsons' work that Homans holds to be the ultimate 'reification' of the social realm to a level beyond individual manipulation and determination. It thus has, Homans argues, no explanatory significance. In contradistinction he advances a conception of human behaviour in which all 'social' relations (including political and economic relations) are reduced from the theoretical point of view to 'elementary psychological processes'.

Yet Homans is not only critical of structural–functional theories of the social realm; he is openly opposed to any theory which operates with the concept of the social as a theoretically discrete element of explanation of social or historical processes. It is the very notion of *social* relations, whether as a theoretical concept or as an ontological presupposition, which is held to be problematic.

Leaving aside the epistemological components of Homans' critique of structural–functionalism (these have already been discussed), the major point of contention lies in the mode which Parsons conceives functional relations and social processes. In the paper 'Bringing Men Back In', Homans chooses the problem of the relation between kinship forms and industrialisation as the clearest example of the futility of structural–functional theory and the explanatory superiority of his own psychological account.

Parsons proposes to explain the determinate relationship between kinship forms and the economy, and in particular the relationship between the nuclear form of family unit and the industrially-advanced economy, by means of the concept of 'structural differentiation'. This concept designates the tendential process that Parsons considers to be endemic to the structure of social systems, and which refers to the process of differentiation of system units, along functionally more beneficial and advanced lines. Thus the emergence and dominance of the industrial economy, itself an index of the process of structural differentiation, is accompanied, he argues, by a parallel process of functional differentiation of the kinship system in which kinship functions become more specialised and isolated, resulting ultimately in the nuclear family unit.[7]

Homans refuses to see this thesis as a worthwhile theoretical

explanation of the relation between kinship forms and industrialisation. The explanation of this relation is, and can only be,
at the level of human individuals. It must start, that is, with 'men'
(hence the title of his paper 'Bringing Men Back In') as the
primary elements of the account.

Consider his counter-explanation. Some 'men' organised
factories because to do so would enhance their material rewards
compared with other economic means. In addition (and fortu-
nately), other men volunteered their labour for factory work, in
preference to agricultural subsistence, because they too are
attracted by the increased rewards offered by industrial production. One consequence of this situation was that the traditional
ties of kinship, extended family networks and so on, were found
to be incompatible with the primary means of earning a living. A
mobile and isolated family unit was shown to be more fitting to
factory-based production.

This is the alternative explanation that Homans offers for the
historical transformations of the family unit in industrial
economies. The central component of that explanation is the
notion of the needs and capacities of 'men':

> the nuclear family tended to become associated with factory
> organisation; and the explanation for the association is
> provided by propositions about the behaviour of men as such.
> *Not the needs of society explain the relationship but the needs of men.*
> ('Bringing Men Back In', op. cit., p. 110, my emphasis)

The 'needs' referred to are the apparently well-established
psychological tendencies (which Homans borrows from learning
theory in behaviourist psychology), of which the primary one is
that man is a 'reward-seeking animal'. It is according to such
propositions, and not to any sociological conceptions, that the
explanation of any human processes must be determined. There
can be no independent discipline of 'sociology' (with an object
and concepts of its own) in the strict sense. There can be no
references at all which cannot in principle be reducible to the
psychological processes of the human individual:

> no matter what we say our theories are, when we seriously try
> to explain social phenomena by constructing even the veriest
> sketches of deductive systems, we find ourselves in fact, and

whether we admit it or not, using what I have called psychological explanation. (ibid., p. 114)[8]

With reference to the work of Parsons it is hardly surprising that Homans finds more comfort in his earlier writings, with their emphasis on the concept of human action, than with the later concepts of personality and social systems. The preference is clear: 'As the theory of action was applied to society, it appeared to have no actions and mighty little action' (ibid., p. 115). The way in which Homans attacks Parsons in this respect is strongly reminiscent of other critiques which have emerged from within ethnomethodology, symbolic interactionism and social phenomenology. While these positions clearly adhere to a distinct conception of the human individual – reference is made to meanings of the individual and to 'common-sense conceptions of the world' rather than to behavioural drives and instincts – the overall project has a strikingly similar effect. This is to deny the theoretical significance of any concept which cannot be reducible to that of the human *individual*. All 'social' processes are in the last analysis merely individual actions or behaviours. Where Homans obliterates the social realm in favour of innate behavioural characteristics or traits, these other positions deny the social in favour of the subjective constitution of the individual's situation by the actor.

Where Parsons, together with Durkheim, argues that a concept of the social *as distinct from* that of the human individual is necessary to sociology as an independent discipline, Homans and a great many others besides openly oppose any such objective. For Homans *any* process involving human individuals can always be explained away by the basic propositions of psychology. Any processes which are not, as yet, explicable in these terms can be so in future given sufficient factual information and 'intellectual machinery'. Homans even denies the pertinence of the term 'reductionist' to refer to his position, for he does not accept that there is a genuine 'sociological' proposition to begin with!

Yet the problems with projects such as this one are all too apparent. One must question whether it is possible to theorise *consistently* variant social or historical forms from a given stock of psychological drives. In particular, how can one logically conceptualise *different* social types and their transformations (e.g.

'agrarian' to 'industrial' societies, to use terms with which Homans operates), from apparently similar and invariant individual mechanisms?

This is indeed precisely the problem that Parsons registers in Homans' project. What Parsons locates as the major shortcoming of individualism/reductionism in Homans' theory is that the attempt to reduce all social processes to individual units 'clearly precludes analysing the conditions under which the component may be independently variable'.[9] If the referent to the explanatory power of psychological propositions is not to be totally fatuous, then these propositions must themselves be capable of extension to incorporate the notions of different economies, societies, etc. Yet this is precisely where Homans' claims can be shown to be unrealised.

Take, for example, his account of industrialisation. Two primary psychological drives are seen to explain the process of the industrialisation of the economy: (a) men are more likely to perform an activity the more valuable they perceive the reward of that activity to be; (b) men are more likely to perform an activity the more successful they perceive the activity is likely to be in getting that reward. Such drives apparently increase the likelihood of the development of labour-saving machinery and increase the availability of men willing to organise factories and others willing to offer their labour. The psychological propositions are thus seen to 'explain' the process of industrialisation.

Unfortunately the explanation fails to account for certain conditions of existence which the process of industrialisation must of necessity imply, and which are indeed *presupposed* within Homans' description. The organisation of a factory presupposes certain minimum conditions. It presupposes capital, whether in money or plant, and how can the *same* psychological drives account for the *differential* distribution of capital without invoking a form of determination extraneous to it? Secondly, it presupposes land, which is not just 'there' for development, but which has to appear for rent and which is thus subject to conditions of ownership and possession – again, relations that cut across any drive toward reward-seeking. Thirdly, the organisation of the factory presupposes the existence of a labour force, not just as individual men, but men who take the form specifically of *labour*.

This final point alone shows the immense difficulty which

Homans finds to consistently maintain his position. It is clearly quite absurd to attempt to account for the appearance of factory labour by a psychological drive toward reward-seeking on behalf of individual labours. Not only is this historically ludicrous, for there is no reason to suppose that initially industrial labour was necessarily accompanied by greater material returns than other forms of labour, and it is also naive to present the appearance of a labour force as a 'choice' on behalf of individuals (this ignores physical expropriation of peasants from land as an effect of political-economic movements). The thesis is actually *internally* contradictory, for it presupposes something which it cannot, in its own (psychological) terms, account for: the existence of a free labour force which is obliged to offer itself in return for its means of subsistence, i.e. wages. In other words, factory labour is only possible given certain conditions and relations which must exist *prior* to its entrance into production.

An account by Marx illustrates precisely this point (note that this *is* an illustration, not a method of criticism in itself). In his analysis of the genesis of industrial capital, Marx refers to the situation of the colonies as the site of capitalist relations and to points made by Wakefield's theory of colonisation. Wakefield reports on a Mr Peel (undoubtedly a reward-seeking animal), whose objective was to set up a productive unit in Swan River, Australia, at a time when Australia was still virgin territory. So scrupulous was this entrepreneur that he took with him from England what he thought to be the complete requirements for industrial production. He took with him property in money, means of subsistence, means of production, and even 3000 men, women and children to work for him. On arriving at Swan River, however, Mr Peel discovered to his amazement that his work-force disappeared and left him with his money, means of subsistence and machinery. The problem lay in the fact that alternative means of subsistence were available for his work-force so that there was no *necessity* for them to work in his factory. It is meaningless then to account for their disappearance in terms of their own reward-seeking drives, for the decisive issue is the very availability of the alternative itself, i.e. as a *social relation*. Wage labour is a social relation which presupposes certain relations of ownership and possession of means of production and means of subsistence. Whatever the psychological traits of individuals, if these relations do not exist then wage-labour itself cannot exist. In the colonies wage-labour was absent as an economic relation, and Marx refers ironically to 'Unhappy Mr Peel who provided for everything except the export of English modes of production to Swan River' (*Capital*, I, p. 766). One does not have to accept Marx's own concepts to appreciate the significance of the point. In the free colonies the bulk of the land was still 'public' in the sense that it did not take the economic or politico-legal form of 'property' as such. Consequently, every settler could turn part of the land into his own 'property' and make it provide his means of subsistence. There was, as yet, no social separation, or its economic and political conditions of existence, of the labourer from his means of subsistence. There was therefore no necessity for him to enter factory production in order to attain his subsistence (or that of his family).

Homans naively fails to offer an explanation of relations which are presupposed in his account. He fails to explain the determination of differential rates of reward, and the distinct forms in which those rewards can be attained (profit, wages, etc.). His 'psychological explanation' far from constituting a superior theory of society is merely evasive with regard to the *conditions of existence* of social phenomena which his theory imputes but does not explain.

## 4.4 Merton's 'Functional Paradigm' and 'Factor' Theories of Social Phenomena

While Homans and others attempt to totally discount the pertinence of a specific concept of the 'social', other positions in sociological theory take a less extreme stance. While denying the degree of 'abstraction' of Parsons' concept of the social system, they talk of a 'moderated' functionalism. While they may approve of concepts such as 'systems' and 'needs', they aim to maintain a closer link with 'reality', and in particular with what they consider to be a more realistic conception of human action. The major author of this tendency is Robert Merton.

Merton is critical of the use that Parsons makes of the concept of system and 'system-units'. For Parsons, the 'units' and 'parts' of the system are to be defined in *terms of the system*. The central theoretical concept is that of a boundary-maintaining system, and the components of that system are conceived as *mechanisms of its functioning*. Merton aims to transform this parts–totality relation in order to produce a more acceptable formulation of functional analysis.

Merton's critique is best represented in the paper 'Manifest and Latent Functions',[10] which, though not explicitly directed at Parsonian functionalism, is quite clearly of indirect significance to it. Merton proposes an inventory of the basic postulates of functional analysis past and present. The three central postulates are seen to be that of the 'functional unity of society', that of 'universal functionalism' and the postulate of 'indispensability'. In all three cases it is argued that functional relationships are established *a priori*, that is, prior to any empirical determination. Consequently, these are held unacceptable on both epistemological and substantive grounds.

It is apparent that elements of all three postulates are seen to dominate Parsons' structural–functionalism, but one has to discover this in explicit form in Merton's brief but revealing reply to Parsons' paper 'The Position of Sociological Theory'.[11] In his reply Merton refers to the concept of 'functional prerequisites' as 'formal' and 'cloudy' in so far as they are not determined empirically or *a posteriori*. He also claims that the concepts of 'order' and 'equilibrium' operate so as to distort the essential nature of the social world, i.e. that it is continually in flux. The general opposition is to the notion of the 'social system as given', which apparently carries with it the ontological assumption of the basic unity of society.

What is paradoxical about Merton's critique is that at no stage does he approach what Parsons himself considers to be the primary role of the concept of the social system – its *theoretical* purpose. That the concept of system and its related concepts of order and equilibrium are not simple ontological statements but theoretical instruments is continually asserted by Parsons:

> If one has the conception of a homeostatically controlled boundary-maintaining system that has some stability and therefore to which some such concept as equilibrium is applicable, then all one means by functional analysis is a set of classifications of such a system. (From 'Cause and Effect' in D. Lerner (ed.), *Cause and Effect in Sociology*, p. 59)

The three postulates classified by Merton do not include a reference to the *theoretical* function of the concept of social system or equilibrium. Merton's own 'functional paradigm', on the contrary, is presented in terms of epistemological and ontological referents in which the theoretical character of the concept 'function' is totally displaced. The elements which Merton intends to add to functional analysis all bear this epistemological or realist emphasis:

> Parsons has not explicitly treated several concepts which point away from the emphasis on the social system as given. Chief among these are the concepts of social dysfunction, manifest and latent functions, functional substitutes and equivalents, the diverse social units subserved . . . by a given function, etc. (Merton's 'Discussion' of 'The Position of Sociological Theory')

The critique of the postulates of functional analysis which Merton advances involves two major changes in reference which are held essential to an unproblematic functionalism. In opposing the postulate of the functional unity of society, (i.e. any *a priori* concept of the social totality), he argues that functional interreltions should be established solely according to the 'specification' of the social units, and that it must be accepted that some units might have 'multiple consequences', and may also be 'dysfunctional'. In other words, 'one cannot assume full integration' (*On Theoretical Sociology*, p. 90) in an ontological sense. In opposing the second postulate, that of universal functionalism, Merton proposes that such a notion be tempered and subjected to a 'codified approach to functional interpretation', that functional relations be established on empirical grounds as empirically-contingent *variables*. Finally, he holds that a functional paradigm must accept the possibility of functional alternatives, equivalents or substitutes and not presuppose consistent or persistent relations between system-parts.

The epistemological problems of Merton's paradigm have already been approached but we can, in this context, point to certain substantive or theoretical problems which this thesis involves. Merton explicitly opposes the very possibility of constructing a 'prior' concept of the social totality, on the grounds of avoiding the 'assumption' of full integration of system-parts. In contrast, he argues for what Isajiw[12] has labelled an 'item-centred' approach.

In this, the parts of the system are to be determined independently of the whole in so far as they are empirically-contingent phenomena and as such must be treated as 'a question of fact, rather than axiom' (*Social Theory and Social Structure*, p. 26). The concepts of the parts of the system must be established independently of the concept of the system itself. Any other method of establishing these concepts is seen to involve an unwarranted 'commitance' to one model, and it is here that Merton locates the potent ideological import of some versions of functionalism.

Merton makes explicit what is behind a now common thesis held by the majority of 'functionalist' sociologists,[13] not to mention its more extreme form held by the anti-functionalists (Dahrendorf, Lockwood, etc.): the 'parts' of the system should be defined independently of the system itself. But apparent here is a paradox which either makes the term 'functionalism' totally meaningless or involves the functional paradigm in contradiction. In the first case, the term 'functionalism' means simply an epistemological relation between independent observable phenomena, and it does not involve any distinctive substantive theory.[14] With respect to the second, the functional paradigm actually conflicts with what is involved in functionalist explanation.

Elements of the latter clearly exist in Merton's work. This is apparent from his discussion of 'manifest' and 'latent' functions and 'dysfunctions', and from the mode in which they are established. Manifest functions are defined as the observed consequences of intended motivations for the 'system', and latent functions as the observed consequences which are unrecognised and unintended. In a similar vein, dysfunctions are defined as those processes which can be observed to create strain or tension on the system. In all three cases the 'consequences' of the function are to be *observed*, to be determined empirically and independently of the (concept of) the system itself. System-units, parts and items are to be established apart from a prior concept of the system for which they have consequences or effects.

The contradiction lies in this: how is it possible to refer to consequences for a system without having a prior concept of the system itself? Two issues are involved here. First, it is not possible to refer to 'units' or 'parts' in any meaningful sense without the concept of the totality of which they are a part. A part must by definition be a part of something, and if it is known to be a part then that presupposes the concept of the object of which it constitutes a part. Secondly, it is not possible to establish theoretically the 'consequences' of parts of the system without some prior conceptualisation of the make-up of the system, such that the existence of a consequence can be specified, and so that the nature of the consequence may be known.

If functional analysis is to have any logical significance at all then it *must* involve 'prior' concepts. To talk of parts, units or consequences without some such concepts is a self-contradiction. Given the explicit (epistemological) rejection of these concepts, Mertonian and related forms of functionalism not only of necessity contradict their protocols laid out in advance but, what is worse, leave open the door to arbitrary untheorised concepts. Merton's opposition to *a priori* conceptualisation means simply that the concepts which are used (of 'parts' and 'systems') are subject to little or no theoretical organisation of systematicity. The limits that such a paradigm can impose on a sociology are obvious. The avoidance of theoretically-systematic concepts, in the hope of avoiding 'commitment' to one system model, clearly presents obstacles to the analysis of what must be central issues in sociological theory – the conditions of existence and reproduction of social phenomena. Merton's 'functional paradigm' is merely a gloss for what is essentially a theoretically disorganised sociology.

A position which may be seen in many ways as a bridge between Mertonian-type functionalism and various forms of non-functionalist or anti-functionalist sociology, is that taken up in the early essays of Alvin Gouldner, best illustrated in the paper 'Reciprocity and Autonomy in Functional Theory',[15] Gouldner demonstrates the ease with which a 'functionalist perspective' can become a mere platitude.

Gouldner opens his account with an explicit preference for Merton's, rather than Parsons', mode of functional analysis:

> The basic gain of the Mertonian strategy is that it prevents either premature commitment to, or premature exclusion of, any given structure as an element in the social system.
> ('Reciprocity and Autonomy in Functional Theory', p. 246)

An epistemological – ontological opposition to Parsons' social theory, similar to that of Merton's, is proposed. 'Empirical potency' is preferred to 'logical elegance' ( = prior conceptual specification of the structure of the system and its relations). The elements of the social system are to be constituted 'inductively' not 'deductively'. Gouldner also offers his own brand of opposition to the 'integrationalist' presupposition of structural–functionalism. The latter is seen to rule out the possible autonomy of system parts and any capacity for internal conflict and social change.

Two areas are held to be most problematic in the functionalist conception of the social system: on the one hand, the issue of 'membership' of the system and the determination of its parts, and on the other, the principle of functional reciprocity. On system membership, Gouldner argues that the 'parts' of the system must be constituted through empirical research and not by means of any *a priori* concept of the social system. System membership can only be validly established according to the empirically contingent.

However, Gouldner's major opposition to Parsons' 'complete' functionalism (as distinct from Merton's 'incomplete' functionalism – its 'incompleteness' is apparently its virtue!), relates to the principle of reciprocity. The postulate of an integrated social system is seen to be synonymous with that of 'symmetrical interchange' or 'symmetrical reciprocity'. This postulate is seen to be empirically misled and effectively to preclude the study of power relations involving constraint and conflict, or the existence of 'degrees' of reciprocity, and so on.

Gouldner's alternative is to propose the notion of 'functional autonomy'. In this, tension is to be regarded as an integral part of functional relations,[16] and the parts of the system, instead of being defined in terms of the system itself, are to be seen as autonomous elements which bear a contradictory status between 'self-maintenance' and the demands of the system:

> To fit the data of social behaviour, the system model required must be such as to facilitate not only the analysis of the interdependence of the system as a whole, but also the analysis of the functional autonomy of its parts, and the concrete strains which efforts to maintain this autonomy may induce. (ibid., p. 256)

It is apparent that such a schema, being so arbitrary as to allow virtually everything, can quite easily be made the front for a mode of explanation more in line with social-psychology and other individualistic sociologies. Gouldner, indeed, sees this as one of its strong points, mentioning its ability to incorporate positions such as that of Erving Goffman. While Gouldner repeats the problematic arguments of Merton's functional thesis (the failure to register adequately the theoretical status of the concept of the social system in Parsons' work,[17] and the similarly absurd attempt to define the 'part' independently of a concept of the totality which makes it a part), it is this individualistic element of his attack which distinguishes his position from that of Merton. What lies behind his criticism of Parsons and his own alternative formulations is an individualist humanism, made explicit in his later works. In this sense, the demand for greater attention to be given to system 'parts' rather than the system itself is merely a gloss for the age-old debate on free-will: ' . . . human beings are not invariably characterised by a total dependence upon any one social system' (ibid., p. 255). 'System parts' in Gouldner's theory are nearly always individual actors, and 'autonomy' is just another word for the asserted capacity of the individual to withstand the pressures of his situational institutions and organisations. The attempt to rebalance functional analysis in the direction of the notion of functional autonomy is not so much a revolutionisation of functional theory, more a humanist polemic for free-will and human individuality. The reference to 'functional' becomes, effectively, superfluous.

Parsons, himself, has rarely directed criticism toward those other positions which, though they refer to themselves as 'functionalist', represent theses far removed from his own conception of structural–functionalism. However, with regard to the question which most marks the distinction between his and others' conception of functional analysis, i.e. that of the mode in which system-parts are to be defined, he has specified the crux of the issue:

> Specific descriptive propositions often refer to particular aspects or properties of an empirically existent set of phenomena. Such propositions are, however, empirically meaningless unless the 'what' is clearly and determinately conceived and defined. (*Essays*, p. 213)

Both Gouldner and Merton, not to mention a host of others,

begin by denying the conditions upon which a conceptualisation of system parts (in the rigorous sense) is possible. The parts, be they reciprocal, autonomous, manifest, latent, or whatever, must by definition be conceived in relation to some other object or totality (even autonomous parts are autonomous *from something*). The fact that such a totality has not only been unproblematised but has actually been denied a significant theoretical status says much for the arbitrary character of much sociological theory, 'functionalist' or otherwise. What is distinctive about Parsons' sociology is that he has explicitly set out to conceptualise the social realm in an attempt to avoid arbitrariness and reductionism.

We are now in a better position to elaborate more fully on the Parsonian theory of the social and, on that basis, to examine the theoretical coherence of its central concepts – the social system, the functional prerequisites, the pattern-variables, etc.

## 4.5 Parsons' Theory of the Social System

Parsons considers the concept of the social system as the 'terminal' concept for sociological analysis – the basis on which to build a theory of social relations and through which to analyse concrete social situations. The concepts of 'order', 'structure', 'equilibrium' and so on, must be considered in terms of this, the *theoretical* function of the concept of the social system. Consequently, it is fatuous to read such concepts as ontological postulates, as many critiques have tended to do, for, as Parsons states:

> Structure does not refer to any ontological stability in phenomena but only to a relative stability – to sufficiently stable uniformities in results of underlying processes so that their consistency within certain limits is a workable pragmatic assumption. (*Essays*, p. 213)

In fact, the concept of the social system is more than a 'pragmatic assumption', and Parsons later refers to it as the 'parent concept' of his sociological analysis.[18] Yet the important point, particularly in light of the many criticisms that the concept of the social system and its related concepts of order and equilibrium have received, is that these concepts are seen by

Parsons to be the means of analysing both relatively stable societies *and* those which are subject to rapid or severe transformation. The concept of equilibrium, for example, is, theoretically speaking, as applicable to the analysis of social stability as it is to the analysis of social change, and as applicable to the analysis of conformity as it is to that of deviance or conflict. Parsons holds only that the same set of concepts be used in the theorisation of both cases and that these concepts be developed and spelt out explicitly prior to any concrete investigation.

This is not to say that those concepts themselves have remained untouched from the time of Parsons' earliest works. On the contrary, the theorisation of the social realm has itself undergone major transformations from *SSA* to the post-1950 works (these points are dealt with more thoroughly in the following chapter). Taking the concept of 'order' alone, it is clear that the so-called 'Hobbesian problem of order' has received quite different answers in these two periods of Parsons' work. In *SSA* social order (via 'social action') is located above all at the *cultural* level – it is made possible by means of common orientation of actors to sets of values (primarily to ultimate values). In the post-1950 works, however, the concept of order is located predominantly at the level of the *social* system itself, and the cultural system becomes a mechanism of the functioning of the social system and a differentiated system of action. The social then becomes a determinate mode of organisation of action elements, and its components and mechanisms determinate features of the social system.

The specifically *theoretical* status of the concept of social system and its related concepts is spelt out quite explicitly by Parsons:

> the structure of a system as described in the context of a generalised conceptual scheme is a genuinely technical analytical tool. It ensures that nothing of vital importance is inadvertently overlooked, and ties in loose ends, giving determinacy to problems and situations. It minimises the danger, so serious to common-sense thinking, of filling gaps by resort to uncriticised residual categories. (*Essays*, p. 217)

The last sentence of this statement could just as easily be used to sum up the consequences of the positions of Merton, Gouldner, etc., and the statement as a whole is a good summary of the status which Parsons ascribes to the concepts of the social system. A central feature of Parsonian theory is that the 'parts' of the social system or the 'units' are defined in terms of the concept of the social system itself, and not independently (empirically or otherwise) from it. The theorisation of system parts is to be established via the concept of the *totality which defines them* and not arbitrarily as 'empirical uniformities' or 'consequences'. More precisely, system parts are to be defined as *mechanisms of significance* for the system.[19]

All social phenomena and social processes are to be conceived in terms of the concept of social system, the notion of a differentiated mode of organisation of action elements. Social units, elements or parts are to be theorised in terms of the social system of which they are components, whether this be a societal subsystem or a social system of a less inclusive nature. They are to be analysed in terms of that *functional relation to the system.*

These points may appear at this stage to be formal and abstract. In order to add weight to this exposition of Parsons' theory of the social, and to draw the full significance of the distinctive forms of analysis which his sociology involves, we might consider a more 'concrete' thesis of his which serves as an illustration of what is involved in specifically 'Parsonian' functionalism.[20] I refer to his analysis of 'political power' and its relation to the notion of the polity as a functional subsystem.[21]

### (i) *The Concept of Power*

Just as it is erroneous to reduce Parsonian theory to an elaborated Weberian approach,[22] it is equally erroneous to confuse Parsons' mode of analysis of political power with orthodox conceptions of power (primarily Weberian) adopted in sociology and political science. Such an equation not only conflates what are theoretically distinct orders of concepts, but it also disguises what is in many ways the great merit of Parsons' sociology: to pose explicitly and consistently the problem of the social conditions of existence and mechanisms of reproduction of social phenomena.

Among others, Poulantzas[23] makes the mistake of tracing the 'zero-sum' concept of power back to a 'functionalist–

integrationalist' conception of the social totality, of which he cites Parsons as the prime representative. Poulantzas equates the 'givenness' of quantity of political power in the zero-sum concept with the 'givenness' of the social system as a fully integrated whole. In other words, the zero-sum concept of power is held to be consistent with Parsons' structural–functionalist theory of society.

Such an interpretation, however, fails to acknowledge the fact that Parsons has directed an explicit critique of the zero-sum concept and has sought to develop a distinct form of analysis of political power. This is most clearly expounded in Parsons' review of C. W. Mills' *The Power Elite*.[24]

It is not strictly necessary to accept Parsons' concept of political power or his discussion of the United States to appreciate the effectivity of his critique of the zero-sum concept of power. This critique, insufficiently acknowledged in discussions of Parsons' concept of power,[25] involves two points of contention. First, Parsons disputes the validity of Mills' 'empirical generalisations' and considers them an inaccurate assessment of the situation in US politics. Secondly, and for us (and for Parsons) more significantly, Parsons levels an attack on the *theoretical conditions* of the concept of power that Mills advances.

The zero-sum concept may be defined in Lukes' terms as the situation in which 'A exercises power over B when A affects B in a manner contrary to B's interests' (*Power: A Radical View*, p. 34). The zero-sum concept of power provides the conceptual basis for not only the so-called elite *vs* pluralist debate on political power, but also the 'countervailing powers' thesis and to a great extent the 'conflict-consensus' debate.[26] In all of these cases the central issue concerns the *distribution of a given quantity of power* at any one moment. Poulantzas provides a good summary of the zero-sum concept:

> It is a matter of conceiving of power as a given quantity inside a society. On this theory, any class or social group *thus has as much power as another does not have*, and any reduction of the power of a given group is directly translated into an increase of the power of another group and so on, in such a way that though the distribution of power changes, the amount of power still remains an unvarying quantity. (*Political Power and Social Classes*, pp. 117–18, emphasis as in original)

It is easy to connect this concept to Weber's definition of power as 'the chance of a man or a number of men to realise their own will in a communal action, even against the resistance of others who are participating in the action'.[27] The significant point is that the question of power is reduced to one simply of its allocation or distribution, a question to be answered 'empirically'. It is a question of the extent to which an individual or group attains a portion of the set quantity of power available in society at a given moment in time, at the expense of other individuals or groups.

Parsons is opposed to the very mode in which the problem of power has been traditionally posed. The zero-sum concept begins with the question of the distribution of power; but according to Parsons this starting point is problematic. Power, he admits, 'has to be divided or allocated, *but it also has to be produced*' (*PSS*, p. 200, my emphasis). In other words, the question of the distribution of power must, *theoretically*, be secondary to the question of the mode in which power is produced and reproduced. Without a theory of the production of power, the question 'what is power?' cannot be answered definitively.

To demonstrate his point, Parsons offers a parallel with economic wealth, i.e. a parallel between power and money. Wealth, of course, is subject to variant forms of distribution, such that at any given time the wealth of one individual or group is at the expense of another individual or group. However, what is theoretically more important are the conditions of *production* of wealth, for these alone can tell us what determines the distribution in the first place, and therefore what the situation is likely to be in the future. The question of wealth distribution is held to be secondary to that of its production. Incidently, in this respect Parsons adopts the orthodox conception of the combination of 'factors' of production as the process which produces wealth, and the notion of 'returns to the factors' as the process of distribution and reproduction of wealth. Whether these are valid concepts is not significant here – what is important is that the question of production is placed before that of distribution.

Parsons applies the same logic to the problem of power. The 'empirical' determination of power relations under the zero-sum concept can, at best, give only a rough approximation of the current distribution of power at any given moment in time. As it does not explain how power is itself produced, it can provide no grounds for assuming the persistence of that distribution nor the possibility of it changing. To return to Mills (and others), the central problem is held to be that of *who* has power, but we are given no explicit theorisation of how this power is itself generated in society – only how power, once in existence, is passed on (e.g. through family connections). To pose the problem of the mode in which political power is generated would be to approach the question of the (social) conditions of the existence of power Without such theorisation the 'problem of power' can only remain at an arbitrary level.

For this reason Parsons' critique of Mills cannot be considered merely as a rebalance of empirical emphasis between, as Giddens claims, conflict and consensus world-views, as a re-emphasis of the relational non-coercive aspects of power as opposed to Mills' essentially coercive-based definition. It is a critique of the theoretical context of Mills' theory, of what Mills himself fails to account for in his theory – *the social conditions of existence of power relations*. The analysis of power relations under the zero-sum concept leaves power as an empirical contingency. It is a particular example of the more general tendency in sociological theory which I have referred to above in the cases of Merton and Gouldner etc. – the absence of the theorisation of determinate conditions of existence of social phenomena.

What then of Parsons' own treatment of political power? His analysis of power is based above all on the concept of the social system and the concepts of the functional prerequisites/functional subsystems. Power is not defined in terms of relations between individuals but in terms of the functional subsystem of which power is the primary 'output' or facility – the polity. The social system is a mode of organisation of action elements differentiated internally according to primary relationships with four functional prerequisites, functional problems which all social systems face.[28] These are 'adaption', 'goal-attainment', 'integration' and 'pattern-maintenance' ($A, G, I, L,$ respectively). Now for each functional problem there is a corresponding functional subsystem which has a primary task of fulfilling one problem. The polity is one such subsystem, for as a subsystem of the total (societal) subsystem it is concerned primarily with the functional problem of goal-attainment – the mobilisation of effective collective action in the attainment of the goals of the collectivity.

It is the functional relation of the polity to the social system as a whole which constitutes Parsons' theory of the social conditions of existence of political power. The concept of the polity is illustrated by means of a parallel between the political and economic aspects of modern societies.

Four reasons are given for the suggested theoretical parallel between the economy and the polity. First, both may be seen as abstract and analytical entities – they refer not to concrete realities as such (business or government) but to analytically discrete areas of investigation. Political theory and economic theory are abstract conceptual schemes which are concerned with phenomena of political or economic significance – Parsons holds that both can be subsumed within the system of concepts of the general social system.

The second parallel is that the polity, like the economy, may be usefully viewed as a functional subsystem of the total social system. While the economy is the subsystem with functional primacy in the adaptation of the environment for the purpose of producing societal resources, the polity is concerned with the processes by which the organisation socially necessary is built up and manipulated, and by which the goals of the collectivity are both determined and resolved.

The third parallel is between the status of 'collective action' for political theory and 'production' for economic theory. Both collective action and production are seen to involve a combination of factors which are directed toward the development of more valuable facilities, the mobilisation of resources, and making 'adjustments to conditions of demand'.

The fourth parallel between the polity and the economy relates to the nature of their 'outputs' and it directly involves the question of power. Power is equivalent to money for Parsons, in so far as both may be conceived as subsystem outputs which take the form of 'generalised symbolic media':

> Power ... is the generalised capacity to secure the perfor-
> mance of binding obligations by units in a system of collective
> organisation when the obligations are legitimised with refer-
> ence to their bearing on collective goals and where in the case
> of recalcitrance there is a presumption of enforcement by
> negative situational sanctions. (*PSS*, p. 361)

At least three points of significance are mentioned in this definition. First, power is defined in terms of the polity, which is in turn defined in terms of the concept of the social system. Power is not some arbitrary relation between individuals but is conceived as a 'mechanism of significance' for the system – it is a determinate social relationship. Secondly, power depends upon certain social conditions for it to be able to operate effectively – in particular, it requires 'legitimation'. Thirdly, power, although primarily a symbolic relationship, is *always* (either implicitly or explicitly) supported by coercion. I have already drawn the significance of the first point; one or two comments on the other two points may be in order in relation to the Parsonian concept of power.

To begin with, the inclusion of legitimation and 'generalisation' within the concept of power is significant in so far as it specifies that power cannot exist or function without its social conditions of existence. Power is generalised in that it cannot be reduced to one contingent act and then extrapolated to social relations in general – this would appear to be the case under the zero-sum concept. Parsons holds that power must involve a degree of general 'compliance', a medium which is accepted as such by the majority of the members of a society/group. The role of legitimation is made parallel with that played by 'confidence' in monetary systems (a central notion in orthodox monetary theory). If money is to operate as a generalised medium sufficient to function in a multitude of discrete transactions, it must have more than intrinsic value. Money must inspire confidence, a mutual acceptance of its status based on its capacity continually to return the goods.

Similarly, power should not be equated with deterrence alone, i.e. physical coercion or the possibility of it happening. For power to have any societal effectivity it must be legitimised; it must, that is, be grounded in the relational system, the normative guidelines provided by the institutionalisation of power.

It is quite erroneous, however, to consider legitimation as the essence of Parsons' concept of power ('conflict' theorists, for example, consider this the exclusive conception of Parsons' approach to power). Parsons stresses that legitimation refers only to the capacity to 'secure binding obligations' – *the capacities themselves are distributed differentially*, and here power differs from money. In other words, the hierarchical aspect of power is written into his very definition as an endemic feature of power relations. On this point Giddens' critique falters.

Another point is that coercion is not held to be a peripheral or incidental element of power. According to the polity–economy parallel, coercion is to power what commodity-money is to money in general (paper money), a 'reserve'. Money and power are symbolic media which provoke confidence and compliance, but they are always backed by a 'material' reserve which can operate in cases of disruption and breakdown. On this point, the 'consensus-conflict' opposition is again misplaced. Note also that the concepts of power and legitimation are seen as *general concepts* not empirical generalisation. They are applicable to the analysis of concrete societies, whether that society be based primarily on the coercive or legitimated elements of power.[29]

Enough has been said to support the statements made earlier concerning Parsons' social theory and its relation to various forms of functionalist and non-functionalist theory. His analysis of power illustrates the explicit attempt to define social phenomena and social relations in terms of their social conditions of existence. The zero-sum concept of power, on the other hand, is theoretically far less complete and far more arbitrary. The parallel between this concept and the sociological projects of Gouldner, Merton and Homans[30] etc. is difficult to ignore. There is an essential *theoretical* distinction between Parsonian structural–functionalism and other forms of sociological theory that cannot be spirited away by claims concerning the validity or otherwise of his empirical generalisations.

If these points are correct, then it is clear that a critical examination of Parsons' sociology must first of all approach the question of the nature of his theory itself. It must begin by considering the internal coherence of that theory, the relations between the concepts of social system, functional prerequisites and subsystems, pattern variables, and so on. Two areas in particular warrant investigation. On the one hand, the question of the internal structure and internal relations of the social system which go to make a boundaries totality – primarily the question of the functional prerequisited. On the other hand, there is the problem of the relations between the social system and the two other systems of action, the personality and the cultural. The following chapter takes up the issue of the functional prerequisites, the mode in which the functional subsystems are constituted, and the systemic relations within the social system. The remainder of this chapter is concerned with a more specific analysis of the relations between the social system on the one hand and the personality and cultural systems, on the other.

### (ii) The Social System and its Conditions of Existence: The Personality and Cultural Systems

In addition to its internal requirements, the social system depends upon relatively consistent relationships with the other two systems of action for its conditions of existence. I will argue that in his attempt to provide an account as to how this consistency operates and is possible, Parsons creates for himself a number of major problems.

To begin with, the personality system is crucial to the functioning of the social system in so far as it provides sufficiently 'socialised' human individuals. Action in the social sense cannot exist without a supply of actors adequately 'motivated' to respond to the conditions and norms of action which are organised according to the exigencies of social existence. For example, the actor's own self-categorisation must correspond in the main to his actual status in the social system, his need-dispositions must be relatively consistent with the roles and role-expectations of the social realm.

In cases such as these, there must be a minimal degree of consistency between the two foci of organisation, need-dispositions and role-expectations, between the personality and the social systems. Yet, as we have already seen,[31] the proposed mechanisms by which this consistency is held to be possible fail to provide an adequate account of this relationship. It is the process of socialisation which is seen to be the mechanism by which the raw human animal is made 'social', but this process in itself presupposes that the human individual is already granted the capacity to respond in this fashion. In the discussion in the previous chapter it was shown that the relationship between the human organism and 'action' proper was highly problematic – in this case the specific relationship between the personality and the social system merely extends that problem. The concept of socialisation, as we have seen, presupposes that which it seeks to explain: the process of socialisation does not produce the social animal, but merely *realises* that which is already there.[32]

There is, however, an extent to which the coincidence of the personality and social systems involves more than this arbitrary endemic tendency. A decisive linkage between the two levels of action is achieved by means of the third, the cultural system, and above all through its component, value-orientations. Both the relations of consistency between the personality and social systems and the internal relations within the social system are made possible above all by culture. Herein lies the question of the second, and the major, extra-social condition of the social system, the culturally provided systems of meaning which create the conditions for socially relevant action. This brings us to the most important part of the critique.[33]

The decisive importance of culture to social relations in Parsons' sociology cannot be denied. At its most elementary level its intervention is crucial to the establishment of social processes. The most primitive form of social system is the interaction between two (or more) actors, the ego–alter relationship. Its conceptual basis is the 'role', what the actor does in his relations with others seen in the context of its functional significance for the system. The primary ingredients of the role are role-expectations, patterns of evaluation which organise reci-procities, expectations and responses to these expectations in ego–alter relations. These patterns of evaluation are precisely the elements of culture which intervene at the social level, patterns of meaning which make interaction on any sustained level possible.

Of course, it is culture which lay at the basis of Parsons' earliest solutions to the 'Hobbesian problem of order', culminating in the thesis of *SSA*. Socially-relevant action is made possible through organised value-orientations, action is oriented to the actions of others and therefore surpasses the state of chaos. But culture is no less crucial to Parsons' later theories, though its status does become transformed. Here we find *two*, not simply one, solutions to the problem of order, the cultural and the 'functional'. If the social system is to survive, its members must fulfil the roles which together allow the successful functioning of the system. These are the functional prerequisites with which the system must come to terms. In respect of the functional pressures, the cultural system now becomes the *mechanism* through which the functional problems are *realised*, the two levels being channelled through the normative system, this being the point of contact between the social and the cultural systems.

Both referents, the functional and the value-orientational, are essential to Parsons' post-*SSA* theories. Denial of the functional dimension constitutes a regression to the earlier, less elaborate, theory of the social sphere, with its more explicitly Weberian emphasis. Parsons' critique of Weber's failure to develop a 'functional' reference testifies to the importance of this aspect of social relations.[34] Failure to acknowledge the dual character of social order has been one of the more obvious shortcomings of critical commentaries.[35]

In fact, the co-operation of the functional and value-orientational aspects of action is reflected at a number of theoretical levels, most particularly within the analyses of functional subsystem *vis-a-vis* institutions, and at another level between the functional prerequisites and the 'pattern-variables'.

In the case of the first relation, institution/functional subsystem, the culture/social reference is represented in the fact that institutions reflect value-standards in complexes of status–role relationships. Their primary effect is the integration of role relationships under a standard value-pattern – for example, the institution of 'property' defines rights of possession and obligations relative to them in the context of integrating action-expectations. Functional subsystems, on the other hand, are defined differently, in terms of the relation between a totality (or boundary) and the functional problems that it faces. They are systems differentiated according to their functional primacy, and their primary referent is to the social system as a system of action (although the concept also applies to the personality and cultural systems when they are taken as objects of analysis).

Institutions are in no sense *equivalent* to the subsystems – for example, the economy is not reducible to the institutions of contract or property. They involve, in fact, a distinct form of determination in so far as their primary components are culturally prescribed value-standards. In contrast, the primary ingredient of the functional subsystem is the functional problem which it attempts to overcome. A subsystem will most likely involve a number of institutions: the polity, for example, incorporates the institutions of authority and legitimation as part of its existence as a functioning totality.

While the two forms of organisation of action are not to be equated as such, nevertheless Parsons relies upon assuming at least a minimum of *consistency* between them. Now, it is this very consistency which presents a number of difficulties for the theory of the social system. In order to make the point I will move on to another level at which cultural elements and social-functional pressures coincide, that of the articulation of pattern-variables with the functional prerequisites.

It may be said, in fact, that it is the relation between the pattern-variable combinations and the functional prerequisites which constitutes the relation between institutions and functional subsystems. The pattern-variables, of course, have been central to Parsons' work from its early stages. They are defined as 'patterns of cultural value-orientation' (*TGTA*, p. 79), patterns which determine the choices with which an actor is presented in any given situation. The actor is not, as has already been stressed in an earlier chapter, a freely constituting human individual, for action in Parsons' sense involves choice only within the existent cultural context. It is a choice between alternatives prescribed prior to the individual and existent over and above him.

Parsons' later works introduce a further limitation to human choice – what is functionally necessary if social action is to be relevant for consistent and effective social relationships. It is important that the choice presented to the actor coincides in significant respects with that which is objectively required by the social system of which the actor is only a part. Parsons' account of the social system relies upon the assumption that the *cultural* specifications of the pattern-variables do indeed meet with the *social* requirements of the system of action itself. A great deal thus rests on the theoretical connection between the two spheres that Parsons offers us.

Before approaching this connection directly it is vital to clarify exactly how the two systems, the cultural and the social, co-operate and are constituted. I have already stressed that the social system is in no sense to be *reduced* to sets of cultural values. Such an interpretation, reflected in those who classify Parsons as a 'consensus theorist', ignores the concept of the social system as a mode of *organisation*, reducing the social to an 'emanation' of the cultural realm, a position repeatedly attacked by Parsons. There is, however, a rather different reading of the theory of the social system which takes the obverse position but which is no less erroneous. This interpretation, instead of seeing the social system as a one-to-one reflection of the cultural system, holds the cultural itself to be a natural product of social relations. This links Parsons' theory to 'German historicism', and equates the theory of action and its formulation of the society–culture relation with certain historicist arguments concerning the society-subject and its ideological representation.

This reading is reflected clearly in Poulantzas' *Political Power and Social Classes*. Poulantzas argues that it is possible to establish certain connections between, on the one hand, the functionalist conception of the social totality and the role assigned by it to ideological (cultural) forms, and on the other, the Lukácsian–Hegelian conception of the social totality as advanced by 'historicism'. In historicism (a term based on a concept of Althusser's), both history and the social totality are conceived of as products of a subject. History creates in its teleological (in the strict sense) development the realisation of the ends of a subject. Lukács' *History and Class Consciousness* is seen as the best representative of the historicist tradition via a Hegelian reading of Marx, for Lukács' history is the product of class-subjects, and knowledge of the social is seen as the condition for the relation of a class to its 'praxis'. In becoming a true subject, a 'class for itself', the proletariat attains a true knowledge of bourgeois society and can, on that basis, 'make its own history'. The social totality and its ideological (distorted or otherwise) representation are interconnected moments of a process which actually constitutes them as such.[36]

Poulantzas proposes the relation between this conception and Parsons' theory of the social system through reference to a mediator, Max Weber:

> What links the theories of Weber to those of functionalism (as Parsons noted) is that the global structure is, in the last analysis, considered as the product of a society-subject which *in its teleological becoming creates certain social values or ends.*
> (*Political Power and Social Classes*, p. 198, my emphasis)

However, this proposed triad of Marxist historicism, Weber and Parsons fails at virtually every linkage. It has already been shown that Parsons and Weber offer quite distinct conceptions of the social totality. The 'social' for Weber is merely a subjective conception held by the actor or actors, and it is not, as it is for Parsons, a specific determinate realm. Further problems exist in the apparent Lukács–Weber connection. At least one major distinction is the agnostic, i.e. non-necessary, relation between knowledge and reality in Weber's epistemology as opposed to the complete teleological determination of knowledge out of reality for Lukács. There is, of course, the further issue of Weber's patent individualism, and one need only compare the distinct conceptions of 'class' adopted by these two authors to appreciate the significance of that point.[37]

Yet it is the linkage between Parsons himself and 'historicist' social theory which is of most immediate significance. Without denying that there is indeed a teleological element in Parsons' of the social system and its relation to culture (indeed these points are elaborated at various levels elsewhere in this book), it is quite misleading to present the processes of the social and cultural systems in Poulantzas' terms. To argue that for Parsons, as in historicism, society creates in its teleological 'becoming' its own social values merely distorts the role of culture that he actually presents. What is clear above all in his work is that the cultural elements generating social values are determined *externally* to the functioning of the 'empirical' systems of action. On this point, the notion of the 'cybernetic hierarchy' of systems of action is quite emphatic: the cultural system governs the other systems. Values are not constituted as an effect of levels of development of social relationships as historicism stipulates. It is rather the levels of development of society which are effects of a process of cultural development. It must not be forgotten that the 'process of rationalisation', held by Parsons to be the major motive force of human advance, is a *cultural*, and not a social, process.

To conceive of values as the product of a society-subject then is not acceptable. Indeed, Parsons has himself castigated such a position as 'sociologism', a tendency reflected in Durkheim's analysis of religion which entails 'ethnical relativism'. Social values and ends are not relative to particular phases in the teleological development of society, but are constituted by a realm distinct from 'empirical' action, the cultural system and, above all its most important component, 'ultimate reality'. Of course, *some* elements of culture *are* determined by the social (e.g. 'social ideologies', see *SS*, pp. 348–59), but the most crucial elements are determined externally.

I have now firmly established the character of the relation between the social and cultural systems. First, the two systems are *distinct* in their determination and constitution. The social system is not a simple reflection of the cultural system, as implied by the 'consensus' category, but a separate sphere of action with discrete organisational problems and solutions. Conversely, the cultural system is not a reflection of the social realm. Secondly, there is some form of determinate *relation* between the social and cultural systems, in the sense that the latter is decisive as a condition of existence of social relations and social development.

In other words, Parsons wishes to maintain both the irreducibility and the coexistential character of the social and cultural systems. What I want to do now is to show how this double emphasis is theoretically unsuccessful. Above all, it entails an idealist teleology in which the attempt to conceptualise distinct systems of action is contradicted and is eventually made ineffective. In order to make these points, it will be necessary to return to Parsons' discussions of the pattern-variables and the functional prerequisites, and the relationship between them.

These two sets of concepts are central to establishing the conditions for the analysis of the relation/convergence between the social and cultural systems. The pattern-variables refer to the value-patterns presented as choices to the actor, the 'ideational' aspects of the structure of action. The functional prerequisites constitute the structure of *systems* of action – what is objectively necessary for the system to operate. It is important to the general theory of action that these two levels of processes are at some stage consistent and that the choices actors make are significant (i.e. beneficial) for the system of action of which they are a part. If the levels do not combine, either the 'active' side of action is negated (the actor does not intervene in any positive sense in the process) or the pertinence of the 'system' as a set of effective relations is denied.

Parsons has continually attempted to establish a determinate relation between the two orders in his social theory, yet some internal analysis will show that he has not succeeded. There is no coherent theoretical relation between the pattern-variable scheme and the set of functional prerequisites. The root of this problem lies in the relation between the concepts of the unit act and systems of action. The pattern-variables are closely related to the elements of the unit act, and the functional prerequisites depend above all upon the differentiation of the three systems of action.

The significance of the concept of the unit act for the

theorisation of the pattern-variables is that the former supplies the concept of the elementary *actor–situation* relation. This can in turn be broken down into two basic components: sets of orientations of the actor on the one hand, and meaningful objects of the situation of action on the other. The two components involve a differentiation of the action complex between the attitudinal sphere of action-orientation and object-categories, which together provide the orientational-modality axis on which the pattern-variables are founded. The orientational set of variables views the relationship of actor to situation from the side of the actor(s), whereas the modality set views the relationship from the side of the situation as consisting of meaningful objects: the former set involves the two combinations of diffuseness-specificity and affectivity-neutrality, the modality set includes the quality-performance and universalism-particularism variables (the self-collectivity dichotomy is significantly dropped in later expositions of the variables).

Parsons clearly acknowledges that his schema in itself cannot exhaust the concepts and categories requisite to the analysis of the social system on the scale attempted in the post-1951 works:

> An action system, however, is not characterised solely by the actor's orientations and modalities of objects significant to the actor; it is also a structural system with analytically independent aspects which the elementary pattern-variable combinations by themselves do not take into account. ('Pattern Variables Revisited: A Response to Robert Dubin' in *STMS*, p. 195)

A clear differentiation is made between the level of the unit act and that of an action-*system*, one involving a theoretically discrete order of problems. Parsons accepts Dubin's categorisation of the two orders as 'Model I' and 'Model II':

> Parsons' Model I essentially 'looks out' to the social system from the vantage of the actor; his Model II 'looks down' at the individual from the perspective of the social system. ('Continuities in Social Theory' in *STMS*, p. 530)

Given that there is no simple relation between the unit-act and the social system, not even by numerical expansion (the social is a mode of organisation of action, not a plurality of acts or actors), then some demonstration is required by which to establish at least a comparability between action-situation relation and the four functional problems; a compatibility which avoids the immediate contradiction between the two perspectives ('looking out'/'looking down'). The 'Pattern Variables Revisited' paper is an attempt to provide precisely this demonstration: it involves an extension of the project of *Working Papers in the Theory of Action*,[38] an attempt to provide a more systematic generalisation of the integration between the pattern-variables and the functional paradigm. However, this complementarity is not established and to this extent Parsons' project is unrealised, which is a point of great pertinence to his theorisation of the social.

To begin with, we may consider what forms of combination of the two levels Parsons proposes. He unites what is claimed to be an exhaustive classification of unit-acts with the four functional problems in a system of combinations – the orientational set of variables (diffuseness-specificity/affectivity-neutrality) are paralleled with the pattern-maintenance function, the modality set (universalism-particularism/quality-performance) with the goal-attainment function. The other two prerequisites are united with *combinations* of the two sets. On the one hand, the combination of the orientation/modality variables involving shared and stable relations between the actor and his situation is claimed to be equitable with the integrative function; on the other hand, that combination involving a stable relation between the system and its environment is made consistent with the adaptive function of systems.[39]

This system of classifications and combinations, however, is hardly theoretically plausible, and at times actually involves word-play. The major flaw appears in the attempt to establish a theoretical connection between the actor–situation relation and the system–environment relation (we may recall that the latter is specific to Parsons' post-1951 works, and its pertinence could not have been produced with the early actor–situation relation alone).

To begin with, we may take the unity that is claimed to exist between the modality set of variables and the functional problem of goal-attainment. It is argued that the two dichotomies that operate within the modality set, particularism-universalism and performance-quality, may be seen as equivalent to the goal-attainment function in so far as they produce a classificatory framework by which the actor(s) can conceive his situation. Even in its own terms this unity is a weak one – such a parallel completely fails to come to terms with the concept of *mobilisation* of societal resources, the major component of the goal-attainment function. We may further note that the goal-attainment function of necessity involves the *orientation* of actors as well as object-categorisation, and to that extent to link it with the modality set truncates much of the significance of the concept. In fact, two sorts of problems come out here. First, the four-functional problems each involve *both* actor and situation, so that to equate them with one or the other involves a severe conceptual distortion (this point thus applies to two of the variable-prerequisite parallels). Secondly, the functional problems involve a great deal which *is not reducible to* the actor–situation relation. On the first point, it would appear to have been possible to invert the parallel between modality/goal-attainment and orientational/pattern-maintenance without altering the argument substantially. In other words, the parallel is an arbitrary one with little or no convincing demonstration.

However, it is the second point that is even more significant for it can be shown that the basic structure of the functional prerequisites cannot possibly be generalised from the pattern-variables – that is to say, that *the actor–situation relation cannot be equated with the system–environment relation*.[40] This is most clear in the case of the adaptive function of the social system. This function involves the adaptation of the environment for the production of societal resources which are to be at the disposal of the social system. Parsons at one stage accepts that the system–environment relation is more than a mere relation internal to the system of action, which is what the actor–situation relation must imply:

> Objects that are constituents of the system must . . . be distinguished from objects that are part of the environment of the system. . . . Adaptation concerns the relations of the whole system to objects which, as such, *are not included in it.* 'Pattern Variables Revisited: A Response to Robert Dubin' in *STMS*, p. 206, my emphasis)

This is a clear acknowledgement that the adaptive function involves a referent external to the objects constituted within the system. However, despite this, Parsons goes on to propose the integration between adaptive prerequisite and the pattern-variable dichotomy, viz. 'that of universalism-particularism', i.e. *object-categorisation*. If this is the case, then the environment of action is not an objective problem which the system faces *but a subjective conception on the part of the actors*. If the environment is a mere meaningful situational object then so is the system itself: the system–environment relation is reduced to one of different subjective conceptions. The effect is to deny the concept of system (in the rigorous sense of that outlined in previous sections) as a theoretical instrument designating specific modes of organisation, and to reduce it to a cultural pattern on behalf of the members. To be more exact, the equation of the adaptive (system–environment) relation with the pattern variable (actor–situation) effectively destroys the whole pertinence of the concept of system.[41]

If this is the case, then Parsons is forced to accept a completely contradictory formulation or to change terrain and actually transform the concept of the social system in conformity with the pattern-variable combinations. This latter tendency is already apparent in his 'Pattern Variables Revisited' paper, and is extended fully in Parsons' later formulation of the 'cybernetic hierarchy', in which the systems of action are no longer simply differentiations of *organisation*, but differentiations of *culture* (in the last analysis, ultimate reality). This latter position (this point is elaborated in the final chapter) effectively denies the earlier stance which has been shown to be distinctive in its rigour and consistency.

In fact, involved in Parsons' attempted integration of the functional prerequisites and the pattern-variables is a serious theoretical slide between the concept of the *means* of action and the concept of the *ends* of action (I use these two themes in the sense of the post-1951 position, i.e. as part of systems of action and not the simple subjective means–end relation of *SSA*). Parsons conflates the actual processes of action with the requirements of the system of action, the mechanisms of the system with the requirements which these mechanisms realise. This point is made clear when it is considered that, as defined in *TGTA*, the pattern-variables in their 'social system aspect' are role-expectations which are in turn patterns of evaluation – these are themselves subject to the requirements of the system (the 'structural' aspect). Thus role-expectations are governed partly by the requirements of the system and partly by available cultural forms (the double referent of the problem of 'order' referred to above). In equating the pattern-variables with the functional prerequisites, Parsons denegates the specificity of the social system as a system, he conflates mechanisms of realisation with that which is realised.

It is thus not possible for Parsons to generalise the pattern-variables to the functional prerequisite (just as it is not possible to generalise the unit act to the systems of action) without inducing a number of theoretical problems and contradictions. The two orders of concept are not logically or theoretically compatible, no *determinate* relation can be established between the actor–situation relation and the problems of the system of action. The coexistence of a 'looking out' and a 'looking down' referent is not possible without in some sense denying the effectivity of one or the other.[42] It is interesting that on this point Parsons chooses to drop the 'self-collectivity' variable in his later developments, for it is at this tangent that the contradiction between the actor–situation relation and the concept of system is most apparent! This variable would show quite clearly the incompatibility of the two levels in so far as it involves the reduction of the 'social' to a mere *orientation* on the part of the actor. It thus denies the organisational specificity of the social system as claimed in the post-1951 works.

We shall see in the final chapter that Parsons does offer an escape from this theoretical impasse although, it will be argued, it is at the expense of even greater problems. At the end of this investigation, we can note yet again the paradoxical character of Parsons' work. In the degree to which it explicitly attempts to theorise social relations and their conditions of existence, it has much to recommend it over and above more commonly accepted sociological conceptions. Yet despite this, the rigour of Parsons' formulation of the theory of social systems only serves to underline the internal problems which permeate it. The crucial relation between the social system and the cultural system, as demonstrated via that between the functional prerequisites and the pattern-variables, has not been successfully theorised.

# 5 The Economy and the Social System

The analyses so far have been almost totally abstract. The critical investigations presented in the previous chapters are pitched at the most general and theoretically fundamental level of the Parsonian theory of action and the social system. There is some justification, therefore, for a more illustrative discussion of the theory, one which, as it were, shows how the concepts developed above actually operate in more 'concrete analyses'.

This is an excellent opportunity to discuss Parsons' analysis of the relation between the economy and the social system. The mode in which this relation has been approached at various times throughout his work tells us a great deal about the changes to which it has been subjected. The central text for this discussion will be, of course, *Economy and Society*, written jointly with Neil Smelser in 1956.

Parsonian theory has elaborated what is undoubtedly the most rigorous and systematic analysis of the economic/non-economic relation that has been produced from within sociology.[1] A critique of such a theory is thus doubly significant, not only as a comment on Parsons but on sociological theory in general and its capacity to theorise the economy.

The structure of this chapter is as follows. The first discussion will elaborate on two issues: on the one hand, Parsons' critique of the mode in which economic theory itself has approached the problem of its periphery – the non-economic areas of the 'social', to 'wants', preferences, propensities and so on; on the other, the distance between previous attempts from within sociology to theorise such issues and Parsons' own concept of structural–functionalism (this includes his own earlier approaches, but in particular the important theses of Max Weber on economy and society). Following this, the second part will direct a critique at the structural–functionalist theory of the economy itself. Two

166

areas are of particular concern in this respect, both of which constitute focal points of Parsons' thesis – on the one hand, the concept of 'structural-differentiation', on the other, that of 'functional subsystem'.

It will be argued that despite the level of rigour that Parsons attains, the structural–functionalist theory of the economic/non-economic relation falls down at two decisive junctures. On the one hand, it is argued that this theory depends on a confusion and conflation of two orders of concepts, those concerning the notions of 'cultural directionality' and 'structural differentiation', orders which, it is shown, are theoretically incompatible. It is also shown that both notions, taken independently or together, involve assumptions which are strategically teleological, despite claims to the contrary. On the other hand, this work locates a number of crucial theoretical problems which surround the concepts of the 'functional prerequisites' and 'functional subsystems'. These concepts, which are very characteristic the structural–functionalist mode of analysis, are shown in the last analysis to reproduce the ambiguities and arbitrariness which they, at one level, appear to surpass. Central in this respect is the notion of the human 'subject' and the humanist way in which the relation between subject and situation (system, requirements of the system, etc.) is elaborated. These theoretical problems are shown to render impossible the project for a coherent mode of analysis of the economic/non-economic relation on the lines of structural–functionalist theory.

*Economy and Society* represents a distinct theoretical position at two levels; it is distinct from the mode in which economic theory has itself approached the problem of its non-economic periphery on the one hand, and it is distinct from the mode in which 'action theory' proper (i.e. Weber's sociology) has conceived this relation on the other. The issues involved will now be outlined and developed.

## 5.1 Economic Theory and Sociology

*Economy and Society* (*ES*) elaborates a critique of economic theory much of which has been the continual concern of Parsonian theory from its earliest theses, culminating in *SSA*.[2] Here the major objective is to demonstrate that the voluntaristic theory of action is the only truly general formulation of the economic/

non-economic relation, one which incorporates all the analytic elements of the action frame of reference. In respect of this, *SSA* argues that previous attempts have ignored or suppressed at least one of these elements. One such attempt, Parsons argues, is utilitarian theory which, it is argued, is characterised by atomism, rationalism and empiricism. It is utilitarianism that is seen to constitute the basic conceptual apparatus of both classical and neo-classical economics in its conception of the non-economic periphery of economic processes.

Two general criticisms are levelled at classical economic theory: either it has tended to depend entirely upon the postulate of the intrinsic rationality of action, in which the means–end relation is conceived in such a fashion as to obliterate the investigation of ends altogehter (i.e. ends become random), or it has formulated the determination of ends in a metaphysical and/or positivistic manner as the 'natural identity of interests', 'needs', hedonism, etc.[3] The critique of economic theory is thus posed in terms of *absences*: either the absence of *any* determination of ends or more generally of the non-economic sphere, or the absence of a particular type of determination, viz. its voluntary element, action oriented to sets of 'ultimate' ends and values.

At the level of *SSA*, however, the critique of economic theory is very limited: there is little or no theoretical demonstration that such absences are theoretically damaging,[4] and there is little offered in terms of an alternative formulation of the economic/non-economic relation. It is not until *Economy and Society* that the problems of economic theory are rigorously posed.

In this text Parsons refers to the tendency within economics of 'resting on *ad hoc* hypotheses about "human nature" which are psychologically and sociologically dubious if not downright untenable' (*ES*, p. 184).

In particular, he locates, three primary tendencies in economic theory in its handling of the non-economic realm[5] which go beyond the mere issue of 'ends'. The first is the use of vague, often anthropological, notions of '*homo oeconomicus*', of 'human nature', and so on. Secondly, there is the tendency to *reduce* the non-economic to the status of a random variant, i.e. a purely dependent variable and thus empirically contingent (Parsons cites Schumpeter's concept of a hypothetical economy, from which deviations are to be measured). The third tendency is to conceptualise the non-economic in terms of an 'empirical generalisation', i.e. as a 'given' (an example being Keynes' notion of 'psychological laws').

As well as the general problem of ambiguity, the effects of such tendencies are in the direction of an individualism – particularly in the theory of marginal utility, but also in such apparently non-individualistic areas as welfare economics[6]– a rationalism in which all action that does not come directly within the scope of economics is defined as somehow 'irrational' and the overall theoretical barrier to the formation of a truly *general* system of concepts for the analysis of the economic non-economic relation. Such consequences Parsons attempts to demonstrate by means of several examples. I will repeat here the two most effective examples.

The first and most extensive is the Keynesian concept of the 'consumption function' and its reliance on the notion of 'propensity'. For Keynes, the problem of the aggregate demand function requires that some explanation be given of the general relation between consumption on the one hand and savings and investment on the other: the objective is thus to formulate a general thesis concerning the factors which determine the sum which is to be spent on consumption when employment is given. Two broad classes are differentiated, the 'objective' and 'subjective' the former includes such factors as changes in the wage-unit, in the difference between net-income and income in general, in capital values, in fiscal policy, and so on;[7] the latter are seen to be general subjective dispositions and social 'incentives'. Within both classes, and in the relation between them, is the assumption of the operation of a psychological mechanism, seen by Keynes to be a 'fundamental psychological law' – the 'propensity'.

Parsons considers such a thesis to be inadequate on both theoretical and empirical grounds. The concept of propensity reduces the non-economic world to single variable, which is itself an expression of a psychological tendency; consumption and savings are conceived in terms of the uni-dimensional relation between the level of income and the psychological expression of it. The problem with such an argument lies at two levels; on the one hand, it depends upon a totally unfounded presupposition as to a psychological law, and on the other, it involves the total absence of any theorisation of the conditions of existence of the non-economic sphere itself, a sphere which Parsons argues is a *socially determinate* realm. The ambiguity and reductionism inherent in the concept of 'propensity' to consume is seen to derive from the absence of the concept of the social conditions of existence of the consumption function:

> What does this function imply about the social structure? In the first place, the only two terms in the consumption function relation – the consumers and their incomes – are linked by the principle that consumption rises as income rises, though not so rapidly. If this principle is all that is given, what are the reasons why the principle should hold? (*ES*, p. 229)

Essentially similar features are seen to be operative in the economic analysis of 'imperfect competition', although they are more acute because of its wider referent. The tendency in this case is to *reduce* the non-economic to an economic object. The theory of imperfect compition refers to a situation in which the assumptions of the perfect market no longer apply – there exists an imbalance of advantages and power on one side of the market. Such imbalances are, however, conceived in purely economic terms – supply and demand (number of sellers, elasticity), cost-curves, monopolistic competition, and so on. The problematic issue is again one of determinacy.

> But what are the *conditions* of imperfection? What are the *sources* of the power imbalance? In terms of our paradigm, what are the conditions to which either ego or alter (or both) must adapt which lead to the relative advantage or disadvantage in the market situation, and to the development of features of the market which are not obvious cases of economic rationality? (*ES*, p. 145)

In these and many other areas of economic analysis (the theory of labour-supply, trade-cycle models, etc.) Parsons locates a primary problem: the theorisation of the non-economic conditions of existence of the economic sphere remains at a level that is unsatisfactory or non-existent. It is in respect of this critique that he proposes the theoretical 'synthesis' between economic theory and sociology.

In this case, Parsons must demonstrate that it *is* sociology and not psychological theory, political science, or any other body of theory that must undertake this regeneration of economics. He attempts this through reference to the apparently 'fundamental' nature of its object – human action. In this respect Parsons claims a set of theoretical 'congruences' between economics and sociology: these relate to the apparent complementarity of their respective 'frames of reference' which is seen to be effective at several levels. First, it is claimed that the economists' conception of supply and demand can be viewed as a special case of the general concepts of performance and sanction, i.e. as a part of the theory of action; secondly, that the distinction between goods and services is a logical equivalent to that of social and non-social objects; thirdly, that in both disciplines there is a notion of 'exchange' or mutual advantage, which in both cases is a central organising postulate; and finally, that there is the reference in both sociology and economics to some mode of organisation or 'system'.

On the issue of this demonstration it might be worthwhile to pose one or two doubts concerning this attempt. For example, the parallel between supply–demand and performance–sanction would appear to disregard the essentially *marginal* determination of choice in the former as opposed to the cultural (value-orientational) determination of choice in the action-conception. Or again, the congruence between the distinction between social and non-social objects and goods and services pays little or no concern to the theoretical differences that hold between the notion of *interaction*, on the one hand, and *utility*, on the other. What Parsons offers by way of theoretical proof of compatibility is hardly sufficient to bridge the gap created by these conceptions – if this is the case, then no amount of word-play can rescue the project from eclecticism.

The project itself is to reformulate certain features and parameters of economic theory according to the exigencies of sociological theory: the objective is to maintain the major categories and concepts of formal economics[8] – in particular its essential feature of measurement in monetary terms – but to subsume them within a specifically *sociological* frame of reference. For example,

the imperfection of markets differs not only in degree *but in sociological type*. The market for consumers' goods differs from

that for labour, and both differ from that for capital funds.
These markets differ in type primarily because the different
markets connect the economy with *different* sectors of the
society: these connections enforce qualitatively *different* limitations on the respective market conditions. (*ES*, p. 3, emphasis
as in original)

The origin of the intervention of this explicitly non-economic
referent Parsons locates in Marshall's notion of 'human services',
which includes a referent to both the marginal response to the
rate of remuneration *and* to a more general 'underlying willing-
ness to work'.[9] In addition, Marshall supplements the orthodox
economic classification of the factors of production (land,
labour, capital), with an additional factor – that of organisation,
a referent to the non-economic sphere of contract. These
notions are, however, of an elementary character: the synthesis
between sociology and economics in *ES* is of a more elaborate
form.

## 5.2  The Economy, 'Action' and the Theory of Social Systems

It is generally recognised that *Economy and Society* offers a
difference in 'emphasis' from the position taken by Parsons in
*SSA* concerning the economic/non-economic relation. In the
latter, the prime objective was to construct a position mid-way
between both forms of theoretical 'imperialism', economic and
sociological – i.e. to include all of the analytical elements. The
prime example in this respect is the thesis of Pareto: here
primary reference is given to 'economic rationality' in the form
of the marginal subject, but in *addition* to a sphere of
'residues' – non-logical action, the object of sociology rather
than economics. This distinction is elaborated by Parsons into
that between rational action and action oriented to 'ultimate
ends', i.e. the position taken by Weber. The complete analytical
programme is thus one of economics *plus* sociology.

   In *ES*, however, Parsons claims 'Our view now is distinctly
different . . .' (p. 6) The distinctiveness of the later position is
seen to lie in the conception that economic theory is not merely
the organisation of a distinct class of 'variables' to which a further
set is to be added, for what is seen to demarcate the two spheres is
not that of variables but of the *parameters* which the two

disciplines must conceptualise – parameters seen in terms of relations of *functional subsystems*:

> Economic theory should, according to this view, be regarded as the theory of typical processes in the 'economy', which is a subsystem differentiated from other subsystems of a society. The specifically economic aspect of the theory of social systems, therefore is *a special case of the general theory of the social system*. (*ES*, p. 6, my emphasis)

But what is the *significance* of this transformation of the theoretical mode in which the economic/non-economic relation is to be conceived? It would appear to be much greater than Parsons himself has made explicit and concerns the implications of the concepts presented in *ES* for a critical reading of *SSA* and indeed of Weberian economic sociology. A few comments on both Weber and the theoretical means of *SSA* would appear to be in order.

As Parsons points out in his Introduction to Weber's *The Theory of Social and Economic Organisation*, it was not Weber's objective to replace economic theory but to add to it an area of relatively underdeveloped conceptualisation – the major one being, for Parsons, the theory of institutional structure. Institutions are seen as the social form of orientational modes, of *types* of action. One such mode is that pertinent to the economy, economically oriented (rational) action:

> Action will be said to be 'economically oriented' so far as, according to its subjective meaning, it is concerned with the satisfaction of a desire for utilities. 'Economic action' is a peaceful use of the actor's control over resources which is rationally oriented, by deliberate planning, to economic ends. *An 'economic system' is an autocephalous system of economic action.* (*The Theory of Social and Economic Organisation*, p. 158, my emphasis)

What is of particular significance in such a thesis is that the 'economy' is defined not as a mode or organisation or structure but in terms of an *orientation*: the economy has an *essence* which is the form of action that it embodies. The distinction between the ecnomy and non-economic spheres is thus in terms of the distinctions between *types* of action. This is clear in Weber's distinction between 'market' and 'planned' economies – these are differentiated in terms of the relative presence of two polar types of meaningful orientation, budgetary and profit-making, the former oriented to 'the security and increase of resources and income', the latter 'to maintaining and improving profitability and the market position of the enterprise' (ibid., p. 199). The economy is thus conceived in terms of the combination of an individualist referent – the vehicle of the economy is the individual actor and his orientations (to profit or toward 'irrational' considerations) – and ideational or 'value' elements which constitute those orientations. The determination of the society–economy relation lies essentially in the realm of values and their effectivity. Weber provides no concept of this relation in terms of determinate totalities, structures or systems.

Parsons' own *SSA* remains, on the whole, little removed from Weber's formulation. There is, however, one major distinctive referent, albeit a rather formalist one: this concerns the epistemological concept of 'emergent properties'. Thus economic rationality is not to be seen simply as the orientation of an individual as in Weber's notion but rather, 'Economic rationality is . . . an emergent property which can be observed only when a plurality of unit acts is treated together as constituting an *integrated system of action*' (*SSA*, pp. 739–40, my emphasis).

The concept of emergent properties signals the theoretical pertinence of the concept of a system of action, which is more than a simple aggregate of individual actions and distinct from a simple mode of orientation, but which involves the concept of a *mode of organisation* of action elements and, consequently, a set of situational exigencies. But beyond this formal notion *SSA* provides no *specific* concept of the social or the economic system – this is clear in the essay written shortly afterwards, 'The Motivation of Economic Activities',[10] in which the economy is still conceived solely in terms of an *institutional* form determinate according to the value patterns which it represents, rather than as a discrete *system* of action. It is the objective of *Economy and Society* to pose precisely this problem and implicitly to overcome the idealism apparent in the earlier position and in the theses of Weber.

A distinct mode of theorisation of the economic/non-economic relation is now found: 'In defining production, utility, wealth, and income, the focal point of reference is for us *SOCIETY* as a system' (*ES*, p. 21).

The objective is no longer to supplement economic theory but to subsume it within the theory of social systems – it involves not the extension of the theses of *SSA* but of transformations of the problem itself.[11] The crucial concept is the notion of the *social system* and its distinction from both the personality and cultural systems. This transforms the conceptualisation of the determination of the social sphere from the orientational reference of *SSA* (social = a type of action) to the boundary reference of the later works in which the social is defined as a collective *actor*:

> A social system having the three properties of collective goals, shared goals, and of being a single system of interaction with boundaries defined by incumbency in the roles constituting the sytem, will be called a collectivity. (*TGTA*, p. 192)[12]

Given the differention of the cultural and social systems, the status of values is displaced: they no longer constitute the social but become *mechanisms of its functioning*.[13] This is clear in the case of economic rationality:

> the concept of economic rationality may designate either a property of a social system or a property of a personality system; but these two references must not be confused. In either case, however, the concept refers to the mode or organisation of the system relative to its values. (*ES*, p. 177)

Economic rationality is not the *essence* of the economy as in the case of Weber but is a mechanism of its functioning and is thus secondary to the exigencies of the boundaried system. The economy is defined as a boundary-maintaining system and as such is subject to two related forms of processes, those relating to the appearance of that system and those concerning its pertinence as a system.

The first process is that of 'structural differentiation', and accounts for the actual presence of the 'economy', defined in the strict sense as the predominantly *market*-based means of fulfilling consumption needs. This process refers to an evolutionary tendency of social systems to fragment along functionally beneficial lines – Parsons' version of the traditional approach to the division of labour. That the economy as such exists as a specific totality is due to a sequence in which all social systems are constrained to comply with certain internal and external requirements. These lead into the second order of process: the synchronic sphere of 'functional imperatives'.

There are four functional imperatives: adaptation, goal-attainment, integration and pattern-maintenance/tension-management (referred to as $A, G, I, L$, respectively). The first two concern the relation between the system and its situation: $A$ refers to the capacity of a system to control its environment for the purpose of achieving certain goals; $G$ refers to the establishment of a relation between the system and its situational objects in terms of the formulation of a specific 'goal-state' in the direction of gratification of the system as a whole. The other two relate to the internal mechanisms of the system: $I$ involves the maintenance of solidarity between the units of the system in the interest of its effective functioning, and $L$ the maintenance of a stable value-system (cultural consistency) and the control of endemic motivational strains (Parsons *does* refer to inherent conflict), which are potentially disruptive of the system. For Parsons, 'Any system of action can be described and its processes analysed in terms of these four functional prerequisites' (*ES*, p. 18).

It is at this level that the concept of 'functional subsystems' emerges. Given these imperatives, Parsons argues, systems will tend to produce subsystems which will be constituted with primary reference to one of the four requirements. Each subsystem may be seen as a boundaried mode of organisation, which articulates with its environment through certain 'boundary interchanges'. The pertinence of the concept of functional subsystem for the Parsonian theory of the economy is obvious – it represents the double referent by which the economy is theorised in *ES*: on the one hand as a subsystem of the total social system, on the other as a social system in itself in which the different economic processes are conceived as differentiations of functional primacy. The schema of functional problems/functional subsystems is applied at both levels of the economic/non-economic relation. A brief exposition of the two levels, the functional differentiation of *society* and the functional differentiation of the *economy*, will be given by way of illustration.

The theory of the functional differentiation of society is Parsons' most distinctive and famous contribution to sociological theory – in particular it serves to distinguish his theory of the economic/non-economic relation from other attempts from within sociology to handle the problem.[14] At this level, the non-economic sphere is explicitly conceived as a *situation* to the economy – not as a 'given' nor as an 'empirical generalisation' but as a functionally determinate system of boundaries and interchanges. The economic and the non-economic are thus viewed as different modes of *organisation*, centred around the differentiation of functional problems. This constitutes the well-known formula of the structure of society; the economy is the subsystem primarily concerned with the problem of $A$, its goal being the *production* of generalised facilities for the disposal of the society; the polity involves the $G$ function in that it mobilises societal resources for the attainment of given collective goals; the $I$ subsystem is concerned primarily with solidarity, or the co-ordination of units in the direction of 'harmony' and control of deviance; finally, the $L$ subsystem is differentiated according to the problem of intra-unit states and processes, with maintaining conformity to the dominant values and with developing sufficient motivation (primarily at the level of personality).

The assertion of functional primacy constitutes the conceptual *autonomy* of each system, but it also presupposes a mode of *relationship* between each system or their functional interdependence. Parsons handles this in terms of the notion of interchange, the mutual exchange of generalised facilities between the systems in the direction of an overall contribution to the system as a whole.[15]

The contribution of each subsystem to the social system is thus conceived in terms of outputs or products which flow into the three situational subsystems in the form of generalised facilities; at the societal level the economy produces wealth, the polity produces political power, the $I$ subsystem produces solidarity, and the $L$ subsystem produces prestige (which relates motivational factors to the common-value system). A further specification (and as will be seen, a significant one), is that such facilities are processed through the further differentiation of the subsystems themselves according to their own functional primacies. Outputs are thus always directed at specific branches of each subsystem and are not distributed by a simple spreading of resources across the board.

Given this theoretical basis, Parsons elaborates the second major level of functional theorisation to be found in *Economy and Society*, the functional differentiation of the economy itself. Very briefly, the economy is conceived in terms of the four universals outlined above, such that its structure is broken into four subsystems whereby the *A* function is fulfilled through capitalisation and investment, the *G* function by production (including distribution and sales), the *I* function by 'organisation', and the *L* function by what Parsons calls 'economic commitments' (cultural, motivational and physical resources). These subsystems are made parallel with the more orthodox classification of the 'factors of production', capital, labour, organisation and land, respectively – the generalised facilities accompanied by their products – profits, wages, rent and interest. The schema is exemplified by Parsons' treatment of consumption.

Consumption, it is argued, must be conceived in terms of *boundary processes*: the relations between this sphere and its periphery must be seen as a process of 'double interchange', the reciprocal distribution of facilities between subsystems which is rigorously governed by the functional requirements of the total system. Consumption is not to be conceived in mechanistic fashion as the mere expression of income or of market position, but as a bounday process between the *A* and *L* subsystems, primarily between the institutional representations of these subsystems located in the household and the enterprise. The whole process is mediated by the value system (internalised and institutionalised) and as such it is claimed that the economy offers consumer goods and services 'in return for which' it receives motivated labour, and conversely, the household offers consumer spending and labour services as its main goal in the reciprocal relation.

It is only in terms of such a schema, Parsons argues, that the conditions of consumption patterns can be analysed. Economic processes and their non-economic relations must be seen as boundary relations – relations which are subject to both levels of systemic effectivity.

It is clear that Parsons' attempt in *Economy and Society* to theorise the economic/non-economic relation is significantly distinct not only from the way in which economic theory handles this problem, but also from the orthodox sociological conceptions often presented in some form as the relations between rational and value-based action, or between Gemeinschaft and Gesselschaft, distinctions which are common coin amongst idealist sociologies. The major concepts in Parsons' case are those of functional prerequisites, modes of organisation, subsystems, boundary interchange, structural differentiation, and so on. But what of the status of *these* concepts?

If Parsons' theory of the economy is to be seen as a theoretically elaborate attempt to conceive the economic/non-economic relation as compared with other attempts (both from within economic theory and sociology) to handle the problem, then it is due primarily to two orders of concepts (both related): on the one hand, the notion of 'structural differentiation', and on the other, that of 'functional subsystem'. In this section the theoretical character of these concepts will be interrogated.

## 5.3  The Concept of Structural Differentiation

As will be demonstrated shortly, the concept of structural differentiation occupies a particularly strategic position in the Parsonian theory of the economy: it supplies the means of establishing the 'economy' as a distinct object for the thoery of social systems, of accounting for the processes which articulate with the economy, and, in a general sense, of explaining the apparent significance of the 'Western' form of economy. This section will argue, however, that this concept is a highly problematic one on two levels. First, that Parsons includes within the one concept *two* processes which are not only confused and conflated, but which are theoretically incompatible – these are, on the one hand, the concept of functional differentiation, and, on the other, the notion of cultural directionality. The two concepts are theoretically necessary to Parsons' project but are logically incompatible. Secondly, it will be further shown that both referents of structural differentiation involve theoretical properties which are in fact *teleological*, the postulate of an immanent tendency whether in the realm of value-systems or in the sphere of systemic 'advance'. As a consequence, it will be claimed that this decisive concept is without any coherent foundation.

One of the major concerns of *Economy and Society* is to approach a problem essentially similar to that posed by Weber in *The Protestant Ethic and the Spirit of Capitalism*: the nature, significance and genesis of the 'Western' or 'market' form of economy. In both cases, the thesis is that such an economy is of 'universal' significance, and that more generally the Western form of society is a decisive landmark in human history,[16] and that, therefore, its analysis is of central concern for sociological theory.

For Weber, the market form of economy represents the dominance of specifically *economic* relations, the dominance of formal, over substantive rationality (the latter remains of course, a persistent element). The market economy, distinguished by the presence of a 'market situation' (exchange for money), 'marketability' (regularity with which objects are exchanged), and 'market freedom' (autonomy of parties in the sphere of price competition), is contrasted to what in many ways is its opposite – the planned economy in which these essential elements are non-existent or 'regulated'. In these cases, the major conditions of existence of the capitalist economy are reducible to the regulation or freedom of an *orientation* of individual actors, and the rational pursuit of self-interest on the basis of monetary (marginal) calculation, i.e. economic rationality. Therefore, what is of prime significance is the *determination* of this orientation, which for Weber lies above all in the realm of 'ultimate values', and in particular the form of values present in the Calvinist branches of the 'Protestant ethic'.

It is clear then that the primary concept in the theory of the market (the concept that is offered to account for the *appearance* of the market form of economy) is the notion of *cultural directionality*. It is at this level that the very basic tendency that constitutes the great bulk of Weber's work becomes pertinent: the so-called 'process of rationalisation'.[17] In relation to this process, a cultural one, the non-cultural conditions of existence of the development of the market economy are little more than supports or obstacles to the domination of rational orientation; concrete elements which may allow or prohibit the expansion of formal rationality as opposed to substantive rationality. What is significant here is that the conditional, or in Parsons' terms the situational, features of the economy and society are not theoretically effective but are merely secondary to the overall notion of an ideational process – hence the study of the world religions. The idealism of this thesis is evident.

If Parsons adopts a similar problem, he provides the means of theorisation which contains significant distinctions from Weber's formulation. The major referent used to account for the market form of economy in Parsons' case is one which is absent in Weber – the concept of *functional differentiation*: 'Societies differ from each other in the degree to which the collectivities of which they are composed are differentiated in terms of functional primacy' (*ES*, p. 16).

The central feature of the concept of functional differentiation is the postulation of a general tendency toward increasing efficiency of the system – a tendency later specified as the 'enhancement of adaptive capacity'.[18] Smelser's work on one concrete example of this process is perhaps most explicit on this issue.[19] For Smelser the essential elements of a theory of social change are the notions of 'complexity' and differentiation; the former implies the 'splitting' of simple structures into more complex organisations, the latter supplies the *significance* of this process, the directionality of *advance*:

> The model of structural differentiation is an abstract theory of change. When one social role or organisation becomes archaic under changing historical circumstances, it differentiates by a definite and specific sequence of events into two or more roles or organisations. (Smelser, *Social Change and the Industrial Revolution*, p. 2)

This general formulation is illustrated for Parsons by the case of the break-up of the European medieval manor. The manor had traditionally been characterised by the unification in it of both economic and non-economic functions, i.e. it occupied the central organisational position with regard to political, social and economic processes. As an effect of the tendency of systems to differentiate, however, the manor was subject to diversification and fragmentation, resulting in the enclosure movements and the development of handicraft. This process of break-up created the conditions for the beginning of a new era of economic development in Europe.[20]

The concept of structural differentiation (the tendency of systems to develop into more advanced structures) is one of the central theses of Parsons' theorisation of the appearance of the market: the market represents the sphere of social relations which have become *specifically* economic (hence one of the conditions of existence of formal economic theory itself, for the latter, grounded in the technique of measurability, is seen to depend upon the *prior* existence of money and markets) – the market is the differentiated structure of action representing the process of increasing adaptive capacity, and it signifies the real differentiation of the *economy* from non-economic structures (the obvious implication being that non-market economies are relatively less advanced and efficient).

However, in itself this concept is inadequate, for some other concept is required to explain why some societies are more differentiated than others, i.e. which invokes a process operative at an even more fundamental level in that it provides the conditions of *success* of the process of structural differentiation itself. Such a concept is to be found, in fact, in the conception of the effectivity of the cultural realm and in the notion of *cultural directionality*,[21] and bears a close relationship to Weber's conception of the evolution of value-systems or the 'process of rationalisation' (as Parsons himself claims in his Introduction to 'Culture and Social Systems' in *Theories of Society*).

The double referent, however, involves major theoretical problems. Parsons appears to operate with the concept of two developmental processes, that of cultural directionality and the functional process of structural directionality. He presents their relationship in terms of the hierarchical effect of the former in creating the conditions of existence of the latter; for example, in an attempt to theorise the appearance of the market economy, the latter is held to be the most advanced and differentiated form of economic activity, but its *appearance* in one society rather than another is subject to the requisite development of adequate value-systems. However, this hierarchy in itself does not escape the central issue of the *theoretical* relationship between the two concepts, for despite expositional attempts to account for their combination (in particular, the epistemological relationship between analytic and concrete), the basic problem remains: *the concept of cultural directionality is not theoretically compatible with the concept of structural differentiation*. In order to demonstrate this point, I shall refer again to certain of Weber's theses on the matter in question, and relate them to Parsons' parallel arguments.

Weber's *The Protestant Ethic and the Spirit of Capitalism* is a thesis which is centred around the role of a specific cultural pattern in determining modes of orientation of action, which in turn are seen to be determinant of the forms of economy adopted by different societies – in this case, the example of the Calvinist variant of Protestant theology. The problems with such a thesis have already been noted, but of particular significance here is the absence of any elaborate theory of the extra-cultural relations of the value sphere, the latter in fact effectively *constitutes* the former. It is the distinction between such a thesis and Parsons' mode of theorisation that is pertinent, for in Parsons' case the concept of the social level involves not only a reference to the process of cultural directionality, but to a very definite extra-cultural realm of determination absent in any rigorous form in Weber. Thus, although Parsons reproduces the Weberian insistence on the effectivity of the Protestant type of value-attitude for the development of the market economy, he is at pains to supplement the ideational level of effectivity with a theoretically distinct one: the effectivity of structural differentiation.

In the case of the latter, there is clearly a notion of directionality but it is, or must be, distinct from a simple cultural directionality: it has a reference to a different system of action, the social system, and the divisions or subsystems within it. The essential issue here is the notion of increasing efficiency of systems to cope with their situations and environments. The relationship between system and situation is not reducible to that between values and orientations, but it involves the theoretical significance of *determinate levels of organisation*, the notion of functional prerequisites, and so on. Values are not expressed in action apart from their relation to the given organisational forms. In short, the cultural level is *functional but not determinant* of the social. In this case the difference between primitive and advanced societies is not, as is the case for Weber in his analysis of the 'East' and 'West', primarily a difference of cultural/ orientational forms; but differences in the capacity of systems in a functional sense. One or two examples will illustrate the crucial point that the two processes of directionality are distinct.

First, take the discussion of the Soviet Union. In Parsons' analysis of Soviet society it is argued that as a social system it must be considered a relatively undifferentiated structure compared with, say, the United States. In particular, there is apparently a 'fusion' of two major spheres of action: the polity and the economy. Parsons' comment on this situation is illuminating:

> How stable, beyond the period of 'forced draft', such a fusion may be is a crucial question about such societies; will *certain 'natural' tendencies* for the economy to differentiate from the polity appear or will they be inhibited? (*ES*, p. 83, my emphasis)

A clear distinction is thus made between the inherent tendency of social systems to differentiate and the value-system within which that system operates – in this case, the values of 'Marxism–Leninism' are seen to be in conflict with the natural forces of social development. Conversely, the case of the 'Western' societies is an example of a unitary relationship between the two levels, cultural and social, that is the value-system is seen to be highly adaptable to the demands of structural differentiation; even in this case, however, the two realms are theoretically discrete.

The second example of this feature of Parsons' thesis has already been referred to above: the treatment of the crucial status of economic rationality shows that orientational patterns in themselves cannot constitute an economy, but are only mechanisms of its functioning. Economic rationality is not the essence of the economy but is *embodied* at specific systemic levels

The significance of the distinction between the cultural and social levels in social development for this discussion is that at the level of the theory of the market economy the two spheres are conjoined: the market form of economy is seen to be the product of the joint operation of the processes of cultural directionality and structural differentiation, as is clear in this comment on Weber:

> We would like to reformulate the process of rationalisation as the tendency of social systems to develop progressively higher levels of structural differentiation under the pressure of adaptive exigencies. (*ES*, p. 292)

This reformulation is central to the thesis of *Economy and Society* concerning the market economy: it refers to the *unification* of the two processes, the complementary relationship between cultural and social processes. Parsons needs to argue both that the two are discrete (the social system has a functional, not a simple, ideational reference) and also that at some stage they can be united (in order to explain why the tendency has been realised in some cases and not in others). I argue that this cannot be coherently achieved, that it is theoretically impossible to maintain both the distinction and the unity of the two processes of cultural directionality and structural differentiation.

Why should a rationalistic orientation to action be equivalent to the functional capacity of systems of action? If the concept of system is to be defined in consistent fashion as a discrete level of organisation, with *its own* conditional requirements, why should this cultural object be seen as complementary to a systemic referent? Not only does Parsons offer no elaborated account of exactly how and why the processes of directionality and differentiation can be at some level conjoined (indeed, they are often presented as expressions of the same process – the 'reformulation' of the process of rationalisation referred to above), but there are indications that the thesis *cannot* be rigorously maintained.

This is so on two grounds. At a very general level, the relation between 'action' defined as a process of orientation toward meaningful objects (primarily values) and the concept of *systems* of action is a problematic one. As has been demonstrated elsewhere,[22] Parsons cannot coherently maintain both the determinacy of value-elements in action and the notion of discrete modes of organisation of action-elements into systems. Consequently, the rigorous coexistence of the double reference of cultural directionality and structural (systemic) differentiation is not theoretically possible. At the level of both the action/system relation and of the two realms of social evolution, cultural and systemic, it is theoretically impossible to resolve the contradiction between the distinct forms of determination.

Another way of making this point with specific reference to the problem of directionality is to consider the effect of the extension of either process in relation to the other. Thus, in the case of the process of rationalisation, just which referent is dominant, the orientational aspect of rationality or the system within which rationality is embodied? If it is the former then the specificity of systems is denegated, the effectivity of systemic requirements is suppressed and they can no longer be considered as 'independent foci of organisation' (*SS*, p. 6). If it is the latter then why should culture be held as a unique sphere of determination of action, as indeed it is in the theory of the development of the market economy? It is clear that the effectivity of one precludes the effectivity of the other, and that the processes of cultural directionality and of structural differentiation, despite the claim that they are concretely cooperative, are *theoretically* incompatible. Parsons' attempt to unite the two processes in *Economy and Society* has no firm foundation: as such it can only result in contradiction or incoherence.

The duality of reference is not the only problem: both processes in themselves are theoretically unacceptable. In the case of cultural directionality the problems are obvious, for the determination of this sphere itself is a non-problem for the theory of action. Its dominant component – ultimate reality – is a realm explicitly conceived as beyond 'natural' determination and thus beyond rational explanation.[23] Thus, in order to account for, say, the development of the value-system of the Protestantism out of more traditionalistic ethics, Parsons is faced with a major dilemma – how to avoid a conception of cultural development which postulates a random order of appearance of ultimate ethics while remaining firm that such an order is beyond rational explanation. Consequently, the process of cultural directionality can only be conceived as some form of absolute realisation of a human essence – the process of rationalisation becomes the realisation of the true nature of 'man'. The problems of such a thesis, problems which are more apparent in the later works (in particular the text '*Societies*') must be evident.

The concept of structural differentiation is more complex in a theoretical sense, but nevertheless does have one property in common with the notion of cultural directionality: it is *teleological*. The notions of 'differentiated/undifferentiated', of related notions of 'advanced/backward', 'developed/underdeveloped', 'complex/simple', and so on, are theorised in a teleological mode with the central property being that of an immanent tendency: 'Our most general proposition is that total societies tend to differentiate into subsystems (social structures) which are specialised in each of the four primary functions' (*ES*, p. 47).

These oppositions, common coin in the sociology of development, are defined in terms of a 'future anterior',[24] the past – simple, primitive, undifferentiated etc. – is conceived purely in terms of its *distance* from, and as an expression of, the future (the present). In Parsons' case, for example, medieval society or communist societies are conceived of as, in certain respects, 'undifferentiated' *in relation to* that which is differentiated. The conception of the United States, and of Western democracy in general, provides the theoretical instruments for the explanation of less differentiated societies: the differentiated society (separation between the market economy, democratic government, nuclear family etc.) and the differentiated economy (separation of production, consumption etc.) provide the indispensable means of theorisation of distinct forms of economy and society. The market form of economy is thus the optimum mode of economic process against which all other economies are to be judged.

This is clearly a case of theoretical *expressivism*: all societies are *more or less realisations* of the concept of the differentiated society. The process of social evolution involves a hierarchy (primitive–intermediate–modern) which signifies the phases of realisation of an essence, moments in the movement of the whole. Each stage in the process of structural differentiation is not conceived of as a *determinate structure*, but rather as a phase in the realisation of the differentiated social system. This concept is thus antithetical to Parsons' own requirements for a concept of the social system.

As well as a conceptual expressivism, the notion of structural differentiation must imply that history has a purpose (consistent with the classical philosophies of history). Although many theories of the economy/society relation invoke this teleological postulate at some level,[25] Parsons' particular attempt involves a more acute property. Not only is history the site of the general tendency toward increasing complexity, but this complexity is itself governed by the more fundamental issue of the *increasing adaptive capacity* of systems. In short, complexity is attained *because* of its future effect. This is more explicit in the case of Smelser: 'when one social role or organisation becomes archaic under changing circumstances it differentiates by a definite and specific sequence of events into two or more roles or organisations' (*Social Change and the Industrial Revolution*, p. 2). Social change is thus a linear order of advance; complexity and

differentiation are the means by which this advance is attained:
Smelser makes this point clear: 'Empirically, we may classify
under-developed or semi-developed economies according to
how far they have moved along this line of differentiation' (*The
Sociology of Economic Life*, pp. 107–8).

The concept of structural differentiation thus requires that
the historical process is assigned the status of the support of an
essential principle, the immanent tendency towards the increasing adaptive capacity of social systems. Such a teleology cannot
provide the means of theorisation of the economy/society
relation as determinate structures and processes for the teleological element is itself antithetical to this requirement. These
points are developed in the following chapter.

## 5.4 The Concept of Functional Subsystems

If the concept of structural differentiation supplies the means of
theorisation of the specificity of the 'economy' in relation to
other systems, a further concept is necessary through which to
think the relations *between* the systems. This is to be found in the
notion of functional interdependence, and in the concept of
functional subsystems in particular.

Parsons' opposition to previous formulations of this problem
of intra-social process has already been noted: in particular the
attempt from within economic theory to explain the exchanges
between the economy and the society, and indeed to explain
economic processes themselves, was claimed to be unacceptable
owing to its reliance on ambiguous notions of the economic
subject. Parsons' critique of Homans' exchange theory illustrates
both the general strain of the opposition and the nature of the
alternative.

Homans argues that concepts such as 'social system' or the
'economy' must be seen as extrapolations from a few well-trusted
psychological processes – they must always be explicitly reducible to psychological propositions, e.g. 'man is a reward-seeking
animal'.[26] The immediate problem of such an absurd thesis is
recognised by Parsons – how, given a set of essential characteristics of the human subject, is it possible to conceptualise rigorously different economies and different social structures? The
starting point of the theory of the economy and society cannot be
the properties of the individual human subject, whether they be

those postulated by marginalist economics, behaviourist psychology or any other essentially individualist conceptions. On the contrary, a distinct referent is necessary in order to allow the theorisation of the economy/society relation: 'Concrete behaviour is not a function simply of elementary properties, but of kinds of systems ... their various structures and the processes taking place within them' (from *Institutions and Social Exchange*, ed. Turk H. and Simpson R. L., p. 35).

Parsons' distinction between elementary properties and 'kinds of systems' is quite clearly an attempt to avoid the reduction of the latter (and subsequently the economy and society) to the former. The concept of the functional system and subsystem is the means by which Parsons attempts to surpass the reliance on any ambiguous notion of the economic 'subject'. The question posed in this section concerns the effectiveness of this project. To be precise: does the concept of the functional subsystem overcome the obvious problems of the postulate of the economic (or any other) 'subject'? It will be argued that, in fact, the distinction between 'elementary properties' and 'kinds of systems' collapses at certain crucial junctures, and that consequently Parsons does not achieve the objective necessary to his theory of the economy. In order to demonstrate this point I will return to the formulation of the functional prerequisites and, in particular, to the function of goal-attainment.

The functional prerequisites refer to the relation between the system and its situation: they concern the internal problems of the system on the one hand, and the relation between it and its environment on the other – thus $I$ involves the internal cohesion of the system, $L$ the stability of units and pattern, whereas $A$ concerns the control of the environment for the purposes of the system, and $G$ concerns the establishment of that state and the mobilisation of resources necessary for its fulfilment.

It is obvious that the functional requirement of goal-attainment and the correspondent subsystem occupy a unique position in relation to the other functional imperatives: whereas the $I, L$ and $A$ prerequisites may be seen as relatively 'automatic' processes of adjustment within the system and between it and the environment, the goal-attainment function involves the *establishment* of the relation between system and environment and the *mobilisation* of the system as a whole in a certain direction – in short it constitutes the 'vital principle' of the system. It is not surprising, therefore, that it is at this juncture that the mode of theorisation is most problematic, for when we turn to the conceptualisation of the *mechanisms* by which the functions are realised (the establishment of a 'goal-state', mobilisation of resources), it becomes apparent that theoretical ambiguity plays a strategic role. Consider the following arguments:

> A goal-state, for an individual actor or for a social system, is a *relation* between the system of reference and one or more situational objects which (given the value system and its institutionalisation) maximises the stability of the system. Other things being equal, such a state, *once present*, tends to be maintained, and if absent, tends to be 'sought' by the action of one or more units of the system.' (*ES*, p. 17, latter emphasis mine)

The ambiguity surrounds this reference to a relation 'once present', for beyond reference to the given value-systems Parsons offers no concept or theory of the precise mechanisms and processes by which this relation between system and situation is to be established. The role of culture is misleading here for, although it is functional in this relation, it can only supply the particular 'contents' of goal-states and/or maintain a given goal-state. If Parsons is to avoid an idealist–emanationist thesis then some distinct concept is required of the mechanisms by which one value-pattern is adopted and not another, and by which these value-patterns are made functional in a certain direction.

If Parsons offers no such concept then what processes *are* implied? The definition of goals and goal-states supplies some indication, for it implies, on the one hand, the capacity to desire:

> With respect to any boundary interchange . . . each participating system pursues a GOAL which is the establishment of a desired or needed relation between the acquisition of input (with due regard to quality and amount) and the corresponding output (*ES*, p. 108)

and, on the other hand, that systems have the capacity for *gratification*:

Goal-states may be negative, i.e. noxious situational conditions, or positive, i.e. a maximisation of favourable or 'gratifying' conditions. (*ES*, p. 17)

It becomes clear that these two capacities are attributes commonly assigned to the *human subject* – taken together they must imply two more definite mechanisms: *recognition mechanisms* and *gratificational mechanisms*. Both features are theoretically problematic.

To take the first, if a system is to have a 'desire' or a need, and if these are to be at some level effective (as functionalism requires of processes within the system), then some feature of the system must be supplied with the means to recognise these needs and, further, to recognise the structure of the situation in order that a goal-state may be established. For example, if the goal of the economy as a social system is the production of goods and services, then a mechanism is required by which the economy can become conscious of its goal and by which it can conceive the way in which the situation may be manipulated in order to achieve this imperative. Each subsystem and system must have a *consciousness*, a means by which systemic needs, situational objects and value-patterns can be sifted and arranged in a particular order or pattern. Functional subsystems are therefore conceived as *human subjects*: they are supplied with the capacities correspondent to those offered in the humanist formulation of the individual human actor.

Can the fact that subsystems have capacities normally assigned to individual human subjects be made theoretically consistent with Parsonian discourse? Two forms of reconciliation can be offered. First, it might be argued that the concept of 'cybernetic hierarchy', already introduced in *Economy and Society* and of great significance in the later texts, overcomes the problem of postulating a recognition structure in so far as the process of inter-system relations can be reduced to 'information-energy' interchange, i.e. an automatic process. Such a thesis is hardly successful in avoiding the consequences outlined above. Either the effectivity of culture is defined in the relatively loose sense as a mechanism of the functioning of the system (as in the case in *ES*) and then the problem remains as before – some mechanism must exist which can interiorise culture patterns, i.e. a recognition structure – or culture is conceived in the later sense as *constitutive*, in which the systems of action become in the last analysis mere 'slices' of an idealist hierarchy of effectivity. This alternative only overcomes the inconsistency of the earlier position in so far as the claimed autonomy of the systems of action is denegated in favour of a full-blown idealist teleology (see chapter 6).

The second form of reconciliation is no more successful than the first. In this case, the claim that the subsystems must involve the capacities of human subjects might be seen as perfectly consistent with the general theory of action, in that it has always been made explicit that social systems are 'actors'. But it is necessary to distinguish, as indeed Parsons does, between the concrete individual actor and a *system* of action – the latter is, of course, 'made up' of individual actors but it is not a mere aggregate of actors (or in the case of the personality system not a concrete human individual), but a theoretically *specific* object. In ambiguously transposing capacities of the individual human subject to the level of the systems and subsystems Parsons contradicts the definition of the systems of action as 'analytically discrete'. Totalities such as the polity, the economy, and more generally the total social system, are thus conceived as human subjects or 'society-subjects'. At the level of the polity this leads Parsons to adopt a thesis central to much classical political philosophy: the polity/state as the collective mind of the society, the neutral body above society which operates for the 'good of all', or in Parsons' case for the fulfilment of collective goals. Each and every structure of society is provided with a human consciousness and the capacity to act on the basis of the faculty.

The ambiguity surrounding the mechanisms of recognition is confounded with the second general feature implicit in the concept of functional subsystem: the capacity to obtain *gratification*. Subsystems are seen to relate to each other, and ultimately to the system as a whole, through a process of reciprocal exchange; the contribution of each subsystem to the functioning of the system is not conceived in terms of a general 'spreading' of products and facilities to all other subsystems, but rather in terms of specific matching – input–output relations are such that the products of one branch go primarily into one other branch. Why, it might be asked, must the functional process take this form? Although the notion of 'spreading' would not be altogether inconsistent with the concept of system, Parsons is emphatic that the process of functional contribution does not operate in this way. This can only be because subsystems are maintained as essentially *human* entities – they operate on the basis of human desires and gratifications (for example, the household receives goods and services for which *in return* it provides labour services for the economy).

Such a thesis is interesting in relation to Parsons' critique of Homans. Homans' form of 'exchange theory' is attacked for several reasons but one in particular concerns its *psychologism*, the reduction of social processes to psychological processes (for example, the explanation of economic mechanisms in terms of 'reward seeking'). Now, although the alternative to a reductionism is, as has been seen, the concept of system and related concepts, when it comes to the problem of the *mechanisms* by which the systems and subsystems articulate and function, it is apparent that Parsons depends upon precisely the same ambiguous psychologism and humanism explicit in the positions he criticises. In short, *Parsons is forced to assign to the mechanisms of the systems capacities he refuses to assign to the systems themselves.*[27] The exact status of these mechanisms becomes theoretically problematic – they are situated mid-way between two forms of determination, the effectivity of culture, on the one hand, and the conditional exigencies of systems of action, on the other. The ambiguous nature of the recognition and gratificational mechanisms is inflated with this contradictory mode of double determination: the crucial role played by these components of the subsystems is conceived in terms which have no coherent theoretical foundation.

In addition to this order of problems, a more concrete set exists over the concept of functional subsystems: this concerns the mode in which economic categories are interiorised within the theory of social systems. It has already been noted that Parsons' claim concerning the 'congruences' between economic theory and the theory of action is devoid of sufficient demonstration, and indeed appears to operate on the basis of word-play; however the actual theoretical link offered is even less convincing.

The articulation of the theory of social systems and economic theory is made at two levels. On the one hand, the economy is conceived as both a social system (in which the differentiated subsystems are made correspondent with the factors of production, land labour, capital and organisation) and as a subsystem of the total social system. On the other hand, the factors themselves are seen to be 'concretely' represented in basic economic *institutions* – enterprise, occupation, contract and property. Both levels are problematic.

In the first case, the parallel between the functional problems and the factors of production has no determinate basis, for there appears to be no rigorous foundation on which to make each parallel between subsystem and factor of production. Why, for example, must the integration of the economic process be fulfilled through the entrepreneur? Why, indeed, should Parsons adopt the orthodox economic set of categories to begin with? There is no theoretical demonstration why one factor should occupy any particular functional role and not another, nor is there a rigorous justification for accepting concepts produced externally to the theory of social systems to begin with.

The second step of interiorisation of economic categories is perhaps more problematic in that it involves a more fundamental order of problems already discussed. Functional subsystems are 'concretised' through the merger with economic institutions (property, contract, etc.) – concrete economic behaviour is functionally determinate only given its mediation by economic institutions; these represent the dominant value- patterns at the social level, and, in particular, economic institutions embody and reflect the value of economic rationality. The major ambiguity here surrounds the relation between institution and functional subsystem, for this relation is another example of *double-determination*. As was shown in the previous chapter, institutions are governed by the cultural configurations of which they are an expression (hence their close relation to the 'pattern-variables'), whereas systems of action are governed by the organisational exigencies of their internal constitution. The concept of institution and those of the functional subsystems have no firm theoretical connection. There are no consistent theoretical grounds for interiorising economic institutions within the functional subsystems.

Given these features of the concept of the functional subsystem it is impossible to consider it as a viable theoretical alternative to existing attempts to conceive economic and non-economic relations. In the last analysis, this concept is no less problematic than those it attempts to surpass. It cannot provide a coherent means of theorisation of the economy/society relation.

## 5.5 Conclusion

As this analysis has shown, Parsons' theoretical attempts to pose the question of the relation between the economy and its social situation tell us a great deal both about the degree of sophistication of his work and, ultimately, its underlying conceptual problems.

*Economy and Society*, it could be said, was written at the time when the distinctively structural–functionalist character of Parsonian sociology was at its zenith. In the works that followed, he chose to pay much more attention to the cultural system and to socio-cultural change – in other words, towards the concept of the cybernetic hierarchy. This chapter has briefly referred to problematic areas which only a developed discussion of the theory of social change can demonstrate in more detail. This leads naturally to the final discussion in this overall investigation.

# 6 The Theory of Social Change and Social Evolution

I come now to the final discussion of this analysis of Parsonian theory. It is fitting to make the theory of social change and social evolution the object of this discussion because of the unique significance of this topic area to Parsons' work in general. To begin with, it is no exaggeration to say that it is over the problem of social change that most of the controversy surrounding his work is centred. Secondly, this area is an extremely good index of the various 'phases' through which Parsonian theory has gone. There have indeed been several major alterations to the theory of action and this is most clearly reflected in the analysis of change.

It is, however, a more general issue which is of most significance here. The role of culture is, of course, the hinge-point of Parsonian theory. It has been shown to be decisive in his analysis of the unit act and, on a different level, in his theory of the social system. In his more recent writings, the cultural system becomes more explicitly presented in terms of socio-cultural *evolution*, and is thus internalised within a theory of development. I will, therefore, take the opportunity to tackle in this discussion of social change and social evolution the more general problem of culture as represented in Parsons' work.

Following a brief outline of the predominant criticisms of Parsons' theory of the social system and an outline of the various phases through which his analysis of social change has passed, I will attempt to assess the theoretical nature of his theory and, in particular, the notion of social 'evolution'. This will involve a discussion of the relationship between the concept of socio-cultural evolution and the Darwinian theory of natural selection, in terms of an examination of Parsons' conception of 'generalised adaptive capacity'. Finally, I will approach more specifically the problem of the cultural system and, in particular, the role of religious elements in that system. I will conclude that, despite Parsons' attempt to avoid an 'idealist emanationism', his theorisation of the cultural system (and its effects on social systems and their evolution) results in a full-blown philosophy of history.

## 6.1 Social Change and Structural–functionalism

What is perhaps most remarkable about many sociological commentaries on Parsons' work is the claim that social change is a non-problem for his social theory. Consider, for example, Gouldner's statement that 'the Parsonian social system . . . is, in brief, a perpetual motion machine', coupled with the argument that 'conflicts and disorder are viewed not as part of the necessary order of things'.[1] Lockwood has also presented a similar interpretation, claiming that 'there are no social processes . . . which systematically make for deviance and social change' in Parsonian theory;[2] and, of course, Dahrendorf sees no indication that Parsons considers social change a real issue for sociology – in the theory of the social system, he says, 'historical change is absent'.[3]

Such readings are commonplace.[4] It is only relatively recently that the obvious anomalies of such interpretations have been spelt out.[5] It is not only with reference to the later work of Parsons that they misrepresent Parsonian theory, but more acutely with reference to the 'structural–functional' period. I will show in more detail later that a theory of social change not only exists in the theory of the social system but is in many ways *central* to it. At this point I will look at the related claims that (a) Parsons leaves no room for *systematic* sources of conflict and deviance, and (b) that he precludes mechanisms of social change in his theory of the social system.

'Conflict' theorists argue that social relations involve inherent sources of strain. Differential interests and scarce resources are seen to induce conflict relationships; these become a normal part of social functioning and lead in turn to social change. Parsons' work is held to ignore such sources of strain, and to rule out inherent sources of conflict and deviance. Thus Gouldner can argue that 'Parsons' ego and alter do not seem to live in a world of scarcity; scarcity seems to have no effect on their behaviour or on their relationships' (*The Coming Crisis of Western Sociology*, p. 237).

However, despite the popularity of such a conception, it is hardly difficult to find in Parsons' work theses which flatly contradict it. On the issue of scarcity, consider the following argument:

> By virtue of the primordial fact that the objects – social and non-social – which are instrumentally useful or intrinsically valuable are scarce in relation to the amount required for the full gratification of the need dispositions of every actor, there arises the problem of allocation. . . . This is the fundamental problem which arises from the interaction of two or more actors. (*TGTA*, p. 197)

There is an inherent source of strain arising from the scarcity that is inevitable given the distinction between the personality (organised around need-dispositions) and social (organised around role-expectations) levels of action. The articulation of the personality and social systems induces an *endemic* area of strain. Further, the relationship between the social and cultural systems provides additional sources of conflict. The two systems are distinct levels of organisation with a degree of autonomy from each other. Again, Parsons is quite explicit on the issue:

> No one system of value-orientation with perfect consistency in its pattern can be fully institutionalised in a concrete society. There will be uneven distributions among the different parts of the society. There will be value conflicts and role conflicts. The consequences of such imperfect integration is in the nature of the case, a certain instability, and hence a susceptibility to change. (ibid., p. 231)

Reading the critiques of Gouldner, Lockwood and the others, it is difficult reconcile these with some on Parsons' statements such as the one above. Yet these are not isolated quotes from Parsons' works – they follow directly from the conception of three systems of action and the definitions of the systems themselves. Deviance, conflict and change are not seen as mere observations (although they may be), but are *systematically* induced, inherent in the relations between the systems themselves.

It is not necessary to labour on this issue. It will be shown quite categorically as this discussion proceeds that social change *is* a central issue for Parsonian theory. I need only at this point register the fact that the traditional critical attacks, accusing that theory of ignoring social change and conflict, are quite misplaced.

Of course, at the root of many of these criticisms are issues which have already been discussed in previous chapters. Many of the criticisms are merely elaborate forms of the empiricist attack on abstract theory dealt with in chapter 2. Thus Smith's opposition to functionalism,[6] although in most ways a more informed analysis of Parsonian theory than those of Gouldner and others, proposes that 'change is simply a difference of the pattern of events over time' (*The Concept of Social Change*, p. 152). Social change is to be analysed according to the empirical recording of events and relations between them. A similar line is taken by Nisbet, who argues that 'social change cannot be dealt with in any illuminating or valid way except in terms of events'.[7]

In addition to the epistemological issue, the various debates over the theory of social change reflect wider controversies on the individual *vs* society question. Again, this problem has already been dealt with previously and there is no need to revive it here. Misrepresentation of Parsonian theory is not the only problem with 'conflict theory' and 'historical sociology'.

As has already been pointed out, it would not be correct to say that Parsons has *one* theory of social change in the sense of a unitary and consistent theory for his analysis of social change has altered in many important respects from the earlier to the latest works. It will help if, before actually confronting that theory critically, the various developments or transformations of it are spelt out clearly.

## 6.2 The Development of the Theory of Social Change

This section will be primarily expositional and will operate with the perhaps unsatisfactory but pragmatically necessary 'phases' of Parsons' work. The demarcation of these phases will begin with the arguments of *The Structure of Social Action*, move on to the 'structural–functional' period, and finally discuss the later theses on social evolution. Such a chronological outline must not, however, assume a 'developmental' conception of theory, as proposed in Parsons' own reflections on his work.[8] The terms 'development' and 'phases' as used here refer only to alterations or transformations of the theory of action: no 'improvement' of that theory is presupposed.

*The Structure of Social Action*, as is well known, is not primarily concerned with an extensive elaboration of a theory of social structure, but rather with the analysis of processes of 'convergence' of several major social theorists. As such, it does not provide much by way of a theory of social change. It has already been shown that *SSA* fails to elaborate any concept of social system or a specific mode of organisation of action elements. The nearest that Parsons gets at this stage is to provide the epistemological concept of 'emergent properties',[9] but these only designate *types* of action, 'historical individuals' (e.g. economic rationality) and not organisations of action.

In *SSA*, in so far as there is an arena that can be designated 'social', it is with reference to the unity of a system of 'ultimate ends'. The only form of social theory to develop out of this is one which makes social structures synonymous with a set of *culturepatterns*. Thus, social change in this respect becomes synonymous with cultural development, and the attempt to classify social types is governed by the need to classify types of culture. With no developed concept of the social system the analysis of social change becomes an idealist exercise in tracing the origins of systems of ideas.

What is interesting about *SSA* with respect to the analysis of change is Parsons' critical position on Darwin. He offers several criticisms[10] but two of them are particularly revealing. First, he accuses Darwinian theory of omitting an element of 'directionality' in its outline of development. Yet in his later works, as we shall see, Parsons claims a close relationship between the theory of action and the theory of natural selection. The paradox is that the connection is seen to lie in their respective mechanisms of development, both apparently dependent on the concept of 'generalised adaptive capacity'.

The second criticism illustrates perhaps even more clearly the differences that exist between the early and late Parsons. He argues that Darwinism, or more accurately 'Social' Darwinism, depends upon a conception of history whereby 'the course of history is determined by an impersonal process over which they [i.e. men] have no control' (*SSA*, p. 113). Darwinism is attacked for failing to allow the voluntary processes of action the determining role in historical development, for supressing the subjective element of action. Again, the impression given is that the relevant objects of analysis of social change are the systems of ideas, expressions and symbols of culture. It is these which define the subjective course of action, and not some systematic prerequisites as in later theses.[11]

It is clear, therefore, that in *SSA* Parsons does not provide much by way of a theory of social change. Even his outline of culture is presented in individualistic terms as 'normative orientation', and not yet as a *system*.[12] We must not forget, however, that culture remains the hinge-point of his conception of social change, and we shall return to this point later.

It is only with the 'structural–functionalist' writings that social change becomes a specific theoretical problem for Parsonian sociology. He dismisses the claim that sociological analysis of change must be restricted to the recording of contingent events, that the ontological peculiarity of change makes a general theory impossible or prohibits the development of abstract concepts. The claim that 'history is flux' is a common counter-assertion against Parsons' theory, but Parsons shows the absurdity of such a claim and the conclusions drawn from it:

> The categorical assertion that any assumptions about struc-
> ture are scientifically inadmissable, because in the last analysis
> everything is in flux, denies the legitimacy of science. In any
> science, and in sociology in particular, the concept of change is
> meaningful only in terms of a definable something, i.e.
> something which can be described in structural forms.[13]

An analysis of social change must be able to say what it is that is changing; it must involve concepts which define the objects which are involved in processes of change. Hence, Parsons sees the static-dynamic opposition as a misplaced dichotomy. It is not simply a matter of a choice between different empirical assess-ments, but rather a question of a theory to account for *both* types of society. Parsons is not proposing a 'static' view of society –

whether a particular society is relatively static or dynamic is a question of concrete particulars – but rather a theory which explains processes in both.

His theory in this case is centred around the concept of the social system as a boundary-maintaining unity. A system thus defined is one in which it can be said that theoretically and empirically there is a significant difference between structures and processes internal to the system and those external to it. This concept, seen as a 'point of reference', enables the identification of sets of interdependent elements which can be defined as mechanisms for the functioning of the system. With regard to the problem at hand, the concept of the social system thus presented becomes the 'terminal' concept, constituting the conditions of existence of the theory of social change.

What characterises the structural–functionalist argument most, however, is the conviction that the concept of the social system in this sense is moulded by the relatively *undeveloped and incomplete* nature of the theory. While we do have terminal patterns or points of reference for the analysis of social relations (i.e. the concept of the boundary-maintaining system), we do not yet, argues Parsons, have 'a complete knowledge of the laws which determine processes within a system' (*SS*, p. 483). In fact, it is this conception of theoretical incompleteness which actually defines the term 'structural–functional'. Parsons claims to overcome the fragmentary knowledge of laws by the operation of two forms of theorisation.

First, the concept of structure designates 'on the basis of the logical requirements of the action frame of reference', the features of the system which can be treated strategically as constants. Out of the ranges of variation to be found in action processes, there will arise certain patterns which can be designated as relatively stable and constant features. These can be described as 'structural categories' of action. Structural analysis as such is precisely the classification of these patterns into categories.

The descriptive/categorical bias of structural analysis is itself partly overcome by the second type of analysis – the 'functional dimension'. The functional dimension formulates the relation between the 'givenness' of the structure and the environmental conditions articulated with it. It gives some sort of knowledge of the mechanisms of the functioning of the system, internally and externally. The problem for functional analysis is an explanation of the mechanisms which make orderly responses to environmental conditions possible. Hence we are given the functional prerequisites, a set of universal exigencies which all systems of action must solve at some stage in order to remain in equilibrium. These complement the structural categories in the 'dynamic' direction.

Having said that, structural–functionalist theory is still seen as an incomplete framework for social analysis. With reference to social change this leads to a very important claim: 'a general theory of the processes of change of social systems is not possible in the present state of knowledge' (*SS*, p. 486). Without a complete knowledge of the laws of social systems, a theory of change must be restricted to a theory of particular sub-processes of change *within* social systems, not of the overall processes of change *of* systems. It is a misrepresentation of this thesis that is perhaps most responsible for the numerous accusations of 'static-bias' which have been directed at Parsons. Change of social systems itself is not denied – rather it is held to be a problem on which we have inadequate knowledge and must, therefore, operate with the next best – the concepts of structure and function.

I emphasise this point for a specific reason. In his later works, Parsons implies that the term 'structural–functionalist' is no longer applicable, given certain theoretical developments.[14] As we shall see, there *are* significant transformations of the analysis of social change in the later texts, and these will be seriously questioned. At this point we must note how certain areas of analysis are excluded from the theory of social change but how later they occupy quite different roles.

In his conviction that a theory of change of social systems was not yet possible at the time when he was writing, Parsons cited three areas which were not pertinent to the theory as it stands. These were the organism, the physical environment and the realm of culture. All three are obviously *factors* in social change in the sense that they are effective in the changing of social systems. However, from the point of view of structural–functional analysis they are not of *theoretical* concern but must be treated as 'givens'.

For example, with reference to the organism and the physical environment, Parsons states that 'we have advanced no theory of the interdependence of social action processes and the biological and physical factors of their determination' (*SS*, p. 488). It is with reference to the role of culture, however, that the differences between structural–functional analysis of change and the later positions is most apparent. Culture, like the biological organism and the physical world, is held to be an *environment* to the theory of change.

Although culture is quite obviously an integral part of the theory of action, it is argued that, from the point of view of a theory of social *change*, it must be treated as a given. The actual dynamics of culture, the factors of development of culture patterns, are no more a part of the theory of change than the biological organism. Culture is a factor of social change but the primary concern of a structural–functional theory of change is with the *effects* rather than the *origins* of culture patterns. Again, as we shall see, this is quite a different thesis to the one proposed in his later writings.

So there we have it. The analysis of social change is here dominated by the concepts of structure, function and system. On this basis, Parsons approaches more specific questions on the factors involved in change and the impact of those factors, leading eventually to descriptions of 'types' of structural change. Let us expound on the question of the factors of social change, as these are useful indices of Parsons' approach to the general question of social change at this stage of his work.

We can recall that the prior theoretical condition for a theory of change lies in the concept of a boundary-maintaining system of interdependent variables. It is the systematic character of these variables which is of most concern to the analysis, not the sources of change themselves. In fact, any form of 'general theory' of change which stipulates in advance primary factors in the genesis of change is antithetical to Parsons' project: 'the view that there is no simple intrinsic priority in the factors of the initiation of change is inherent in the conception of the social system which we have advanced here' (*SS*, p. 493).

There are no inherently primary sources of impetus to change in social systems – hence his opposition to all 'dominant-factor' theories, materialist or idealist.[15] Parsons states clearly that 'there is no necessary order of teleological significance in the sources of change'.[16] The impetus to change may come from a set of cultural patterns, but it may equally arise from population changes, the climate, technology, and so on. According to Parsons, such factors may concretely determine change in any particular case, but a factor-primacy is not written *into the theory itself*. Structural–functional analysis of social change is primarily concerned, therefore, with what Parsons calls 'tracing the repercussions' of the factors of change. This is best illustrated by looking at his discussion of 'vested interests'.[17]

For there to be any form of social equilibrium, the institutionalisation process must produce an integration of the need-dispositions of actors with a set of culture patterns – in particular, patterns of value-orientation. However, given a disturbance at the system level (social, personality), there will inevitably be some form of 'lag' before the other systems again come into line. Thus a disturbance at the level of role-expectations will create some form of disequilibrium at the level of need-dispositions. The integration of need-dispositions thus creates an 'inherent' resistance to change at the social level. Social change thus not only alters role-expectations but must do so by eventually overcoming the resistance to change which is inevitable in an equilibrating system.

'Vested interests' are a good example of this inherent resistance to change. They refer to an interest in maintaining a specific level and pattern of gratification from an existing system of role-expectations. They will always be a problem for any social change. Change will disturb the existing possible balance of gratification, and there will always be, as a result, some form of opposition and strain. Eventually this strain must be overcome by the processes making for equilibrium.

This is an example of the major theoretical role that structural–functionalism takes *vis-à-vis* a theory of change. It relates above all to an analysis of the *impact* of forces of change rather than to the sources of change themselves. In fact, Parsons goes as far as to outline five variables according to which impact will vary:

(i) the magnitude of the disturbance;
(ii) the proportion of the units in the system at the relevant levels which are affected;
(iii) the strategic character of the units' functional contribution to the system;

(iv) the incidence of the disturbance on analytically-dis-
     tinguishable components of the system's structure;
 (v) the level of effectiveness of the mechanisms of control.

These five elements are seen to provide the conceptual means
with which to overcome the 'formless empiricism' of many other
analyses of social change, without lapsing into a 'dominant-
factor' theory. The former is held to provide virtually no
*explanation* of social change, the latter to deny the *interdependence*
of the variables involved in change.

However, this attempt to avoid 'dominant-factor' analyses
should not be overestimated. While Parsons appears to argue
that no one source of change holds a primary position, nevertheless one component of change *is* singled out and assigned a
unique significance. This brings us back to the concept of *culture*.

While Parsons does not, at this stage, go as far as to claim that
culture is the most important factor or source of change, he still
places it in a central position for analysis. He does, in fact, go as
far as to say that culture, primarily by means of value-patterns, is
the major organisational factor in *determining the impact* of the
factors of change. The significance of culture is clear in the
following statement:

> It may be difficult to define magnitude of impact: however,
> given approximate equality of magnitude, the probability of
> producing structural change is greater in proportion to the
> position in the order of control at which the impact of its
> principle disturbing influence occurs. This principle is based
> on the assumption that stable systems have mechanisms which
> can absorb considerable internal strains, and thus endogone-
> ous or exogoneous variabilities impinging at other levels in the
> hierarchy of control may be neutralised before extending
> structural changes to higher levels. It follows that the crucial
> focus of the problem of change lies in the stability of the value
> system.[18]

We see again the unique status of culture to the theory of
action. While there may be no primary source of change,
nevertheless the decisive role of culture is written into the theory
of action itself. In this case, it is culture which determines the
*direction* of social change.

Despite Parsons' continual emphasis that there is no primary source of change, he still maintains some notion of 'order of importance' of the variables. There is, written into the theory of change itself, a *hierarchy* of variables and this is reflected in the concept of 'directionality'. If culture is not the primary source of change, it does at least determine, in the main, the *direction* of change, given the initial impetus.

An example of this directionality is the 'process of rationalisation'. As shown in the previous chapter, Parsons' use of this concept is not exactly equivalent to Weber's, in the sense that social change is not simply an ideational tendency but a *systemic* process. Nevertheless, the process of rationalisation is cited as an important example of the direction in which social change tends: 'there seems to be no doubt that there is an inherent factor of the directionality of change in social systems, a directionality which was classically formulated by Max Weber in what he called the 'process of rationalisation' (*SS*, p. 499).

An important facet of culture in comparison with other factors is its capacity to be 'transmitted without loss'. Culture – knowledge, moral standards and expressive symbols – can be preserved and perpetuated far in excess of its particular relationship to the social and personality systems. 'There is', Parsons states 'in culture the possibility of indefinite cumulative development' (*SS*, p. 498). Culture is unique in the sense that its most fundamental component – value-orientations – has the capacity to 'govern' action, and in addition it can accumulate and therefore outlive particular societies. It can thus control the directions that change takes. Change is not then a random process from one state of the system to another.

Before leaving this issue there is one question still to be asked. Parsons argues that directionality is written into the concept of action in the sense that action is 'oriented' in a certain direction. Orientation is an inherently directional process. Yet here he appears to conflate two system-levels, the cultural and the social.[19] Orientation is above all a cultural process (or at least the value-orientational component). To transplant the directionality inherent in value-orientation in order to explain a *social* process would seem to take little regard of the particular organisational processes of the social system. The direction contained in the cultural symbol or expression is surely, in terms of Parsons' own theory, not equivalent to the direction of the social system.

We can leave this issue until later, as it refers to more basic theoretical questions. At this juncture we can move on to explain the position taken in Parsons' most recent writings, which we refer to as the 'Social Evolutionist' position.

## 6.3 Social Change as Social Evolution

Parsons maintains that his later theses on social evolution do not radically depart from his earlier positions. His theory itself, he holds, has been subject to an 'evolutionary' process. We must therefore consider the extent to which this claim is true.

There is one basic thesis with which to begin. It is argued that the concepts of social change are fundamentally the same as the concepts for the analysis of systems in equilibrium. In other words, the processes which operate so as to change a system are the same as those which serve to maintain it. The only difference lies in the intensity, distribution and organisation of the component elements of the processes in question. Change results from certain combinations of these elements.

The primary change process, from the point of view of Parsons' later 'evolutionary perspective', is the *'enhancement of adaptive capacity'*. This process defines that social change is not simply a transformation of an existing state of affairs, but that it also involves *advance*. Thus 'social change' becomes 'social evolution'; the evolutionary process is not just change of organisation but change in a definite direction, toward a higher level of socio-cultural existence: 'Our perspective clearly involves evolutionary judgements – for example, that intermediate societies are more advanced than primitive societies' (*Societies*, p. 110).

Such evolutionary judgments guard against 'cultural relativism', a form of analysis which views cultures in their own terms, not in terms of a *general* explanation of social development. Such a theory, Parsons points out 'regards the Arunta of Australia and such modern societies as the Soviet Union as equally authentic "cultures", to be judged as equals in all basic respects' (ibid.). Different societies cannot be treated as 'equal' because of the existence of an evolutionary scale of primitive–advanced forms. Societies are not simply to be analysed, they are to be *judged*.[20] Cultural relativism, of course, is only a problem if, at the beginning, we accept an evolutionist standpoint.

So what essentially distinguishes primitive from advanced societies is the degree to which the enhancement of adaptive capacity is realised. This capacity may be generated from within the society by forming new structures, or it may originate from outside the system by means of cultural diffusion. An example of the latter is a 'seedbed' society – a society which, although it may itself have ceased to exist, nevertheless continues to be effective through a continuance of elements of its culture. Societies following seedbed societies take advantage of the cultural advances they have made and which have spread geographically and historically.

Regardless of whether the enhancement of adaptive capacity originates inside or outside the system, the process and its effects can be theorised according to the same paradigm. Four basic categories are prescribed: differentiation, adaptive up-grading, inclusion and value-generalisation. Briefly, these categories can be explained as follows.[21]

Differentiation is the division of a unit or structure into two or more units or structures. These structures differ according to their structural characteristics and in their functional significance to the system. Differentiation only takes on evolutionary significance (i.e. is 'progressive') if each newly-differentiated component has greater adaptive capacity than its predecessor. Thus, the differentiation of the political system from the economy was only advantageous because it allowed a better handling of political problems, i.e. it increased the adaptive capabilities of the societies in which it occurred.

Adaptive up-grading refers to an increase in the range of resources available to a social system. The handling of system problems in any particular situation depends upon a number of social resources. If these resources are increased (for example, if there is an increase in the number of productive units in the economic system), then there will be an improvement in the adaptive capacity of the system as a whole.

Differentiation and up-grading together constitute a further functional problem: the integration of the action elements so produced. Inclusion refers to the incorporation of the more complex range of elements and structures within the *existing* normative system. Social systems will vary in the extent to which their normative systems can effectively cope with the upsets and transformations which accompany differentiation and adaptive up-grading. For example, some systems may be unable to cope with increased democratic control of political decision-making, given a 'traditionalistic' emphasis. Those normative systems which are better equipped will obviously improve the capacity for advance.

Finally, the process of value-generalisation refers to the capacity of the system to *change* its value-system. Given the other processes, it will be necessary for the value-patterns to have a greater level of generality than before in order to legitimise the wider range of goals and functions of its units. In short, value-generalisation is the converse of inclusion and involves the development of wider values, constituting a higher level of effectivity and autonomy of values over normative patterns.

Now, these four processes do not occur at random. They do not appear concretely according to contingent occurrences. In fact, they are incorporated within a conception of a determinate *order*. We are here brought back to the concept of the cybernetic hierarchy. What is unique about the social evolutionary thesis is that the *whole* action complex is theorised in terms of the hierarchy. The cybernetic relation is one whereby systems high in information but low in energy 'control' systems which are low in information but high in energy.

This places 'ultimate reality', which is the major environment to the action complex, at the top in the hierarchy of control, with the systems of action following in order of effectivity.

> The cultural system structures commitments *vis-a-vis* ulti-mate reality into meaningful orientations toward the rest of the environment and the systems of action, the physical world, organisms, personalities, and social systems. In the cybernetic sense, it is highest within the action system, the social system ranking next, and the personality and organism falling respectively below that. The physical environment is ultimate in the conditional, as distinguished from the organisational, sense. (*Societies*, pp. 9–10)

It must be noted that the status of the cybernetic hierarchy is greatly enhanced in this conception compared with its formula-tion in the earlier writings (with significant consequences). In the outline of social change given in *The Social System* and similar texts, culture was given primacy in the analysis of the *impact* of the forces of change. In other words, in so far as there was any reference to a cybernetic hierarchy or determinate order, it was always *given* the sources of change. However, in the theses of *Societies* and other related texts there is a quite different status. The cybernetic hierarchy is no longer limited to an operation *within* the systems of action, but is operative in *determining the systems themselves*. The hierarchy is now placed outside the systems, no longer restricted to a process of order of the impact of social change.

It is, above all, this thesis which most clearly labels Parsons' evolutionist position. Is this conception of socio-cultural evolution the general theory of change which was claimed in the *Social System* to be 'not yet possible'? Parsons himself clearly alludes to something on those lines: 'Developments since the emergence of the four function paradigm and the analysis of generalised media, in particular, have made the designation "structural–functional" increasingly less appropriate'.[22]

Clearly, the concept of the three (or four) 'differentiated' systems of action takes on a different significance. Earlier, this differentiation between personality, social and cultural systems was proposed as a 'pragmatic' starting point, equivalent to the concept of 'emergent properties'.[23] Now, however, the differentiation of action systems becomes *part of the evolutionary process*. The appearance of the personality, social and cultural systems as differentiated systems of action becomes part of a historical tendency.

History becomes the site of an increasing differentiation between the four major systems of action. Thus, a primitive society is one in which there is a low level of differentiation between the social and cultural systems, as well as between the biological organism and the personality system.[24] This is in addition to the further differentiation *within* the social system of the four functional subsystems.

It comes as no surprise that Parsons proposes a scheme of evolutionary 'stages'. 'An evolutionary perspective implies both a criterion of evolutionary direction and an evolutionary scheme of stages' (*Societies*, p. 26). Three major stages are advanced: primitive, intermediate and modern.

The means of demarcation of these stages (the mode in which they are periodised) is above all in terms of the degree to which the cultural and social systems are differentiated. The criteria of the divisions between stages of evolution of societies lie in the level of development of the code structures of the normative system. Norms are, for Parsons, the contacting bridge between social and cultural systems. In primitive societies there is apparently little differentiation between the social and cultural systems, primarily because there is an undeveloped language system. For there to be a transition from the primitive to the intermediate stage of society, it is imperative that an elaborated and formal system of codes be developed. In particular, the development of a written language is held to be the watershed between these two stages of evolution. The symbolic contents of a culture can, with writing, be embodied in forms separate from particular action contexts. These act to stabilise and standardise social relations. This then allows the separate development of the social and cultural *systems*.

In similar fashion, the watershed between intermediate and modern societies is facilitated by the formation of a legal code – a legal system. While the written language furthers the independence of the cultural system from the conditional exigencies of society, laws further the independence of norms from particular political and economic interests. By formalising the normative system law allows wider transactions and more consistent relationships.

The basic thesis behind all this is clear. History is the process of increasing subordination of the conditional by controlling factors. Implicitly, it is the process of suppression of 'non-human' factors by cultural ('purely human') factors. History is not simply a process of differentiation and increasing complexity, but of advancing stages of humanity. Human action is distinguished by the intervention of values in behaviour – the more those values dominate and the more explicitly and consistently they operate, the more 'human' that action is. History in Parsons' social evolutionary theory is the process of expansion and development of humanity.

This point will be expanded further at a later stage. At this stage it is necessary to expand a little more on the mechanism of this evolution – that of increasing generalised adaptive capacity.

The basis of the concept of generalised adaptive capacity is given in the paper 'Evolutionary Universals in Society'. This concept, Parsons claims, is an essential concept to *all* evolutionary theory, both organic and socio-cultural. In fact, it is seen as the site of the *continuity* between biological evolution and social development.

In his very early writings, Parsons was at pains to demarcate the humanities from any form of biological determinism. Insistence on the biological or physiological determination of human behaviour denies the essentially voluntary character of action. However, now Parsons is claiming a continuity of biological and sociological theory. This is not, of course, a programme for extending biological concepts into sociology – more the opposite, as will be shown – but at least the theory of social evolution takes a different approach to the question of their relationship.

There is an apparent 'watershed' between human and 'subhuman' development. Both phases of evolution can be analysed in terms of the development of enhanced and generalised adaptive capacity. This involves the degree to which the system in question can evolve mechanisms to increase its resources, through which to come to terms with its environment and to improve its functioning.

Central elements to this capacity are 'evolutionary universals', elements again seen to be common to both biological and social development. They are defined as 'any organisational development sufficiently important to further evolution that, rather than emerging only once, it is likely to be "hit upon" by various systems operating under different conditions' (*STMS*, p. 491).

For an example of this take vision. Vision, because of its function in mediating organised information from the organisms' environment, is the most 'generalised' mechanism of sensory input. It thus occupies a unique role as a potential mechanism of adaptation of the organism to its environment. This mechanism is therefore likely to be 'hit upon' by different systems in different conditions. As such, it is an 'evolutionary universal', generally beneficial to evolutionary advance. Other examples of this are the hand and brain – both mechanisms being seen as being vitally important not only physically but also with regard to producing and manipulating cultural codes. They thus have a double significance for evolution.

Adaptation according to this interpretation is not passive but an *active* process. Adaptation is not 'merely passive "adjustment" to environmental conditions, but rather the capacity of a living system to cope with its environment' (*STMS*, p. 493). This is seen to be perfectly consistent with Darwinian evolutionary theory.

What is distinctive about socio-cultural evolution, however, is its greater 'flexibility'. The peculiar nature of its particular adaptive processes mean that adaptation in social evolution involves a more generalised capacity to cope with the environment. The reason for this lies in the concept of culture. Owing to the conditions of unique organic endowment, man derives the capacity to create and transmit culture. Culture then becomes *more* important to man's development than his genetic structure. Parsons goes as far as to say (not, of course, alone), that the gene has been replaced by the 'symbol' as the primary feature of human adaptation.

Genetic adaptation, of course, continues to operate. But not only is it supplemented by the symbolic mechanism of adaptation, it is increasingly subordinated to it. As human evolution develops, the relative importance of symbolic, as opposed to genetic, adaptation will also increase.

Symbolic adaptation is far more than just passive compliance with the environment. It bears a unique relationship to the evolutionary process because, not only does it intervene (via norms) in the relation between man and his environmental conditions, but it actually can *constitute* that relation. In fact, it can operate so as to determine the ways in which adaptation 'should' be developed and extended. Symbolic adaptation can even come to terms with environmental conditions which do not yet exist, as in the case of 'uncertainty'.[25]

Parsons argues that the gene is being replaced by the symbol as the primary mechanism of human evolution. The central component of symbolic adaptation is the core of ultimate beliefs: 'Within the relevant range, cultural innovations, especially definitions of what man's life *ought* to be, thus replace Darwinian variations in genetic constitution' (*STMS*, pp. 494–5).

Consistent with Parsons' general theory of culture, the basis of the symbol is the realm of religious beliefs. Religion is, and always has been, the major determining feature of orientation, and as such takes the primary place in the genesis of socio-cultural evolution. It is not surprising, therefore, that religion is seen to be the primary evolutionary universal. In fact, religion occupies a unique situation in evolution for it is not 'hit upon' as most other evolutionary universals are but is ever-present in human systems.

For religion to operate effectively, however, it must do more than simply exist. It has to be implemented in action systems, and must therefore involve communication. The second primary evolutionary universal is thus, for Parsons, language. Two other universals complete the 'minimal' set – minimal in the sense that no known human society has existed without them. First, there is kinship, a form of social organisation which is necessary for adaptation because it both reproduces the species (biological adaptation) and also constitutes an important 'support' of cultural adaptation. Secondly, technology becomes an evolutionary universal because it enables the active control and manipulation of the physical environment. The four universals – religion, language, kinship and technology – constitute the essentials of specifically 'human' existence.

Further universals are necessary if the social system is to surpass this 'primitive' basis of existence. For example, a further two are necessary for the process of breaking out of the primitive stage – these are social stratification and systems of cultural legitimation. Another two allow a progression even further than breaking out – administration (via bureaucracy) and money/markets. Finally, two universals are held, more than any others, to be indices of 'modernism' – these are systems of generalised norms and the 'democratic association'.

By way of illustration, I will consider more fully the democratic association. This is defined as a form of social organisation in which there is elective leadership and a fully enfranchised membership. There are and have been various forms of democracy, but nevertheless four components are essential for democracy to attain the status of an evolutionary universal: first, leadership must be institutionalised in the form of elective office; secondly, there must be full franchise, or 'the institutional participation of members in collective decision-making through the election of officers and often through voting on specific policy issues' (*STMS*, p. 516); thirdly, it is necessary to have institutionalised procedural rules for voting etc.; and finally, the democratic association requires the institutionalisation of voluntary status by members and leaders.

The democratic association is considered to be an evolutionary universal because, Parsons argues, the more complex and expanded the society in question, the more important an effective political organisation becomes. This is crucial not merely in the technical sense of saving the adminstrative forms available, but also because of the importance of expanding 'consensus'. Parsons goes as far as to say:

> No institutional form basically different from the democratic association can, not specifically legitimise authority and power in the most general sense, but mediate consensus in its exercise by particular persons and groups, and in the formation of particular binding policy decisions. (*STMS*, p. 516)

That communism cannot achieve this level of consensus is shown, for Parsons, by the fact that communist states make an explicit attempt to 'educate' the people – proof that it does not 'trust' the people it has educated. Communism, therefore, can only legitimise itself – it cannot mediate consensus. As such, societies based on communist methods of political processes are limited in the degree to which they continue to evolve.

These are the basic principles of Parsons' social evolutionary position. Clearly, there are points of difference between this thesis and his structural–functionalist writings. As has been shown, in the latter he avoids reference to a 'primary source' of change and attempts to restrict analysis to the impact of forces. However, it has now been shown that there is an explicit primacy given to the cultural system, not just in *directing* social change but initiating it. We have also seen a somewhat different approach to the conceptualisation of the 'differentiation' of action systems. Earlier in Parsons' work these systems were presented as 'pragmatic' units of analysis; but now they 'appear' according to stages of the evolutionary process – differentiation itself, for example, between the cultural and social systems is a product of historical order.

All this should not, however, mislead us as to the fundamental connection between not only these two phases but between all phases of the Parsonian theory of action. In this respect the concept of culture is the focal point. There is also a theoretical link between the concept of social evolution and the notion of the functional prerequisites. Of course, Parsons was later to make this connection explicit – indeed he claims it to be the basis of his later position. Yet there is an inherent evolutionism even in its early form.

The concept of universal functions and the processes by which they are realised involves an inborn assumption of advance. For example, consider Parsons' analysis of structural differentiation.

> Differentiation ... entails a process by which new kinds of unit, as distinguished from more of the same kind, come to be established. Here it is possible to state a very important principle, namely, that the new kind of unit, e.g. collectivity or role, will subserve what, from the point of view of the adaptive exigencies of the system of which it is a part, is a *higher order* function than did the unit out of which it originates.[26]

So we have a conception of 'evolution' written into the conception of functional differation. Together with the theory of culture, this notion places social evolution in a crucial position in the theory of action. It is this principle which Parsons chooses to elaborate (with certain additional concepts) into the theory of socio-cultural evolution as detailed in his later writings.

We can now proceed to a more critical level and question three basic areas of the theory of social evolution. First, there is the issue of the apparent continuity between the respective theories of biological/organic and socio-cultural evolution as claimed by Parsons. Secondly, we can question Parsons' particular interpretation of the term 'evolution' and criticise his treatment of the evolutionary process. Finally, there is the overall problem of culture and its theoretical role in Parsonian theory, not just in the analysis of social change but in his theory of the social system in general.

I will argue that, despite Parsons' contention that his own theory of evolution respects the central elements of Darwinian theory, there is an inherent incompatibility between the two bodies of concepts. The hinge-point of this incompatibility is located at the level of the respective conceptions of 'development'. Parsons' theory of evolution will be shown to involve a central teleology in which transformations operate according to immanent laws of 'human progress' – an assumption incongruous with the concept of adaptation advanced in Darwin's theory of natural selection. Far from being continuous or even analogous with a theory of biological transformations, it is shown that the theory of social evolution reproduces a neo-religious conception of human development.

## 6.4 Parsons and Darwinism

It has been shown that a basic feature of Parsons' theory of socio-cultural evolution is the notion of *advance*. Evolution is not simply a process of transformation but one of progression to a 'higher' level of existence. Another feature of his theory is that, it is claimed, he borrows heavily from Darwinian theory.

Parsons is quite explicit in his claim to allegiances with Darwinism. He argues that the concept of an evolutionary universal should 'be formulated with reference to the concept of adaptation, which has been so fundamental to the theory of evolution since Darwin' (*STMS*, p. 493). The basis of the concept is the notion of enhancement of generalised adaptive capacity, and this is held to be a *general* concept of all evolutionary theory: 'I have tried to make by basic criterion congruent with that used in biological theory, calling more "advanced" the systems that display greater generalised adaptive capacity' (*Societies*, p. 110).

To be more accurate, there are two points at which the respective theories are seen to meet. First, Parsons (amongst others[27]) proposes the notion of an evolutionary process between the 'sub-human' and human stages. It is apparently possible to treat the developments within human society (the passage from primitive to modern-industrial society) in equivalent terms to the development between 'pre-human' and human society. There is a *continuity* between biological and social development, not simply a parallel process.

Secondly, as we have seen, a conceptual analogy is upheld with reference to the respective mechanisms of adaptation. Namely, the gene and the symbol are held to be equivalent mechanisms of adaptation, in the sense that both are the means by which the unit in question enhances its capacity to come to terms with the environment.

Given these proposals, a very basic question must be asked. Can it, in fact, be argued that there are theoretical continuities between these concepts of socio-cultural evolution and the theory of natural selection? More specifically, can this notion of a process of *progress* in evolution, the transformation to higher levels of existence, be made compatible with Darwinian evolutionary theory? Posed in these terms, it is not difficult to show that Parsons' claims are not successful.

Darwin's discussion on differential organisation of species

demonstrates this point. For Darwin, natural selection acts exclusively by the preservation and accumulations of variations beneficial to the organic and inorganic conditions to which each creature is exposed. This relation between variation and conditions of the environment is the mechanism of adaptation.

Darwin admits that this mechanism will operate in the main so as to increase and widen the level of 'organisation' of many species. In other words, the effect of natural selection will be primarily to increase the differentiation and specialisation of the organs. However, Darwin argues that in no sense can this 'tendency' be distorted into any conception of a *necessary* process toward evolutionary *advance*. Any increase in the level of organic organisation of a species is always relative to the environment and to the production of variations. Indeed, in certain cases, the metamorphosis of a given organic structure may contradict this tendency altogether, and Darwin cites examples of species in which the mature animal is in fact of lower organic complexity than its larva.

Thus, although a high level and increasingly higher level of organisation of species – i.e. developed differentiation and specialisation of the organs – is the predominant tendency in natural selection, it is *not* possible to deduce from this 'generalisation' a conception of any necessary advance toward complexity. Any such generalisations are *only* tendencies, they do not provide the theory of the mechanism of adaptation (as shall be argued is the case with Parsons). The limitations to this notion of generalisation are made clear in arguments such as the following:

> we can see, bearing in mind that all organic beings are striving to increase at a higher ratio and to seize on every unoccupied or less well-occupied place in the economy of nature, that it is quite possible for natural selection gradually to fit a being to a situation in which several organs would be superfluous or useless: in such cases there would be retrogression in the scale of organisation. (*Origin of Species*, p. 118)

This statement illustrates a crucial feature of the Darwinian theory of natural selection. This process refers to the mechanism of combination between the effects of inheritance and the ecological sources of a determinate 'selection pressure'. The theory is not a philosophy of a general historical process of advance of species. Higher levels of organisation (itself a misleading term, as Darwin pointed out[28]) are referred to as illustrations of the theory of natural selection, *but they are not the theoretical basis of that theory*.

Any 'complexity' is to be analysed solely in terms of the *specific* combination of variant forms with environmental conditions of life of the organism. Complexity, as such, is a function of selection pressures relative to a range of variants. Evolution is *not* the process of advancement from simple to complex forms. In fact, the interpretation of evolutionary theory as the outline of the passage from simple (primitive) to complex (advanced) forms is closer to the Lamarckian theory of development, and this was openly opposed by Darwin.

It was Lamarck's error, argued Darwin, to propose the notion of an innate and inevitable tendency toward perfection in all organic beings. Lamarck was thus presented with the problem of 'accounting' for the existence, and continued existence, of more simple organic forms, a problem which he could only overcome through the speculative notion of the continual spontaneous production of new and simple forms in every generation. In opposition to such a conception of evolution and to the problems it generates, Darwin argued:

> On our theory, the continued existence of lowly organisms offers no difficulty; for natural selection, or the survival of the fittest, *does not necessarily include progressive development* – it only takes advantage of such variations as arise and are beneficial to each creature under its complex relations of life. (*Origin of Species*, p. 118, my emphasis).

The theory of natural selection is an analysis of the mechanism by which species are transformed. It is not an 'historical generalisation', nor a simple description of historical tendencies. The mechanism which is the object of the theory is the relation between random variations in characteristics (thought in terms of the laws of inheritance[29]) and the selection pressures of the ecological conditions of life of the organism.

Neither in Darwinian theory nor in the more recent genetic theory of populations is there a place for a concept such as 'generalised adaptive capacity' as formulated by Parsons. The latter is explicitly presented as a definite process of progress and complexity, inevitable and irrepressible tendencies in the evolutionary process. Indeed, and this one point in itself demonstrates the total incompatibility of the two discourses, the concept of *generalised* adaptive *capacity* refers to the process of increasing control and *separation* between the environmental conditions of life and the structure of the organism! Such a thesis is totally foreign to the theory of natural selection – it proposes a process of developing freedom from environmental effectivities, eventually denying the theory of the mechanism of transformation which is the core of the theory.

In fact, Parsons' concept of generalised adaptive capacity, when advanced as a 'general' concept of evolutionary theory, is little more than a play on words. Parsons justifies the pertinence of the concept of adaptation to the form of theoretical project which he proposes (one which is to overcome the consequences of 'positivist' theories [heredity/environment]), through the claim that adaptation refers to more than a 'passive' adjustment to environmental conditions. The structure in question, rather than being a simple effect of external conditions, is subject to adaptation – this involves a process far more active than a cause–effect relation, 'but rather the capacity of a living system to cope with its environment' (*STMS*, p. 493).

It is true to say that Darwin did not conceive of adaptation as a mere effect of the environment, i.e. it is not a process of ecological determination. Adaptation is the operation of random variations *in relation to* the environment, and it is the mechanism which functions in this relation. However, Parsons' argument is somewhat different. He uses this process to refer to the *separation* of the structure from its environmental conditions. The 'non-passive' nature of adaptation in Parsons' sense is used to refer to its capacity to *master* the environment. He slides from the conception that adaptation involves the organism 'coping' with its environment to the thesis that 'This capacity includes an *active* concern with mastery, or the ability to *change* the environment to meet the needs of the system' (*STMS*, p. 493, my emphasis).

By means of an (inadvertent) play on words Parsons achieves his objective – to insert the theory of *action* into the concept of adaptation. The latter becomes an active mastery of the environment, effectively cancelling any determination by the environment in the transformation of populations.

Yet all this is quite incompatible with the theory of natural selection. Darwin did not propose any conception of a necessary tendency toward a 'generalised capacity'. Any capacity (in the biological sense) referred to in Darwinian theory is posed according to particular cases in the operation of a general law. The notion of an inevitable tendency of 'progress' presupposes a pre-determined order of appearance of variant forms (i.e. a teleology) – clearly conflicting with the notion of random variation which is so central to the theory of natural selection. In fact, Parsons goes as far as to claim an advance over Darwinian theory in overcoming one of its more 'indecisive' areas – the analysis of the production of variations. This, he argues, need not be left to random variation, for it is possible to explain from the beginning the *genesis* of variations.[30]

Parsons' claims regarding the continuity between the theory of socio-cultural evolution and the theory of natural selection hold little water. His concept of generalised adaptive capacity and the processes which enhance it are clearly distinct from Darwin's concept of adaptation. The gene–symbol analogy is little more than word-play, allowing the insertion of the concept of *action* into the analyses of adaptation.

## 6.5  Social Evolution as Teleology

These points concerning the incompatibility of Parsons' theory of evolution and the theory of natural selection have implied something which I now intend to demonstrate more definitively. Namely, that the concepts of the evolutionary universals, generalised adaptive capacity, and the whole mode of analysis of social development, constitute an essentially *teleological* theory of history.[31]

The basis for Parsons' concept of evolution is summarised by the statement that 'To be an evolutionist, one must define a general trend in evolution' (*Societies*, p. 110). This is the classical starting-point of all teleological conceptions of history: the general trend is the means of conceptualising the mechanisms and processes which apparently constitute it. Evolution is a process of realisation of a pre-given objective, the different stages being merely degrees of realisation. Parsons' conception of socio-cultural evolutionary stages from primitive to modern societies is consistent with precisely such a notion.

The evolutionary process is toward the enhancement of adaptive capacity. Generalised adaptive capacity refers to an evolutionary constitution in which the structure of the human level becomes separated from its environmental conditions of existence. This is the process of the differentiation of systems of action and their relationship to the environment. Therefore, in this conception and its derivatives we have the grounds for a definite teleology.

Adaptation can be 'generalised', i.e. it can operate so as to encompass more and more conditional problems, and perhaps more significantly, non-existent environments (e.g. 'uncertainty'). Generalised adaptive capacity is thus defined according to its *potential* preceding its actual involvement in particular conditions.

The problem, therefore, is this: how do we *know* what this capacity has the potential to cope with? If the adaptive relation is not defined in Darwinian terms as the *specific* relation of the organism to its particular ecological conditions of life, but rather in terms of its (future) potential, how can we know that this capacity exists? Parsons' answer is simple: we start from an already realised level of development and read backwards.

The levels of adaptive capacity are known by means of a concept of the present (final?) phase of development of the evolutionary process. We are able to judge whether this capacity is greater or smaller by measuring its correspondence/non-correspondence with the present level of evolutionary development. Hence, we are given the notion of the stages of socio-cultural evolution – modern, intermediate and primitive. Thus, the modern phase is characterised by two levels of differentiation: between its social and cultural systems, and within the social system between the subsystems of polity, economy, community and pattern-maintenance. This is used to define less developed phases. What makes a society 'primitive' is the degree of advancement in it of pre-given outcome, the fully differentiated systems and subsystems.

The historical past is defined according to its stage of realisation of the present. The source of change (tendencies toward functional differentiation on evolutionary lines) is known through its effect (fully differentiated systems). The mechanisms of the past are read in terms of the future effectivity. They have a *Purpose*.

Parsons, of course, claims that empirically his theory implies no *necessity* of evolution – some societies are seen to take retrogressive steps (e.g. the Soviet Union). However, his *theory* writes necessity into the structure of processes of change. The concepts for the analysis of change (dominated by the concept of the advanced social system), *theoretically* impute a notion of necessity, in the sense that history is periodised according to the degree of realisation in it of the fully advanced form. A 'lower' level of socio-cultural development is known as such only in its comparison with the concept of the highly-evolved system.

The teleology of Parsons' conceptualisation of social evolution is particularly apparent in his concept of the evolutionary universals. These are conceived, as we have seen, as those processes which increase the long-run adaptive capacity of the system. In other words, they are conceived in terms of their future effect. The origins and mechanisms of these universals are reduced to their relation to their future outcomes.

Again, this is clear if we look at Parsons' account of vision as a universal. He argues that vision is of unique potential significance for the adaptation of the organism to the environment, and as such is likely to be 'hit upon' independently in disparate organisms. The process is derived from a concept of its (future) function. This is a rather different method of conceptualising such organisms from that advanced by Darwin. This method defines a process from a conception of its process, and builds a theory out of a tendency or trend. Darwin argued that this approach would make it impossible to explain the 'exceptional' cases where the tendency is, in fact, reversed – as in the case of the loss of vision in bats. It does not provide a knowledge of the mechanisms in question and then relate them to an empirical situation, but instead derives the mechanism *from* the tendency. Exceptions to the rule become inexplicable – a criticism that Darwin pointed out in Lamarck's conception (see p. 220).

The only way Parsons attempts to resolve this problem (i.e. the loss of vision in certain species) is to claim quite simply that such species 'have not subsequently given rise to important evolutionary developments'. Yet this is merely to beg the question, resorting simply back to the tendency of which the conception makes the explanation impossible. In other words, these exceptions are seen to have little significance because they do not correspond with the general tendency! It is a circular argument which merely avoids the problem of explaining the mechanisms in question.

For Darwin, on the other hand, 'problems' such as the loss of vision in bats or the loss of flight in certain bird species are as equally explicable according to the theory of natural selection as are the common characteristics.[32] The 'tendency' of evolution is not used as the basis of the theory – this exists in the theory of adaptation – and as such, deviations from that tendency are not inexplicable.

The evolutionary universals are defined according to a teleological conception of their future function. The mechanisms involved are reduced to their future effect. Thus, social stratification is classified as a universal because of its role in 'breaking-out' of the primitive level of social relations. It is situated in terms of its future significance for adaptation. As such, it becomes an inevitable process, even if it may at some stages be undeveloped.

Despite Parsons' claims that there is no place in his theory of socio-cultural evolution for a conception of inevitable and necessary outcome, it can be seen in cases such as this that necessity is written into the concept. Processes and mechanisms are theorised according to their future adaptive significance, and their *concept* is governed by their relation to the outcome. This applies even in the straightforward conception of simple–complex societies – 'simplicity' is always simple relative to that which is complex. In Parsons' case, the teleology is even more inescapable. Both the concepts of generalised adaptive capacity and that of the evolutionary universals are theorised in terms of their teleological significance.

Having said this, it must be said that the status of such 'Darwinian' concepts in Parsons' theory of evolution should not be overestimated. That Parsons claims some formal analogy or even continuity with the concepts of Darwinian evolutionary theory is, of course, quite significant, but it should not be thought of as *the* most important issue. Parsons' theory of socio-cultural evolution is subordinate to his theory of *action*. The concept of adaptation, for example, although apparently 'borrowed' from biology is essentially consistent with Parsons' traditional action concepts. What is more important than the validity of the gene–symbol analogy is the nature of the role of the symbol itself. It is to these more general issues which I shall now turn.

## 6.6 Religion, Culture and Social Evolution

The theoretical distinction that Parsons claims between biological and social evolution lies in the apparent capacity of man to create and transmit culture. The gene has been replaced by the symbol as the major sphere of man's adaptation to his enviornment.

> A set of 'normative expectations' pertaining to man's relation to his environment delineates the ways in which adaptation should be developed and extended. Within the relevant range, cultural innovations, especially definitions of what man's life *ought* to be, thus replace Darwinian variation in genetic constitution. (*STMS*, pp. 494–5)

The evolutionary process 'may be formulated in terms of the emergence and handling of evaluative problems' (*TS*, p. 986). The implication is clear: religion is the major sphere of concern for the theory of social (and cultural) evolution. The symbol is above all based in the realm of religious beliefs. Religion is the primary evolutionary universal. Parsons goes as far as to say that the existence of religion *defines* 'human-ness'.[33] Social and cultural evolution is itself subordinate to 'religious evolution' (a thesis carried even further by Bellah). For example, Parsons argues that:

> ... cultural development is essential for the evolutionary advance of social systems. For example, religious developments underlie all major processes of value generalisation. ... Sufficient levels of value generalisation ... are prerequisites to major steps of inclusion in the structure of a societal community. (*SMS*, p. 281)

Religion is of unique significance to culture, culture is of central significance to the social system, and so on down the line. The theory of social evolution is not just an observation of a general tendency, but an attempt to pin-point the *vehicle* of evolution, the prime mover of social and cultural change and religious belief systems.

It is somewhat paradoxical that, given the continued centrality of religion to Parsons' theory of action, we do not find particularly elaborate accounts of the mechanisms and processes involved in the genesis of religious beliefs, values etc. We are forced to decipher features of this analysis from his more general discussions on culture.

Parsons claims that the concept of culture has undergone certain developments and sophistications since its appearance in *The Structure of Social Action*. In this, culture was conceived 'crudely' as a pattern of 'eternal elements'

> its feature was thus a 'structural' one, and one only properly the domain of the formal disciplines such as logic, mathematics, structural linguistics, the systematics of stylistic form, the purely logical structure of a theological system, and the formal analysis of legal norms. (*TS*, p. 964)

Such a conception involved definite limitations to the concept of culture as an integral feature of the theory of action. In particular, Parsons argues, it ignores a crucial aspect of culture, namely that it is a *system*. It is a system in the same sense of other systems of action, in that it is organised around the exigencies of its functioning.

If culture is conceived of as a system, then it should be possible to theorise the processes by which 'complexes of meaning' are created and maintained, and which eventually function to facilitate the other systems. This should remove much of the mystery that has always surrounded Parsons' conception of culture, a mystery that has arisen mainly owing to his opposition to cultural relativism. His earlier formulations involved a definition of culture as 'non-interactional', i.e. not interacting with the empirical systems (social and personality). Culture existed 'above' the other systems and could not be treated in the same way as them.

The question, therefore, is: does this more elaborate analysis of culture which is proposed in the later works overcome the more obvious theoretical problems of the earlier accounts of culture? In particular, is there now an analysis of the *creation* of cultural patterns which, before, the definition of 'eternal elements' made impossible? I shall argue that the 'functional' analysis of culture tells us little more than the earlier definition, and that there is still a very signficant realm of culture which remains unexplained.

Parsons' major extensive discussion of culture is his Introduction to the section 'Culture and the Social System' in his *Theories of Society*. In this, the major distinctive feature of the analysis of culture is the formal subjection of the cultural system to theorisation by means of the four-function paradigm. The problem of conceptualisation of the processes of creation and/or maintenance of culture patterns referred to above, is posed in terms of the 'dimensions of cultural configuration', i.e. the analysis of cultural variation.

Two dimensions of the cultural system are seen to be externally oriented (in that they refer to the categories of meaning of the objects), and two dimensions concern patterns of orientation to and disposition to objects. The first two dimensions are classified under the categories of, on the one hand, adaptive meaning relationships to objects, i.e. the cognitive reference of objects (science etc.), and, on the other hand, of goal-attainment (the meaning which objects have as objects of goal-attainment, over and above the cognitive relationship – in this context expressive symbols are particularly pertinent).

The other two dimensions of the cultural system concern the cultural specifications of relations of orientation/disposition *to* such meaningful objects. These refer, on the one hand, to the integrative feature of the system (i.e. sets of evaluative problems, e.g. moral principles), and on the other hand to the pattern-maintenance dimension (which concerns the fundamental grounding of the orientation of meaning).

These four dimensions apparently constitute the conditions for the analysis of processes of creation and maintenance of patterns of cultural variation. At this stage, the analysis appears basically consistent with the theorisation of the 'empirical' systems of action. However, a crucial distinction exists between the two levels of functional analysis. The functional analysis of the empirical systems is based on the notion of differentiation within the system, resulting in a classification of the simplicity and complexity of differentiation. The functional analysis of the cultural system, however, involves an additional concept: a *hierarchy of effectivity* within the system in terms of which certain dimensions within it take primacy over others. The four dimensions of the cultural system exist in a relationship of determinacy; they constitute an order of effectivity.

The highest determining level of the four dimensions is the pattern-maintenance dimension, which is followed in order of importance by the integrative, goal-attainment and adaptive dimensions. It is the pattern-maintenance dimension which is of most significance here.

This dimension 'concerns the most general world-views or definitions of the human condition that underlie orientations to more particular problems' (*TS*, p. 970). If this constitutes the fundamental grounding of meaning, one element within it is of unique importance: ultimate reality.

> The highest level of the problems of meaning is that of the conceptions of ultimate reality, in the religio-philosophical sense. This concerns the major premises in which the non-empirical components of a culture's total belief system is rooted. (*TS*, p. 970)

The problems with the concept of ultimate reality have already been reviewed in the chapter on Action. The point to be made here is that the elaboration of the analysis of culture on the lines of the four-function paradigm does not alleviate the problem. It is still the case that ultimate reality (the highest level of determinacy of culture and of the whole action complex) is itself *beyond the realm of scientific investigation*.

In fact, Parsons places limits to knowledge throughout his formulation of the cultural system. For example, take the case of cognitive knowledge, which holds the lowest place in the hierarchy of effectivity within the cultural system. Not only is this level least effective in relation to the other levels of culture, but within that dimension there is an additional hierarchy. 'Data' constitute the lowest-order level of meaning of external objects, 'problems' the next, and the structure of the theory itself is one level higher. Yet above all that, we have a higher level of meaning, the frame of reference.[34] This level is itself beyond scientific proof:

> theory itself is relative to the level of the frame of reference that is not empirically provable, but is necessary in order to

give meaning to problems and to theory itself. This hierarchical order is one of the levels of generality of conceptual components. It is also a hierarchy of control, in that the meaning of problems controls interest in the meaning of facts. (*TS*, p. 965)

The situation of cognitive knowledge at the bottom of the meaning-hierarchy, and the additional notion of a realm of knowledge itself beyond investigation (the frame of reference), is extremely significant. It means that, while the ultimate reality component can impose meaning on cognitive systems and can eventually govern (via the other dimensions) the developments within science, the latter cannot in turn impose its scientific definitions on ultimate reality. Ultimate reality cannot be subjected to scientific investigation, it cannot have 'meanings' given to it by rational cognitive systems. It is both beyond scientific investigation and constitutive of the whole cultural complex. Ultimate reality in the 'religio-philosophical' sense:

> ... must be characterised *as a limit of the intelligible*. Logically, it involves the premises on which lower-order commitments of meaning must rest; but the relevance of any such ultimate grounding need not be confined to the cognitive. The highest level signifies the limiting point at which cognition, cathexis, and evaluation merge, because they are all somehow models of differentiation from a common matrix. (*TS*, p. 971)

For all its subjection to functional analysis, the cultural system is still unique. Its most fundamental levels are beyond rational and scientific investigation. As a system, it is not determined by environmental exigencies – it does not have an interactional relationship as do the other systems. It constitutes but is not constituted by any specifiable mechanism. To refer to the effectivity of culture as a process of differentiation hardly pin-points the process by which culture relates to the other system: it would be more accurate to refer to it as a form of *emanationism*. Parsons offers no explanation of the processes by which ultimate reality is itself constituted. He precludes this by the insistence that ultimate reality is unique – it is not determined by the empirical world (this would involve a relativist conception of culture) and cannot be known through the concepts of a science.

By means of an elaborate and systematic attempt to theorise human action, Parsons eventually produces a conception of evolution which is almost theological. There is a unity – ultimate reality – from which the primary determining forces of human activity originates, but which is itself above that activity. The systematisation of the analysis of culture has not answered the problem which existed in *The Structure of Social Action*. The objective to advance and defend a conception of action which avoids non-voluntaristic conceptions does so only to the extent that it really does situate the realm of religious beliefs in a place over and above the empirical world.

Parsons' conception of the evolutionary process is openly founded upon the conception of the effectivity of the cultural system, and, in particular, its role as mediator of the major environment of the action complex: ultimate reality. The concept of the cybernetic hierarchy of effectivity ensures that this process be theorised above all in terms of developments within the sphere of culture and religion. It invokes the domination of the theory of social change by a conception of religious evolution.

In the cybernetic hierarchy, the differentiation of action into systems is a function of the evolutionary process. This process, in turn, is a function of the formulation and handling of evaluative problems. Religion is the nucleus of social and cultural evolution. We now have a problem. Given that social change originates above all in the realm of religious beliefs (thus presupposing that those beliefs themselves must be subject to change or development), how is it possible to account for these transformations? As we have seen, Parsons precludes the analysis of the genesis of religious beliefs in his definition of ultimate reality. Yet, clearly, some further explanation is needed to account for the appearance of variant forms of religious belief systems.

Two alternatives seem possible. First, the appearance of variant forms of ultimate reality (and through that the appearance of different types of culture) is to be seen as a random process. In this case, different religions will appear at random and for a variety of contingent empirical reasons. Different religions will have different degrees of adaptive suitability, and these will tend to persist while others disappear. The second alternative would be to argue that the appearance of new religious systems is itself subject to an even more fundamental process – one which controls the forms of belief that appear and which imposes a form of order on their appearance.

It must now be clear that the first alternative would be incompatible with Parsons' theory of action. The realm of ultimate reality is defined as one beyond empirical determination (to argue otherwise would be to invoke cultural relativism). More importantly, a random appearance of religious beliefs would not allow *evolution*. If social systems do not appear at random, but are subject to a tendency toward progress, it is because cultural systems themselves take on an evolutionary order. For Parsons, the variant forms of 'ultimate reality' must of necessity be theorised according to a definite conception of order and evolutionary advancement. New forms of culture are not simply different but *superior*:

> a higher-level cultural system . . . would have developed a pattern-system capable of comprising a more extensive range of particularised meanings than a lower-order one, and a more differentiated system of meanings – i.e. a range both 'wider' and involving what, qualitatively speaking, are more different kinds of particularised meanings. (*TS*, p. 981)

Parsons' frequent references to Weber's concept of the 'process of rationalisation'[35] make it clear that he adopts some notion of immanent tendencies toward advanced forms of culture. He similarly adopts the thesis that the increasingly rational nature of culture in all its forms (expressive symbolism, scientific knowledge, technology, etc.) is due above all to developments within the value-system. It follows, therefore, that ultimate reality does not simply appear but is generated in a serial order. If societies can be classified on an evolutionary scale it is because, in the final analysis, forms of ultimate reality reflect a more fundamental process of evolutionary progress.

Parsons is by no means completely explicit on this issue, but it would seem that this more fundamental process involves a development of the *human essence*. Socio-cultural evolution is more than a process of increasing efficiency in social relations – it is a developmental process involving transformations of a human project. It is the passage from an 'animal' existence ('proto-cultural' phase) to the highest level of human existence – the form of socio-cultural organisation represented in Western societies:

> We agree entirely with Weber ... in his judgement that the development of what he called Western society in the modern era is of 'universal' significance in human history and in the corollary of that judgement: that the development has not been random but definitely directional. (*SMS*, p. 139)

The teleological, and ultimately speculative, character of this thesis and the arguments which have flowed from it must now be clear. The theory of socio-cultural evolution, and also in less explicit form the earlier texts, is based upon a philosophical anthropology, a conception of a tendential process in human development.

Social change relies above all on cultural change. Cultural change depends above all on transformations of the system of religious beliefs, which are the primary organising feature of culture. Religion, in turn, is the symbolic reflection of stages in the realisation of a human project. The system is thus complete, but it is a system whose foundation is ultimately speculative.

# Conclusion

It is not possible to summarise here the points made above or to attempt some 'explanation' as to where the conceptual problems argued for above originated from. I have maintained that there is no 'core problem' from which Parsons' difficulties stem, but that there is a series of points at which theoretical shortcomings can be designated. The conclusion of this work is, therefore, that Parsonian theory, whether epistemological or sociological, is not a coherent body of concepts on which to base a social theory.

Having said that, I do not intend this work as some form of 'final word' on the works of Talcott Parsons. While I have aimed my criticisms primarily at the most abstract level of his work, it must still be the case that whole areas, primarily 'empirical' or at least more concrete, have not been treated fully. For example, while I have argued that the conceptual basis of the 'evolutionary universals' is ultimately teleological and philosophical, there still remains the problem as to why Parsons chooses certain areas of human existence (e.g. electoral democracy, legal systems etc.) and not others as universals as such. Are the arguments he provides as justification for their inclusion, logically coherent even accepting the general concepts? Questions such as this arise at frequent points in Parsons' analyses and warrant further investigation.

Despite this, I must reiterate that I have not randomly chosen certain regions of his theory at the expense of others, but have attempted to direct analysis and criticism to the conceptual *conditions* of his various theses. It is not possible to discuss effectively certain arguments (say, about the value-system of contemporary United States) without at some stage coming to terms with the general question of values and their intervention in social systems. These are precisely the sorts of issues that this book has tackled.

One final statement: if it has been possible to arrive at, and demonstrate, the unfavourable conclusions about Parsons' work

234

which are presented above, it has a great deal to do with the rigour and scope of Parsons' own theory. Parsons can indeed be shown to have produced a number of major theoretical problems, but this is due, to a great extent, to the nature of his attempt. It is a merit of his work that he has sought to answer questions where others have not even seen the possibility of a question.

# Notes

NOTES TO CHAPTER ONE: MODES OF CRITIQUE

1. Alvin W. Gouldner, *The Coming Crisis of Western Sociology*.
2. Gouldner, in particular, is guilty of major misrepresentations of Parsonian theory. Some of these distortions have been pointed out by J. K. Rhoades in his 'On Gouldner's *Coming Crisis*' in *Varieties of Political Expression in Sociology* (ASR publication).
3. The term 'grid-reading' follows that used by Althusser to refer to a certain reading of Marx, see 'From Capital to Marx's Philosophy' in Althusser and Balibar, *Reading Capital*.
4. The relation between science and philosophy has been of particular concern to the work of Althusser, and has been subject to several alterations in position. Althusser has advanced explicit attempts to provide a means of a reading of theoretical discourse which do not reproduce the problematic tendencies of classical philosophy and its derivates. The most important one is perhaps the notion of Theory (with a capital 'T') as the theory of the mechanism of production of the knowledge effect. The advantages and shortcomings of the Althusserian position are discussed below.
5. For an extended discussion of the variant forms of epistemology and the consequences of them for the theorisation of knowledge, see Barry Hindess, 'Transcendentalism and History: the Problem of the History of Philosophy and the Sciences in the Later Philosophy of Husserl', *Economy and Society*, 2 (Aug 1973) pp. 309–42.
6. See A. V. Cicourel, *The Social Organisation of Juvenile Justice*, and J. Douglas, *The Social Meanings of Suicide*. See also the critique of these positions in relation to the production of social statistics, in Barry Hindess, *The Use of Official Statistics in Sociology*.
7. Other famous examples are D. Foss, 'The World View of Talcott Parsons' in M. R. Stein and A. Vidich (eds), *Sociology on Trial*; R. Dahrendorf, 'Out of Utopia', *American Journal of Sociology*, 64[2] (1958) pp. 115–27. While there would appear to be no reason why criticisms according to ideological characteristics of a theoretical position cannot be effectively advanced, it would seem that these and other examples are both theoretically and politically backward.
8. D. Lockwood, 'Some Remarks on "The Social System"', *British Journal of Sociology*, 7[2] (1956), and Dahrendorf, op. cit.; other essentially similar critiques include L. Coser, *The Functions of Conflict*; A. G. Frank, *The Sociology of Development and Underdevelopment*; A. W. Gouldner, 'Reciprocity and Autonomy in Functional Theory' in L. Gross (ed.), *Symposium on*

*Sociological Theory: Inquiries & Paradigms*; W. Hield, 'The Study of Change in Social Sciences', *British Journal of Sociology* (Mar 1964); I. L. Horowitz, 'Consensus, Conflict and Cooperation' in N. J. Demerath and R. A. Peterson (eds), *System Change and Conflict*; C. Morse, 'The Functional Prerequisites' in M. Black (ed.), *The Sociological Theories of Talcott Parsons*; see also the papers by Lopreato and Martel in H. Turk and R. L. Simpson (eds), *Institutions and Social Exchange*. Apart from 'conflict' theory it is not difficult to find similar realisms in discussions of Parsons' pattern-variable schema.

9. Note that the notion of 'Utopia' has a more extensive usage for Dahrendorf than the definition of the social, for as will be pointed out later, it also refers to an epistemological question.

10. Gouldner, *The Coming Crisis*, p. 224. A very similar humanist opposition is presented by D. Wrong, 'The Oversocialised Conception of Man in Modern Sociology'; see also D. Foss, op. cit.

11. Lockwood, op. cit., p. 282.

12. This notion is most rigorously outlined in J. H. Turner's analysis of Parsons, *The Structure of Sociological Theory*: 'Assertions that the maturing system of concepts adequately mirrors features of actual social systems represent a fundamental challenge to the strategy and substance of Parsons' form of functional theorising' (p. 46).

13. See R. Carnap, 'The Methodological Character of Theoretical Concepts' in *Minnesota Studies in the Philosophy of Science*, I, pp. 38–76. On this subject, it might be pointed out that any form of conventionalist theory of knowledge would strictly preclude the operation of an effective realist mode. In conventionalist philosophies we find the denial of the possiblity of demarcating between meaningful and meaningless statements, any statements of knowledge being merely ways of 'saving the phenomena' (see P. Duhem, *To Save the Phenomena*). Within such a conception, the realist opposition would be impossible, in so far as no one conception of the world could be deemed any more realistic or valid than another. The paradox is that most exponents of the realist critique propose a theory of knowledge which is generally some form of vulgarisation of conventionalist philosophy.

14. *A System of Logic*, pp. 371–2.

15. These two are, of course, often combined in exposition. For example, Merton presents his thesis of 'theories of the middle range' in conjunction with the proposal for the specification of functions as 'observed consequences'; that is, a combination of his epistemology with the substantive concept of social functions (see R. Merton, *Social Theory and Social Structure*). In this case, the exact problem becomes confused.

16. C. W. Mills, *The Sociological Imagination*, and Dahrendorf, op. cit. A very similar thesis is maintained by Bottomore in *Sociology as Social Criticism*.

17. This is hardly surprising as Mills' polemic against Parsons serves to reinforce the anti-theoretical tendencies of sociology, and further pardons the sociological audience of the difficult task of actually reading Parsons!

18. Merton, op. cit. References here are to the edition published in *On Theoretical Sociology*. For a very brief and concise statement of Merton's position, see also his 'Discussion' in reply to Parsons' paper 'The Position of

Sociological Theory', *American Sociological Review*, 13 (1948) pp. 156–68. See also Gouldner, op. cit.

19. See 'Manifest and Latent Functions' in *Social Theory and Social Structure*.
20. For example, R. Nisbet, 'The Problem of Social Change' in R. Nisbet (ed.), *Social Change*, and A. D. Smith, *The Concept of Social Change: a Critique of the Functionalist Theory of Change*.
21. G. Homans, 'Bringing Men Back In' in Turk and Simpson (eds), op. cit., and Turner, op. cit. Similar positions can be found in the various assessments of the 'functionalist method', for example, Harry C. Bredemeier, 'The Methodology of Functionalism', *American Sociological Review*, 20 (Apr 1955).
22. The most famous exponent of this particular methodology is, of course, K. Popper. See *The Logic of Scientific Discovery*, and in particular the concept of 'falsifiability' in chapter 4.
23. Many sociological theses depend in similar fashion on this conception. This is particularly clear in 'systems theory', see, for example, W. Buckley, *Sociology and Modern Systems Theory*.
24. Discussions on the variant forms of epistemology may be found in Althusser, op. cit., and Hindess, *Official Statistics* op. cit.
25. The work of Alexandre Koyré is perhaps the most distinctive in this respect. A concise account of his position is given in his 'The Origins of Modern Science' in *Diogenes*, no. 16 (Winter 1956) pp. 1–22.
26. See B. Hindess, 'Transcendentalism and History', op. cit.
27. For instance, the position of the British empiricists, Hume and Berkeley, and taken to its extreme in Ernst Mach's *The Analysis of Sensations*.
28. This mode of critique is not, however, exclusive to *SSA*. Elements of it are repeated in Parsons' later essays on Durkheim, Weber and Marx. See Part I of Parsons' *Sociological Theory and Modern Society*.
29. The grid-reading is a part of a more inclusive conception of discourse which has been labelled the 'History of Ideas'. For a discussion on this issue, see K. Williams, 'Unproblematic Archaeology', *Economy and Society*, 3 (1974).
30. A major consequence of an evolutionist conception of knowledge is that forms of 'knowledge' such as witchcraft and theology must be seen as subject to the same tendency to advance.
31. A term used by Althusser to describe the teleological character of many readings of the relation between the 'Young' and 'Mature' Marx. See *For Marx*, p. 54.
32. Enno Schwanenberg, 'The Two Problems of Order in Parsons' Theory: an Analysis from Within', *Social Forces*, 49 (1971) pp. 569–80.
33. Alan Dawe, 'The Two Sociologies', *British Journal of Sociology*, 21 (1970) pp. 207–18 (reference here to the edition published in *Sociological Perspectives*, ed. Thompson and Tunstall; this quote from p. 543).
34. Consider R. Aron's treatise on sociology in *Main Currents in Sociological Thought*. Another major exponent of the role of the 'metaphysics' of the author in the constitution of theory is E. Gellner in *Concepts and Society*.
35. Note that this reference to the role of the 'problem of order' is used by Parsons himself in his attempts to describe his theoretical development; see 'Unity and Diversity in the Modern Intellectual Disciplines: the Role of

the Social Sciences', *Daedalus*, 94[1] (Winter 1965) pp. 39–65. Similar interpretations are to be found in the papers by Devereux and Williams in Black, op. cit.

36. See K. Menzies, *Talcott Parsons and the Social Imagery of Man*.

37. It is necessary at this point to distinguish between Menzies' thesis and that argued by Hindess and Savage ('Talcott Parsons and the Three Systems of Action' in *Parsons Reconsidered*, ed. H. Martins – see also following chapters of this book). For Menzies, the Parsonian schema can be reduced to two simple totalities characterised by two *world-views*; the complexity of Parsons' discourse as a system of *concepts* is effectively denegated. Consequently, it is not surprising that Menzies makes a number of significant distortions of Parsonian theory – for example, his equation of Parsons' functional mode of analysis with a Mertonian conception of function as 'observed consequences' (hence the notion of a 'positivist' programme). On this point see later chapters.

38. 'The Changing Foundations of the Parsonian Action Schema'; *American Sociological Review*, 28 (1963), and 'The Impossible Theory of Action', *Berkeley Journal of Sociology*.

39. Thus Turner and Beeghley, in 'Current Folklore in the Criticism of Parsonian Action Theory', *Sociological Inquiry*, 43 (1974), argue that Scott's interpretation of *SSA* as 'idealist' misrepresents Parsons' position – while this point appears quite correct, I will attempt to show below that Scott's reading is not simply an effect of oversights but related to his conception of discourse in general.

40. The problem of identifying discourse by means of a more or less arbitrary selection of statements in a text is most apparent in the case of the sciences. Consider, for example, the explicitly theological statements supplied by Newton of which Koyré says: 'Newton's insistence on God's "presence" in the world and on the analogy between his action upon it and the way in which we move our own bodies is rather amazing. It leads him to certain assertions that one does not expect to find from his pen', *Newtonian Studies*, p. 93. Problems of equal severity are thus inherent in the reduction of discourse to methodological statements.

41. The immediate tendency of such readings is generally to assume (not surprisingly) no significant metamorphoses in the development of Parsons' work; see Williams and Devereux in M. Black, op. cit. It is clear that such conceptions of discourse induce a number of difficulties – it implies, in particular, that the existence of a 'problem' involves only one 'solution'.

42. 'There remains a huge gap between his intentions and his achievement', *Ideology and Social Knowledge*, p. 150.

43. For example, of the type claimed by Hindess and Savage, op. cit.

44. See Buckley, op. cit., and L. von Bertalanffy, *General Systems Theory*. An analogous example is the notion of a 'structuralist method' – see C. Lévi-Strauss, *Structural Anthropology*; similar problems apply to such a thesis.

45. This discussion on the role of presuppositions is a brief form of that by Barry Hindess in *Philosophy and Methodology in the Social Sciences*, chapter 7.

46. For example, that an anthropology of 'man' is incompatible with Marx's

notion of the 'Departments of Production'; see 'Marx's Critique' in Althusser and Balibar, *Reading Capital*.

47. One example is the attempt to supplement the concepts of the sciences with philosophically advised concepts, such as that of 'structural causality' with reference to Marxism. This attempt has been criticised by Hindess and Hirst in *Pre-Capitalist Modes of Production*.

48. Althusser's approach to the discourse of the sciences is heavily influenced by the work of Gaston Bachelard, and to a lesser extent by Georges Canguilhem. An exposition of both positions from the point of view of an Althusserian reading is given by D. LeCourt, *Marxism and Epistemology*.

49. See 'From Capital to Marx's Philosophy'.

50. The general category of Ideology is proposed in the paper 'Ideology and Ideological Stata Apparatuses' in *Lenin and Philosophy and Other Essays*.

51. This contradiction is clearly related to Althusser's attempt to unite questions of discourse with the concepts of Marxism – social formation, political-ideological relations, etc.

52. Althusser cites the empiricist definition of the object of Political Economy given in the Lalande Dictionary. In similar fashion, Hirst uses Durkheim's *The Rules of Sociological Method* to demonstrate the empiricist character of his sociology in general. See Hirst, *Durkheim, Bernard and Epistemology*.

53. This must also apply to the notion of a 'recurrent reading' in the sense in which it has been used in Althusserianism. An example of this is Ranciere's 'The Concept of Critique and the Critique of Political Economy' in *Theoretical Practice*, nos 1, 2, 5 – a translation of the French edition of *Lire Le Capital*.

54. It would seem that in his later works Althusser attempts to apply this connection between discourse and the extra-discursive to the sciences themselves, or at least to Marxism. See Althusser's *Politics and History*.

55. 'Pattern Variables Revisited', in Parsons' *Sociological Theory and Modern Society*.

NOTES TO CHAPTER TWO: THE EPISTEMOLOGY OF ANALYTICAL REALISM

1. See chapter 3.

2. This is particularly necessary in an analysis of Parsons' work. As will be seen later in the text, Parsons frequently resorts to epistemological oppositions, such as that between the 'analytical' and 'concrete', to account for what are, in fact, theoretically problematic relations in his social theory. An example of this is his attempt to co-ordinate the functional prerequisites and the pattern-variables ( see later chapters).

3. A. F., Whitehead, *Science and the Modern World*.

4. See *SSA*, p. 16.

5. This brief account will be expanded in chapter 4.

6. These include discussions of deviance, medical sociology, economic relations, occupational sociology, to mention but a few.

7. In *Theories of Society*.

8. This concept is discussed at greater length in the final chapter.

9. In particular, I have already criticised the conventionalist view of science

indirectly through the discussion on modes of critique, and I have also criticised logico-deductive methodology.

10. Dahrendorf, 'Out of Utopia', *American Journal of Sociology*, 64[2] (1958) pp. 115–27.
11. C. W. Mills, *The Sociological Imagination*, pp. 33–59.
12. Ibid., p. 35.
13. The clearest example of this tendency is perhaps to be found in E. Mach, *The Analysis of Sensations*.
14. L. Kolokowski, *Positivist Philosophy*.
15. Carnap, in particular, has attempted to face this contradiction positively.
16. See A. V. Cicourel, *The Social Organisation of Juvenile Justice* and J. Douglas, *The Social Meanings of Suicide*. For a critique of these views, see B. Hindess, *The Use of Official Statistics in Sociology*.
17. R. Merton, *On Theoretical Sociology*, p. 39.
18. Parsons, 'The Position of Sociological Theory', *American Sociological Review*, 13 (1948) p. 166. See also Merton's 'Discussion' to this paper.
19. *On Theoretical Sociology*, pp. 57–8.
20. Merton's 'Discussion' in *American Sociological Review* (see note 18).
21. K. R. Popper, *The Logic of Scientific Discovery*, and T. S. Kuhn, *The Structure of Scientific Revolutions*.
22. A. Koyré, *Metaphysics and Measurement*.
23. *On Theoretical Sociology*, p. 78.
24. D. Hume, *An Enquiry Concerning Human Understanding*, p. 17.
25. D. Willer and J. Willer, *Systematic Empiricism: a Critique of Pseudo-Science*.
26. W. W. Isajiw, *Causation and Functionalism in Sociology*.
27. In fact, Weber appears to accept a traditionally empiricist conception of the methodology of the *natural* sciences in terms of the recognition of 'uniformities'. This comes out in his conception of 'causal adequacy'. See Weber's *The Theory of Social and Economic Organisation*, pp. 99ff.
28. *SSA*, p. 621.
29. Most explicitly proposed by C. Lévi-Strauss, *Structural Anthropology*.
30. See Bershady's *Ideology and Social Knowledge*.
31. See 'On Building Systems Theory' in Parsons' *Social Systems and the Evolution of Action Theory*.
32. Bershady, op. cit., pp. 69–71.
33. This, of course, is not peculiar to analytical realism. While the significance of an ontology may be more apparent in rationalist positions, it also plays decisive roles in many other epistemological theses, from the regularity of Nature in Mill to the randomness of nature in the probabilistic methodologies of contemporary sociology. This is spelt out clearly in D. and J. Willer, op. cit.

## NOTES TO CHAPTER THREE: THE STRUCTURE OF ACTION

1. *The Coming Crisis of Western Sociology*, chs 5–8.
2. 'The Changing Foundations of the Parsonian Action Schema', *American Sociological Review*, 28 (1963).
3. See B. Hindess and S. P. Savage, 'Talcott Parsons and the Three Systems of Action', in H. Martins (ed.), *Parsons Reconsidered*.

4. The best example of this polemic is to be found in 'deviance theory'. Perhaps the most influential work in this respect is D. Matza's *Becoming Deviant*, and an example of the extreme anti-determinism to which such positions will go is S. Box's *Deviance, Reality and Society*. These branches of deviance theory are explicit derivatives of Schutz and Garfinkel.
5. Cf. A. Schutz, *The Phenomenology of the Social World*; Harold Garfinkel, *Studies in Ethnomethodology*; and G. H. Mead, *Mind, Self and Society*.
6. This is not to say that those forms of sociology which operate with the notion of free-will succeed in consistently maintaining this postulate. In so far as these conceptions of action propose the centrality of the actor's 'common-sense' interpretations of the social world, the actor is no longer strictly 'free' – he acts *in terms of* a set of conceptions, and in that respect his freedom is circumscribed.
7. Weber has been slotted into a number of different categories, all of which claim to pin-point the 'true' Weber. Whereas the ultra-humanists claim that the genuine essence of Weber lies in the notion of the free constitutive subjectivity of the human individual (see Schutz's analysis of Weber, op. cit.), other commentators argue that the 'subjective' sphere is only a factor in the Weberian conception of action, and that an equally significant role is played by various 'material' elements of social, economic and political life. This latter position is held by Gerth and Mills in their Introduction to *From Max Weber: Essays in Sociology*, and J. Rex, *Key Problems in Sociological Theory*. An interesting example of such an argument is to be found in the article by J. Cohen, L. E. Hazelrigg and W. Pope, 'DeParsonising Weber', *American Sociological Review*, 40[2] (1975) pp. 229–41. Here Parsons is attacked for taking what is the third 'interpretation' of Weber in his insistence on the centrality of values and complexes of meaning. While the idea of a 'true' interpretation is clearly an awkward one, the two non-Parsonian interpretations are tasked to explain the Weber thesis on the 'Protestant Ethic' and on the massive importance given to systems of religious values.
8. See also his *The Sociology of Religion*.
9. J. Douglas makes this quite explicit – Weber is seen to have made an important contribution to sociology with his emphasis on the subjective meaning context of action, but is criticised for referring to 'complexes of meaning' which are realms of action over and above direct subjective manipulation by individuals. Cf. Douglas, *The Social Meanings of Suicide*, pp. 238–9.
10. See *SSA*, p. 732.
11. *SSA*, p. 44.
12. In the *International Journal of Ethics*, 45 (1935) pp. 282–316.
13. See chapter 5.
14. A clear statement on this point is given in the paper by Parsons on 'Pareto's Central Analytical Scheme', *Journal of Social Philosophy*, I [3] (1936) pp. 244–62; see in particular pp. 250–1.
15. See *SSA*, pp. 91–2.
16. E. Kant, *Foundations of the Metaphysics of Morals*, p. 96.
17. This point distinguishes Weber's form of methodological relativism from Gouldner's attempt to extend the basic thesis to incorporate *personal* values (Gouldner, *The Coming Crisis of Western Sociology*). It is a distinction

(admittedly a blurred one) between cultural relativism and personal relativism.

18. Parsons, 'Evaluation and Objectivity in Social Sciences: an Interpretation of Max Weber's Contributions' (1964) in *Sociological Theory and Modern Society*.

19. See G. Kolko, 'A Critique of Max Weber's Philosophy of History',*Ethics* LXX (1959) pp. 21–36.

20. *The Theory of Social and Economic Organisation*, p. 91.

21. From 'The Place of Ultimate Values in Sociological Theory', op.cit.

22. But note the argument in Hindess and Savage, op. cit.

23. Cf. *Societies*, ch. 2. The problems of this notion are discussed in the later chapter on social change.

24. See chapter 4.

25. This issue is taken up in its most general form in B. Hindess, 'Humanism and Teleology in Sociological Theory'.

26. See *SSA*, ch. XIII.

27. The problem of the relation between the social system and the cultural system is elaborated later.

28. For an account of this relationship in terms of the 'pattern-variable' schema, see Parsons' *Toward a General Theory of Action*.

29. See '*Social Structure and Personality* (1964), in particular the paper 'The Super-ego and the Theory of Social Systems'.

30. See 'Social Structure and the Development of Personality: Freud's Contribution to the Integration of Psychology and Sociology' in *Social Structure and Personality*. For a secondary discussion, see A. Baldwin, 'The Parsonian Theory of the Personality' in M. Black (ed.), *The Sociological Theories of Talcott Parsons*.

31. This argument, with reference to the social system, is developed later, but in this case the ego–*alter* relation is held to be immanently sensitive to values.

NOTES TO CHAPTER FOUR: ACTION AND THE THREE SYSTEMS

1. See Parsons' critique of Durkheim's conceptions of the individual personality in 'The Super-ego and the Theory of Social Systems', *Working Papers in the Theory of Action* (1952) p. 16.

2. Parsons is opposed to a 'social relativism' of culture which reduces the cultural realm to a social order. This is clear in his critique of Durkheim's sociologistic conception of ethics and religion, developed in *SSA*, vol. 1. He is equally against a psychologistic analysis of culture such as that found in Homans' social psychology (see below).

3. See *TGTA*, pp. 54–6.

4. For example, action subjectively orientated to the actions of others.

5. This important point is developed in the next chapter in the discussion of the distinction between Parsons and Weber.

6. The clearest and most concise account of Homans' position is to be found in the paper 'Bringing Men Back In', in Turk and Simpson (eds), *Institutions and Social Exchange*. (See also his 'Commentary' in the same text.) His critique of functionalism in particular is to be found in the paper

'Structural, Functional and Psychological Theories' in N. J. Demerath and R. A. Peterson (eds). *Systems Change and Conflict* (New York: Free Press, 1967).

7.  This particular thesis is developed in *Family, Socialisation and Interaction Process* (1955), which Parsons wrote with Bales *et al.*

8.  Substantively similar arguments to this can be found in R. P. Dore's notion of 'methodological individualism' expounded in the paper 'Function and Course', in Demerath and Peterson, op. cit., and to some extent in Bredemeier's paper 'The Functional Analysis of Motivation', also in Demerath and Peterson, ibid.

9.  From 'Levels of Organisation and the Mediation of Social Interaction' in Turk and Simpson (eds), op. cit. (See also the 'Commentary' in the same text.) It is interesting that this problem is in many ways that faced by marginalist economic theory, an area of economics which Homans regards as a model for the social sciences. Marginalism cannot explain the *general* change in the level of prices etc., without making reference to features external to the process that it considers constitutive of prices in a market economy, i.e. marginal utility.

10. In *Social Theory and Social Structure*; references here are to the edition in *On Theoretical Sociology*.

11. This paper and Merton's 'Discussion' are published in the *American Sociological Review*, 13 (1948) pp. 156–71.

12. See Isajiw, *Causation and Functionalism in Sociology*. This text contains an excellent discussion of the Parsons–Merton debate.

13. Some examples of positions close to Merton's are: Gideon Sjoberg, 'Contradictory Functional Requirements and Social Systems' and Ernst B. Hass, 'Functionalism and International Systems' [both in Demerath and Peterson (eds), op. cit.]; Lewis Coser, *The Functions of Conflict*.

14. In this sense (and in this sense *only*) Davis' critique of the functionalist school (in 'The Myth of a Functional Analysis', in Demerath and Peterson (eds), op. cit., is correct. If functionalism is simply another mode of expressing cause–effect relations, then it *is* no different from other descriptions of the knowledge process. Where Davis is wrong is in including *Parsonian* functionalism within the general conception of the school.

15. In Gross (ed.), *Symposium on Sociological Theory: Inquiries & Paradigms* (New York: Harper and Row and John Weatherhill, 1967).

16. Elsewhere referred to as the 'functionalist theory of conflict' (see L. Coser, op. cit.).

17. Parsons certainly does not preclude 'functional autonomy'. For example, the simple fact that he refers to the functional subsystems as systems in their own right, i.e. as having *their own* functional problems, shows that the social system is no simple integrated unity. He also considers conflict, tension and deviance as central problems for sociology, where he differs is in respect of the theoretical means with which these are solved.

18. See Parsons' 'Commentary' in Turk and Simpson (eds), op. cit., p. 38.

19. On this important concept, see *The Social System* (1951) pp. 201–2. See also Isajiw, op. cit., where it is argued that the major distinction between Parsonian and Mertonian functionalism lies precisely in this distinction between the concepts of 'mechanisms of significance' for the system on the

one hand, and 'observed consequences' for the system on the other. A distinction which hinges around different ways in which system parts are to be constituted – theoretically in the former, empirically in the latter.

20. A fuller illustration of structural–functionalism is given in the following chapter on Parsons' theory of the economy.

21. See 'On the Concept of Political Power' in *Politics and Sociological Structure* (1969).

22. See chapter 5.

23. See *Political Power and Social Classes*, pp. 117–18.

24. 'The Distribution of Power in American Society' in *Politics and Social Structure*.

25. While Poulantzas equates the two approaches to theorising political power, other authors have tended to misplace the distinction and have failed to acknowledge the impact of Parsons' critique. Most common in this respect had been the tendency to reduce the issue to a simple ontological debate between 'consensus' and 'conflict' theories. See A. Giddens, ' "Power" in the Recent Writings of Talcott Parsons', *Sociology*, 2 (1968) pp. 257–72, and S. Lukes, *Power: a Radical View*. Giddens' otherwise accurate account of the distinction between Parsons' and the zero-sum concept of political power reduces the difference to one of 'world views' (ontologies), ignoring the significant theoretical questions provoked by Parsons' critique of the zero-sum concept.

26. Major texts in these areas are C. W. Mills, *The Power Elite* and G. W. Domhoff, *Who Rules America?* on the 'pluralist' side, R. Dahl, *Who Governs?* and D. Riesman, *The Lonely Crowd*; the 'countervailing power' thesis is developed by J. K. Galbraith, *The New Industrial State*.

27. Gerth and Mills (eds), *From Max Weber: Essays in Sociology*.

28. The functional prerequisites are discussed more fully in chapter 5.

29. This, for Parsons, depends upon how high those societies are on the 'socio-evolutionary scale'. This issue is dealt with in later chapters.

30. The work of Blau is, in fact, an explicit attempt to translate Homan's exchange theory into an analysis of power.

31. See chapter 2 above.

32. This should not be interpreted as a claim that, for Parsons, socialisation is invariably successful. His writings on deviance testify that this is not the case (see *The Social System*, chapter vii).

33. In this chapter, I take up only a part of the issues raised by the cultural system, viz. that most relevant to the *social* realm. In the final chapter I will take up the question of that system in general.

34. See Parsons' 'Introduction' to Weber's *The Theory of Social and Economic Organisation*.

35. For example, the 'consensus' categorisation.

36. It may be noted at this juncture that the action sociology of Alain Touraine involves what is, in one respect, a historicist conception of social relations and social values. Touraine places the concept of 'historical subject' at the centre of his analysis of social movements, and indeed offers this as the basis of his differences with functionalist sociology. See Touraine, 'Toward a Sociology of Action' in A. Giddens (ed.), *Positivism and Sociology*.

37. The relation between Weber and Lukács, and to a certain extent Weber

and Parsons, is discussed in 'Parsons, Weber and Historicism', P. Q. Hirst and S. P. Savage in *Luften für Kritiska Studier*, 4 (1976).

38. To this extent, the critique of this paper may be equally applied to the *Working Papers*.

39. No elaborated classification of all these relations will be given here, as it is primarily the *basis* of these papers which will be questioned. For exposition and classification, see figure in *STMS*, p. 198.

40. Parsons has, in fact, independently insisted on an important distinction between situation and environment. He argues that the latter is 'external to the knowing mind', while the situation entails a *subjective* conception. See 'Systems Analysis: Social Systems', *International Encyclopedia of the Social Sciences*, (ed.) Sills, D. E. (New York: Macmillan, 1967) vol. 15.

41. In this respect, Parsons comes dangerously close to a social phenomenology (though with culture, not the individual, the dominant element), thus denying much of what he has done to distinguish himself from such a position. For example, in the paper 'Social Stratification Revisited' he actually argues that the functional prerequisites and the pattern-variables are one and the same issue (in *Essays in Sociological Theory*).

42. I want to emphasise that I am not basing this argument on any apparent contradiction of 'world views' on the lines of Menzies' argument (*Talcott Parsons and the Social Imagery of Man*), but on strictly conceptual grounds. Parsons has hardly denied the divergence of views which he attempts to combine; simple assertion does, therefore, not suffice as an effective critique. It is the theoretical character of the 'combination' which is of most significance.

NOTES TO CHAPTER FIVE: THE ECONOMY AND THE SOCIAL SYSTEM

1. The term 'sociology' as used here is not intended to cover Marxist theory which, in terms of its basic concepts, remains external to sociological discourse.

2. Parsons' early theses on economics and sociology centre around two major areas – the conception of capitalism in Weber and Sombart, and the theories of Alfred Marshall: see 'Economics and Sociology: Marshall in Relation to the Thought of his Time', *Quarterly J. Economics*, 46 (1932) pp. 316–47. *SSA* represents the most general summary of such theses, but since this text the only significant paper prior to *Economy and Society* is 'The Motivation of Economic Activities', published in *Essays in Sociological Theory*.

3. *SSA*, pp. 699–70.

4. The 'proof' of the validity of the voluntaristic theory of action oscillates between dogmatic assertion and the ambiguous and teleological postulate of an immanent progress in the development of theoretical systems. The whole analysis of the 'analytical elements' depends on this thesis.

5. See *Economy and Society*, p. 91. See also N. Smelser, *The Sociology of Economic Life*, chs 1 and 11, and Parsons' reply to Morse's paper in M. Black (ed.), *The Sociological Theories of Talcott Parsons*, in the essay 'The Point of View of the Author', p. 351.

6. This is seen to be so because, despite the reference in welfare economics to

'social' utility, the social is conceived as no more than an aggregate of individual utilities (see *ES*, p. 32).

7. See J. M. Keynes, *The General Theory of Employment, Interest and Money*, pp. 91–5.
8. For example, with reference to labour-supply, Parsons argues that there is still a great significance in the traditional practice of drawing labour-supply curves – what must be formulated, however, is a specification of the conditions of the labour market which does not collapse into the orthodox reductionism and psychologism common to economic theory: 'our purpose here is not to establish the facts of the market in the narrow sense but to provide determinate sociological standards whereby the facts of the market may be established before rather than after the fact' (*ES*, p. 156).
9. For example, 'the two great forming agencies of the world's history have been the religious and the economic'. From Marshall's *The Principles of Economics*, p. 1. See also pp. 752ff. for Marshall's notion of the two parameters to economic life – the sphere of 'satisfaction' and the realm of 'ideals'.
10. In *Essays in Sociological Theory*, and also in N. J. Smelser (ed.), *Readings in Economic Sociology*.
11. It is, thus, not a mere extension of the analysis from 'micro' to 'macro' levels as claimed by D. Martindale in *The Nature and Types of Sociological Theory*, pp. 421–5.
12. Although it must be emphasised that not all social systems are collectivities – the latter are those systems characterised by solidarity (shared value-orientations). However, this issue will be discussed further later in text.
13. See *Social System*, p. 201.
14. This includes the 'substantivist' conception of the economy as represented in *Trade and Markets in the Early Empires*, edited by K. Polanyı, C. Arensberg and H. W. Pearson. Although there may be levels of similarity between Parsons' conception of the economy and the substantivist notion of the market as formal economising, the determination of this sphere in the latter is not approached by means of the concept of structural differentiation but in altogether more ambiguous terms. On this point, see A. Jenkins' paper ' "Substantivism" as a Comparative Theory of Economic Forms', in B. Hindess (ed.), *Sociological Theories of the Economy*.
15. Although this is an exchange process, distinct in major respects from so-called 'exchange-theory'. For a discussion on these distinctions, see the various arguments in Turk and Simpson (eds), *Institutions and Social Exchange: the Theories of George Homans and Talcott Parsons*.
16. *The System of Modern Societies*, pp. 139ff.
17. For a discussion of this concept, see G. Kolko, 'A Critique of Max Weber's Philosophy of History', *Ethics*, LXX (1959–60) pp. 21–36.
18. See *Societies: Evolutionary and Comparative Perspectives* (1966), and 'Evolutionary Universals in Society' in *Sociological Theory and Modern Society*.
19. *Social Change in the Industrial Revolution*.
20. See *ES*, p. 82.
21. For the sake of brevity the concept of structural differentiation will be

referred to as 'differentiation' and the concept of cultural directionality as 'directionality'.

22. B. Hindess and S. P. Savage, 'Talcott Parsons and the Three Systems of Action' in H. Martins (ed.), *Parsons Reconsidered*.

23. The unique character of the cultural realm has, of course, always been a central postulate of Parsons from his earliest writings, but the only really elaborate attempt to confront explicitly the problem of culture and its primary element 'ultimate reality' is his Introduction to the section 'Culture and Social System', in *Theories of Society* (1961), edited by Parsons, Shils, Naegele and Pitts.

24. This is a concept used by Althusser to designate the mode of reading dominant in readings of the relationship between the 'Young' and 'Old' Marx (see *For Marx*, pp. 54 and 54n). Althusser has demonstrated the expressivist and teleological character of such a formulation.

25. It might be worthwhile to note the existence of a theoretical position which does not, at least in certain of its formulations, define the economic–societal relation in a teleological fashion – this is a position the outlines of which are given in Marx's Introduction to *A Contribution to the Critique of Political Economy* (1857). See, in this respect, Marx's opposition to the notion of production-in-general and the alternative concept of *modes* of production. For a recent elaboration of these points, see *Pre-Capitalist Modes of Production* by B. Hindess and P. Q. Hirst.

26. See 'Bringing Men Back In' in Turk and Simpson (eds), op. cit.

27. For a detailed analysis of the systemic relations in Parsons' work, see M. H. Lessnoff, 'Parsons' System Problems', *Sociological Review*, 16[2] (July 1968) pp. 185–215.

NOTES TO CHAPTER SIX: THEORY OF SOCIAL CHANGE
AND SOCIAL EVOLUTION

1. Gouldner, *The Coming Crisis of Western Sociology*, p. 353.

2. D. Lockwood, 'Some Remarks on *"The Social System"* ', *British Journal of Sociology*, 7 [2] (1956), and in Demerath and Peterson (eds), *System, Change and Conflict*.

3. 'Out of Utopia' in Demerath and Peterson (eds), ibid.

4. Other examples include Barrington Moore Jr, 'The New Scholasticism and the Study of Politics' in *World Politics* (Oct 1953); Pierre L. van den Berghe, 'Dialectic and Functionalism: Toward a Synthesis', *American Sociological Review*, 28 (Oct 1963); C. Morse, 'The Functional Prerequisites' in M. Black (ed.), *The Sociological Theories of Talcott Parsons*.

5. See Guy Rocher, *Talcott Parsons and American Sociology*, and John K. Rhoades, 'On Gouldner's *Coming Crisis*' in *Varieties of Political Expression in Sociology* (an *American Sociological Review* publication). Unfortunately Rhoades corrects Gouldner's mis-reading only to produce another incorrect interpretation – see his conception of Parsons' concept of system as an ideal-type.

6. A. D. Smith, *The Concept of Social Change: a Critique of the Functionalist Theory of Change*.

7. R. Nisbet, 'The Problem of Social Change' in Nisbet (ed.), *Social Change*.

8. See 'On Building Social System Theory: a Personal History' in *Social Systems and the Evolution of Action Theory*.
9. See *SSA*, pp. 739–40.
10. See *SSA*, pp. 110–14.
11. On this point see the chapter on the Economy.
12. This is a point that Parsons himself admits. See the Introduction to 'Culture and the Social System' in *Theories of Society*, op. cit.
13. 'A Paradigm for the Analysis of Social Change' in *Theories of Society*, op. cit., p. 194.
14. See Parsons' review of Bershady's *Ideology and Social Knowledge* in *Social Systems and the Evolution of Action Theory*.
15. See *TGTA*, p. 70.
16. 'A Paradigm for the Analysis of Social Change', op. cit., p. 147.
17. For a more extensive example, see his discussion of agricultural change in 'Some Considerations on the Theory of Social Change', in *Rural Sociology*, vol. 26 (1961).
18. 'A Paradigm for the Analysis of Social Change', op. cit., p. 198.
19. In a similar fashion to the identification of societies with pattern-variable combinations.
20. Parsons' position here runs counter to much contemporary anthropology, particularly the work of C. Levi-Strauss. In *The Savage Mind*, Levi-Strauss argues that it is not only in terms of cognitive systems the terms 'primitive' and 'advanced' are inapplicable. The evidence shows, he argues, that so-called primitive societies are no less complex and elaborate than modern industrial societies. For a discussion of the relation between Parsons' evolutionism and more classical evolutionist theory, see J. D. Y. Peel, *Herbert Spencer: The Evolution of a Sociologist*.
21. For an elaboration, see *Societies*, pp. 22–3, and *The System of Modern Societies*, pp. 26–7.
22. *Social Systems and the Evolution of Action Theory*, p. 49.
23. See 'Talcott Parsons and the Three Systems of Action' by Hindess and Savage in H. Martins (ed.), op. cit.
24. See *Societies*, p. 25. A similar blatantly evolutionist thesis is proposed by Bellah in *Religious Evolution*, and by Eisenstadt, 'Social Change, Differentiation and Evolution', in *American Sociological Review*, 29 (June 1964).
25. See *STMS*, p. 493.
26. 'Some Considerations on the Theory of Social Change', op. cit., p. 229.
27. See *Readings in Pre-Modern Societies* (1972), edited by Parsons and Lidz. In particular, Hallowells' paper 'The Protocultural Foundations of Human Adaptation'.
28. See Darwin, op. cit., pp. 117–19.
29. Accounted for by Darwin by the now discredited concept of 'blending'. This feature of the theory of natural selection was to be transformed by genetic theory and the concept of mutation. Dobzhansky has shown that the concept of blending would, in fact, operate so as to reduce rather than increase variation – one-half in every generation, forming genetically uniform individuals. For a general discussion, see 'Mendelian Populations and Their Evolution', in Dunn (ed.), *Genetics in the Twentieth Century*.
30. See *Societies*, p. 111.

31. The term 'teleology' in this context refers to more than action governed by the conscious intentions of the actor, i.e. to more than its traditional sociological definition. It refers also to non-conscious processes as well – to any process which invokes the notion of process-with-a-Purpose.
32. See *Origin of Species*, chapter 5.
33. See his Introduction to Weber's *The Sociology of Religion*.
34. A developed discussion of Parsons' epistemology is given in chapter 2.
35. See, in particular, 'Religion in Post-Industrial America: the Problem of Secularisation', *Social Research*, 41[2] (1974).

# Bibliography

BIBLIOGRAPHY OF THE WORKS OF TALCOTT PARSONS

**1928**

'"Capitalism" in Recent German Literature: Sombart and Weber, I', *Journal of Political Economy*, 36[6], pp. 641–61.

**1929**

'"Capitalism" in Recent German Literature: Sombart and Weber, II', *Journal of Political Economy*, 37[1], pp. 31–51.

**1930**

Translation of Max Weber's *The Protestant Ethic and Spirit of Capitalism* (London: Allen & Unwin; New York: Charles Scribner's Sons).

**1931**

'Wants and Activities in Marshall', *Quarterly Journal of Economics*, 46[1], pp. 101–40.

**1932**

'Economics and Sociology: Marshall in Relation to the Thought of his Time', *Quarterly Journal of Economics*, 46[2], pp. 316–47.

**1933**

'Malthus', *Encyclopedia of the Social Sciences*, 10, pp. 68–9.

'Pareto', *Encyclopedia of the Social Sciences*, 11, pp. 576–8.

**1934**

'Some Reflections on "The Nature and Significance of Economics"', *Quarterly Journal of Economics*, 48, pp. 511–45.

'Society', *Encyclopedia of the Social Sciences*, 14, pp. 225–31.

'Sociological Elements in Economic Thought, I', *Quarterly Journal of Economics*, 49, pp. 414–53.

**1935**

'Sociological Elements in Economic Thought, II', *Quarterly Journal of Economics*, 49, pp. 645–67.

'The Place of Ultimate Values in Sociological Theory', *International Journal of Ethics*, 45, pp. 282–316.

'H. M. Robertson on Max Weber and his School', *Journal of Political Economy*, 43, pp. 688–96.

**1936**

'Pareto's Central Analytical Scheme', *Journal of Social Philosophy*, 1[3], pp. 244–62.

'On Certain Sociological Elements in Professor Taussig's Thought', in Viner, J. (ed.), *Explorations in Economics: Notes and Essays Contributed in Honor of F. W. Taussig* (New York: McGraw-Hill) pp. 352–79.

**1937**

*The Structure of Social Action* (New York: McGraw-Hill; repr. New York: Free Press, 1949).

'Education and the Professions', *International Journal of Ethics*, 47, pp. 365–9.

**1938**

'The Role of Theory in Social Research', *American Sociological Review*, 3, pp. 13–20; an address delivered before the Annual Institute of the Society for Social Research at the University of Chicago (1937).

'The Role of Ideas in Social Action', *American Sociological Review*, 3, pp. 653–64; written for a meeting on the problem of ideologies at the American Sociological Society's annual meeting in Atlantic City (1937), and reprinted in *Essays in Sociological Theory* (1949).

**1939**

'The Professions and Social Structure', *Social Forces*, 17[4], pp. 457–67; written for presentation at the annual meeting of the American Sociological Society in Detroit (1938), and reprinted in *Essays in Sociological Theory*.

'Comte', *Journal of Unified Science*, 9, pp. 77–83.

**1940**

'An Analytical Approach to the Theory of Social Stratification', *American Journal of Sociology*, 45, pp. 841–62; reprinted in *Essays in Sociological Theory*.

'The Motivation of Economic Activities', *Canadian Journal of Economics and Political Science*, 6, pp. 187–203; originally given as a public lecture at the University of Toronto, and reprinted in *Essays in Sociological Theory*, and in Dubin, R. (ed.), *Human Relations in Administration: the Sociology of Organisation* (Englewood Cliffs: Prentice-Hall, 1951).

**1942**

'Max Weber and the Contemporary Political Crisis', *Review of Politics*, 4, pp. 61–76, 155–172.

'The Sociology of Modern Anti-Semitism' in Graeber, J. and Stuart Henderson, B. (eds), *Jews in a Gentile World* (New York: Macmillan) pp. 101–32.

'Age and Sex in the Social Structure of the United States', *American Sociological Review*, 7, pp. 604–16; read at the annual meeting of the American Sociological Society in New York (1941); reprinted in *Essays in Sociological Theory*, and in Wilson, L. and Kolb, W. (eds), *Sociological Analysis*, and in Kluckhohn, C. and Murray, H. A. (eds), *Personality in Nature, Society and Culture* (New York: Alfred A. Knopf, 1953).

'Propaganda and Social Control', *Psychiatry*, 5, pp. 551–72; reprinted in *Essays in Sociological Theory*.

'Democracy and Social Structure in Pre-Nazi Germany', *Journal of Legal and Political Sociology*, 1, pp. 96–114; reprinted in *Essays in Sociological Theory* (rev. edn, 1954).

'Some Sociological Aspects of the Fascist Movements', *Social Forces*, 21, pp. 138–47; written as the Presidential Address to the Eastern Sociological Society at the 1942 meeting; reprinted in *Essays in Sociological Theory* (rev. edn, 1954).

**1943**

'The Kinship System of the Contemporary United States', *American Anthropologist*, 45, pp. 22–38; reprinted in *Essays in Sociological Theory*.

**1944**

'The Theoretical Development of the Sociology of Religion', *Journal of the History of Ideas*, 5, pp. 176–90; reprinted in *Essays in Sociological Theory*, and in Wiener, P. and Noland, A. (eds), *Ideas in Cultural Perspective* (New Brunswick, N. J.: Rutgers University Press, 1962).

**1945**

'The Present Position and Prospects of Systematic Theory in Sociology', in Gurvitch, G. and Moore, W. E. (eds), *Twentieth Century Sociology* (New York: Philosophical Library); reprinted in *Essays in Sociological Theory*.

'The Problem of Controlled Institutional Change: an Essay on Applied Social Science', *Psychiatry*, 8, pp. 79–101; prepared as an appendix to the 'Report of the Conference on Germany after the Second World War'; reprinted in *Essays in Sociological Theory*.

'Racial and Religious Differences as Factors in Group Tensions', in Finkelstein, L. *et al.* (eds), *Unity and Difference in the Modern*

*World* (The Conference on Science, Philosophy and Religion and Their Relation to the Democratic Way of Life) (New York).

**1946**

'The Science Legislation and the Role of the Social Sciences', *American Sociological Review*, 11, pp. 653–66.

'Population and Social Structure', in Haring, D. G. (ed.), *Japan's Prospect* (Cambridge, Mass.: Harvard University Press) pp. 87–114; this book was published by the staff of the Harvard School for Overseas Administration; the essay was reprinted in *Essays in Sociological Theory* (revised edn, 1954).

'Certain Primary Sources and Patterns of Aggression in the Social Structure of the Western World', *Psychiatry*, 10, pp. 167–81; reprinted in *Essays in Sociological Theory*, and also reprinted as 'The Structure of Group Hostility', in Lanyi, G. and McWilliams, W. (eds), *Crisis and Continuity in World Politics* (2nd edn, New York: Random House, 1966, 1973) pp. 220–3.

'Some Aspects of the Relations between Social Science and Ethics', *Social Science*, 22, pp. 213–17; read at the annual meeting of the American Association for the Advancement of Science in Boston (1946).

**1947**

'Science Legislation and the Social Sciences' *Political Science Quarterly*, 62[2] June.

*Max Weber: The Theory of Social and Economic Organisation*, co-edited and translated with A. M. Henderson (Oxford: Oxford University Press; repr. New York: Free Press, 1957) and Introduction reprinted in *Essays in Sociological Theory* (first edn, 1949).

**1948**

'Sociology, 1941–6', *American Journal of Sociology*, 53, pp. 245–57; co-author Bernard Barber.

'The Position of Sociological Theory', *American Sociological Review*, 13, pp. 156–71; paper read before the annual meeting of the American Sociological Society, New York City (1947); reprinted in *Essays in Sociological Theory* (first edn, 1949).

**1949**

*Essays in Sociological Theory: Pure and Applied* (New York: Free Press).

'The Rise and Decline of Economic Man', *Journal of General Education*, 4, pp. 47–53.

'Social Classes and Class Conflict in the Light of Recent Sociologi-

cal Theory', *American Economic Review*, 39, pp. 16–26; read at the meeting of the American Economic Association (1948); reprinted in *Essays in Sociological Theory* (revised edn, 1954).
**1950**
'The Prospects of Sociological Theory', *American Sociological Review*, 15, pp. 3–16; Presidential Address read before the annual meeting of the American Sociological Society in New York City (1949); reprinted in *Essays in Sociological Theory* (revised edn, 1954).
'Psychoanalysis and the Social Structure', *The Psychoanalytic Quarterly*, 19, pp. 371–84; the substance of this paper was presented at the meeting of the American Psychoanalytic Association in Washington, D. C. (1948), and the paper was reprinted in *Essays in Sociological Theory* (revised edn, 1954).
'The Social Environment of the Educational Process', *Centennial* (Washington, D.C.: American Association for the Advancement of Science) pp. 36–40; read at the AAAS Centennial Celebration in 1948.
**1951**
*The Social System* (New York: Free Press).
*Toward a General Theory of Action* (Cambridge, Mass.: Harvard University Press); editor and contributor with Edward A. Shils and others (repr. New York: Harper Torchbooks, 1962).
'Graduate Training in Social Relations at Harvard', *Journal of General Education*, 5, pp. 149–57.
'Illness and the Role of the Physician: a Sociological Perspective', *American Journal of Orthopsychiatry*, 21, pp. 452–60; presented at the 1951 annual meeting of the American Orthopsychiatry Association in Detroit; reprinted in Kluckhohn, C. and Murray, H. A. (eds), *Personality in Nature, Society and Culture* (2nd edn, New York: Alfred A. Knopf, 1953).
**1952**
'The Super-ego and the Theory of Social Systems', *Psychiatry*, 15, pp. 15–25; the substance of this paper was read at the meeting of the Psychoanalytic Section of the American Psychiatric Association in Cincinnati (1951); reprinted in Parsons, T., Bales, R. F. and Shils, E. A., *Working Papers in the Theory of Action* (New York:Free Press, 1953 and 1967), and in *Social Structure and Personality* (1964).
'Religious Perspectives in College Teaching: Sociology and Social Psychology', in Fairchild, H. N. (ed.), *Religious Perspectives in*

*College Teaching* (New York: Ronald Press) pp. 286–337.

'A Sociologist Looks at the Legal Profession', *Conference on the Profession of Law and Legal Education*, Conference Series, no. II. (Chicago, Ill.: Law School, University of Chicago Press) pp. 49–63; this paper was presented at the first symposium on the occasion of the Fiftieth Anniversary Celebration of the University of Chicago Law School (1952); reprinted in *Essays in Sociological Theory* (rev. edn, 1954).

**1953**

*Working Papers in the Theory of Action* (New York: Free Press); in collaboration with Robert F. Bales and Edward A. Shils; re-issued in 1967.

'Psychoanalysis and Social Science with Specific Reference to the Oedipus Problem', in Alexander, F. and Ross, H. (eds), *Twenty Years of Psychoanalysis* (New York: W. W. Norton) pp. 186–215; the substance of this paper was read at the Twentieth Anniversary Celebration of the Institute for Psychoanalysis in Chicago (1952).

'A Revised Analytical Approach to the Theory of Social Stratification', in Bendix, R. and Lipset, S. M. (eds), *Class, Status and Power: A Reader in Social Stratification* (New York: Free Press) pp. 92–129; reprinted in *Essays in Sociological Theory* (rev. edn, 1954).

'Illness, Therapy and the Modern Urban American Family', *Journal of Social Issues*, 8, pp. 31–44; co-author with Renee C. Fox; reprinted in Jaco, E. G. (ed.), *Patients, Physicians, and Illness* (New York: Free Press, 1958).

'Some Comments on the State of the General Theory of Action', *American Sociological Review*, 18[6], pp. 618–31.

**1954**

'The Father Symbol: an Appraisal in the Light of Psychoanalytic and Sociological Theory', in Bryson, Finkelstein, MacIver and McKeon (eds), *Symbols and Values: An Initial Study* (New York: Harper & Row, 1954) pp. 523–44; the substance of this paper was read at the meeting of the American Psychological Association (1952) in Washington, D. C.; reprinted in *Social Structure and Personality* (1964).

*Essays in Sociological Theory: Pure and Applied* (rev. edn, New York: Free Press).

'Psychology and Sociology', in Gillin, J. P. (ed.), *For a Science of Social Man* (New York: Macmillan) pp. 67–102.

'The Incest Taboo in Relation to Social Structure and the Socialisation of the Child', *British Journal of Sociology*, 5[2], pp. 101–17.
**1955**
*Family, Socialisation and Interaction Process* (New York: Free Press); co-author with Robert F. Bales, James Olds, Morris Zelditch and Philip E. Slater.
'"McCarthyism" and American Social Tension: a Sociologist's View', *Yale Review* (Winter 1955) pp. 226–45; reprinted under title 'Social Strains in America', in Bell, D. (ed.), *The New American Right* (New York: Criterion Books, 1955).
**1956**
*Economy and Society* (London: Routledge and Kegan Paul; New York: Free Press); co-author with Neil J. Smelser.
*Éléments pour une théorie de l'action* (Paris: Plon), with an introduction by François Bourricaud.
'A Sociological Approach to the Theory of Organisation', *Administrative Science Quarterly*, 1, Pt I (June 1956) pp. 63–85; Pt II (Sep 1956) pp. 225–39; reprinted in *Structure and Process in Modern Society* (1960).
**1957**
'The Distribution of Power in American Society', *World Politics*, 10 (Oct 1957) pp. 123–43; reprinted in *Structure and Process in Modern Societies* (1960).
'Malinowski and the Theory of Social Systems', in Firth, R. (ed.), *Man and Culture* (London: Routledge and Kegan Paul).
'Man in his Social Environment – as Viewed by Modern Social Science', *Centennial Review of Arts and Sciences* (East Lansing, Mich.: Michigan State University Press) pp. 50–69.
'The Mental Hospital as a Type of Organisation', in Greenblatt, M., Levinson, D. J. and Williams, R. H. (eds), *The Patient and the Mental Hospital* (New York: Free Press).
'Réflexions sur les Organisations Religieuses aux États-Unis', *Archives de Sociologie Des Religions* (Jan–June) pp. 21–36.
*Sociologia di dittatura* (Bologna: Il Mulino).
**1958**
'Authority, Legitimation, and Political Action', in Friedrich, C. J. (ed.), *Authority* (Cambridge, Mass.: Harvard University Press); reprinted in *Structure and Process in Modern Society*.
'The Definitions of Health and Illness in the Light of American Values and Social Structure', in Jaco, E. G. (ed.), *Patients,*

*Physicians and Illness* (New York: Free Press); reprinted in *Social Structure and Personality* (1964).

'Social Structure and the Development of Personality', *Psychiatry*, 21, pp. 321–40; reprinted in *Social Structure and Personality*.

'General Theory in Sociology', in Merton, R. K., Broom, L. and Cottrell, L. S., Jr, (eds), *Sociology Today* (New York: Basic Books).

'Some Ingredients of a General Theory of Formal Organisation', in Halpin, A. W. (ed.), *Administrative Theory in Education* (Chicago, Ill.: Midwest Administration Center, University of Chicago); reprinted in *Structure and Process in Modern Societies*.

'Some Reflections on the Institutional Framework of Economic Development', *The Challenge of Development: a Symposium* (Jerusalem: The Hebrew University); reprinted in *Structure and Process in Modern Societies*.

'Some Trends of Change in American Society: Their Bearing on Medical Education', *Journal of the American Medical Association* (May) pp. 31–6; reprinted in *Structure and Process in Modern Societies*.

'The Pattern of Religious Organisation in the United States', *Daedalus* (Summer) pp. 65–85; reprinted in *Structure and Process in Modern Societies*.

'The Concepts of Culture and of Social System', *American Sociological Review*, 23[5], pp. 582–3; co-author with A. L. Kroeber.

**1959**

'An Approach to Psychological Theory in Terms of the Theory of Action', in Koch, S. (ed.), *Psychology: A Study of a Science*, vol. 3 (New York: McGraw-Hill) pp. 612–711.

'The Principal Structures of Community: a Sociological View', in Friedrich, C. J. (ed.), *Community* (New York: Liberal Arts Press); reprinted in *Structure and Process in Modern Societies*.

'Voting and the Equilibrium of the American Political System', in Burdick, E. and Brodbeck, A. (eds), *American Voting Behavior* (New York: Free Press).

'Durkheim's Contribution to the Theory of Integration of Social Systems', in Wolff, K. H. (ed.), *Émile Durkheim, 1958–1917: a Collection of Essays, with Translations and a Bibliography* (Columbus: Ohio State University Press).

'Implications of the Study' (on Marjorie Fiske's 'Book Selection and Retention in California Public and School Libraries'), *The*

*Climate of Book Selection: a Symposium of the University of California School of Librarianship* (Berkeley, Calif.: University of California Press).

'Some Problems Confronting Sociology as a Profession', *American Sociological Review*, 24[4], pp. 547–58.

'The School Class as a Social System', *Harvard Educational Review* (Fall 1959); reprinted in *Social Structure and Personality*, and in Halsey, A. H., Floud, J. and Anderson, C. A. (eds), *Education, Economy and Society* (New York: Free Press, 1961).

'An Approach to the Sociology of Knowledge', *Proceedings of the Fourth World Congress of Sociology at Milan, Italy* (Sep 1959) vol. 4.

**1960**

'Mental Illness and "Spiritual Malaise": the Roles of the Psychiatrist and of the Minister of Religion', in Hofmann, H. (ed.), *The Ministry and Mental Health* (New York: Association Press); reprinted in *Social Structure and Personality*.

*Structure and Process in Modern Societies*, a collection of essays (New York: Free Press).

'In memoriam, Clyde Kluckhohn, 1905–1960', *American Sociological Review*, 25[6], pp. 960–2.

'The Mass Media and the Structure of American Society', *Journal of Social Issues*, 16[3], pp. 67–77; co-author with Winston White.

'Pattern Variables Revisited: a Response to Professor Dubin's Stimulus', *American Sociological Review*, 25[4], pp. 467–83.

'Toward a Healthy Maturity', *Journal of Health and Human Behavior* (Fall); reprinted in *Social Structure and Personality*.

'Social Structure and Political Orientation', *World Politics*, 13[1], pp. 112–28; a review of Lipset, S. M., *Political Man*, and Kornhauser, W., *The Politics of Mass Society*.

'Review of Reinhard Bendix's *Max Weber: an Intellectual Portrait*', *American Sociological Review*, 25[5], pp. 750–2.

**1961**

*Theories of Society* (New York: Free Press) vols 1 and 2, co-editor with Edward A. Shils, Kaspar D. Naegele and Jesse R. Pitts.

'Some Principal Characteristics of Industrial Societies', in Black, C. E. (ed.), *The Transformation of Russian Society since 1861* (Cambridge, Mass.: Harvard University Press); reprinted in *Structure and Process in Modern Societies*.

'The Link between Character and Society' (co-author with

Winston White), in Lipset, S. M. and Lowenthal, L. (eds), *Culture and Social Character* (New York: Free Press); reprinted in *Social Structure and Personality*.

'The Contribution of Psycho-analysis to the Social Sciences', *Science and Psycho-analysis*, 4.

'The Cultural Background of American Religious Organisation', *The Proceedings of the Conference on Science, Philosophy and Religion, 1960*.

'The Point of View of the Author', in Black, M. (ed.), *The Social Theories of Talcott Parsons* (Englewood Cliffs, N. J.: Prentice-Hall).

'The Problem of International Community', in Rosenau, J. N. (ed.), *International Politics and Foreign Policy* (New York: Free Press).

'Polarization of the World and International Order', in Wright, Q., Evan, W. M. and Deutsch, M. (eds), *Preventing World War III* (New York: Simon and Schuster, 1962); also in the *Berkeley Journal of Sociology* (1961).

'Youth in the Context of American Society', *Daedalus*, 91[1], pp. 97–123; reprinted in Erikson, E. H. (ed.), *Youth: Change and Challenge* (New York: Basic Books, 1963), and in *Social Structure and Personality*.

'Some Considerations on the Theory of Social Change', *Rural Sociology*, 26[3], pp. 219–39.

'A Sociologist's View', in Ginzberg, E. (ed.), *Values and Ideals of American Youth* (New York: Columbia University Press).

Comment on 'Preface to a Metatheoretical Framework for Sociology' by Llewellyn Gross, *American Journal of Sociology* (Sep 1961).

'In memoriam, Alfred L. Korber, 1876–1960', *American Journal of Sociology*, 66[6], pp. 616–17.

Comment on 'Images of Mand and the Sociology of Religion', by William Kolb, *Journal for the Scientific Study of Religion* (Oct.)

'Discussion of Trends Revealed by the 1960 Census of Population', *Proceedings of the Section on Social Statistics* (Washington, D. C.: American Statistical Association).

**1962**

Foreword to *Herbert Spencer: The Study of Sociology* (Ann Arbor, Mich.: University of Michigan Press, Ann Arbor Paperback Series).

'In memoriam, Clyde Kluckhohn, 1905–60' (co-author with

Evon Z. Vogt), *American Anthropologist* (Feb 1962); reprinted as Introduction to a new edition of Kluckhohn's *Navajo Witchcraft* (Boston, Mass.: Beacon Press).

Comment on 'The Oversocialised Conception of Man' by Dennis Wrong, *Psychoanalysis and Psychoanalytic Review* (Summer).

Review of *Law and Social Process* (Hurst) in *Journal of the History of Ideas* (Oct–Dec).

'The Ageing in American Society', *Law and Contemporary Problems* (Winter).

'The Law and Social Control', in Evan, W. M. (ed.), *Law and Sociology* (New York: Free Press).

'In memoriam, Richard Henry Tawney, 1880–1962', *American Sociological Review*, 27[6], pp. 880–90.

Review of *Reason in Society* by Paul Diesing, *Industrial and Labor Relations Review* (July).

*La struttura dell' azione sociale*, Introduction by Gianfranco Poggi (Bologna: Il Mulino); Italian translation of *The Structure of Social Action*.

**1963**

Introduction to Max Weber's *The Sociology of Religion* (Boston, Mass.: Beacon Press); translated by Ephraim Fischoff from *Wirtschaft und Gesellschaft*.

'Social Strains in America: a Postscript (1962)' in Bell, D. (ed.), *The Radical Right* (Garden City, N. Y. Doubleday).

'Christianity and Modern Industrial Society', in Tiryakian, E. A. (ed.), *Sociological Theory, Values, and Sociocultural Change: Essays in Honor of Pitirim A. Sorokin* (New York: Free Press).

'Social Change and Medical Organization in the United States', *Annals of the American Academy of Political and Social Science* (March).

'On the Concept of Influence', with rejoinder to comments, *Public Opinion Quarterly*, 27[1], pp. 37–62, 87–92; reprinted in *Sociological Theory and Modern Society* (1967).

'On the Concept of Political Power', *Proceedings of the American Philosophical Society*, 107[3]; reprinted in *Sociological Theory and Modern Society*.

'Death in American Society', *The American Behavioral Scientist* (May).

**1964**

'Some Theoretical Considerations Bearing on the Field of Medical Sociology'; written for a symposium that did not appear; published as chapter 12 of *Social Structure and Personality*.

*Social Structure and Personality*, a collection of essays (New York: Free Press).

'The Ideas of Systems, Causal Explanation and Cybernetic Control in Social Science', in Lerner D. (ed.), *Cause and Effect* (New York: Free Press, 1965); presented at the Fourth Hayden Colloquium, Massachusetts Institute of Technology (1964).

'Evolutionary Universals in Society', *American Sociological Review*, 29[3], pp. 339–57.

'Max Weber, 1864–1964', *American Sociological Review* (April).

'Sociological Theory', *Encyclopedia Britannica*.

'Some Reflections on the Place of Force in Social Process', in Eckstein, H. (ed.), *Internal War: Basic Problems and Approaches* (New York: Free Press).

'Levels of Organization and the Mediation of Social Interaction', *Sociological Inquiry* (Spring).

'Die Jungsten Entwicklungen in Der Strukturell–Funktionalem Theorie', *Kolner Zeitschrift fur Soziologie und Sozialpsychologie*, 16[1], pp. 30–49.

'Youth in the Context of American Society', in Borow, H. (ed.), *Man in a World at Work* (Boston, Mass.: Houghton Mifflin); modified version of an article previously written for *Daedalus* (1961).

'Evaluation and Objectivity in the Social Sciences: an Interpretation of Max Weber's Contributions'; an address delivered at the Weber Centennial (April 1964); published in German with discussion in Stammer, O. (ed.), *Max Weber und die Soziologie Heute* (Tübingen: Mohr, 1965); English version published in the *International Journal of the Social Sciences* (1965); reprinted in *Sociological Theory and Modern Society*.

**1965**

'Unity and Diversity in the Modern Intellectual Disciplines: the Role of the Social Sciences', *Daedalus*, 94[1], pp. 39–65.

'An American's Impression of Sociology in the Soviet Union', *American Sociological Review*, 30[1], pp. 121–5.

'Full Citizenship for the Negro American?', *Daedalus*, 94[4], pp. 1009–54; reprinted in Parsons, T. and Clark, K. (eds), *The Negro American* (Boston, Mass.: Houghton Mifflin, 1966).

**1966**

*Societies: Evolutionary and Comparative Perspectives* (Foundations of Modern Sociology Series; general editor: Alex Inkeles) (Englewood Cliffs, N. J.: Prentice-Hall).

'The Political Aspect of Social Structure and Process', in Easton, D. (ed.), *Varieties of Political Theory* (Englewood Cliffs, N. J.: Prentice-Hall).

*The Negro American* (Boston, Mass.: Houghton Mifflin); co-author with Kenneth Clark.

'Die Bedeutung der Polarisierung fur das Sozialsystem: Die Hautfarbe als Polarisierungsproblem', in Silbermann, A. (ed.), *Militanter Humanismus* (Frankfurt: S. Fischer).

**1967**

'The Nature of American Pluralism', in Sizer, T. (ed.), *Religion and Public Education* (Boston, Mass.: Houghton Mifflin).

'Social Science and Theology', in Beardslee, W. A. (ed.), *America and the Future of Theology* (Philadelphia, Penn.: Westminster Press).

*Sociological Theory and Modern Society* (New York: Free Press).

'Death in American Society', in Shneidman, E. (ed.), *Essays in Self-Destruction* (New York: J. Aronson, 1971).

Comment on Kenneth Boulding's, 'An Economist Looks at the Future of Sociology', 1[2] (Winter).

**1968**

'Components and Types of Formal Organization', in Le Breton, P. P. (ed.), *Comparative Administrative Theory* (Seattle: University of Washington Press).

Comment on 'The Future of the Nineteenth Century Idea of a University', by Sir Eric Ashby, *Minerva* (Spring).

*American Sociology*, a collection of essays edited by Talcott Parsons (New York: Basic Books).

'Commentary' on Clifford Geertz's 'Religion as a Cultural System', in Cutler, D. R. (ed.), *The Religious Situation: 1968* (Boston, Mass.: Beacon Press).

Entries on 'Christianity'; 'Émile Durkheim'; 'Interaction: Social Interaction'; 'Vilfredo Pareto: Contributions to Economics'; 'Professions'; 'Systems Analysis: Social Systems'; 'Utilitarians: Sociological Thought', in Sills, D. E. (ed.), *International Encyclopedia of the Social Sciences* (New York: Macmillan).

'The Position of Identity in the General Theory of Action', in

Gordon, C. and Gergen, K. J. (eds), *The Self in Social Interaction* (New York: John Wiley).

*The American Academic Profession: A Pilot Study*; co-author with Gerald M. Platt (Cambridge, monograph).

'The Academic System: a Sociologist's View', *The Public Interest*, 13 (special issue).

'On the Concept of Value-Commitments', *Sociological Inquiry*, 38[2].

'Cooley and the Problem of Internalization', in Reiss, A. J., Jr, (ed.), *Cooley and Sociological Analysis* (Ann Arbor, Mich.: University of Michigan Press).

'Sociocultural Pressures and Expectations', *Psychiatric Research Reports* (Feb); a paper presented to the American Psychiatric Association.

'Order as a Sociological Problem', in Kuntz, P. G. (ed.), *The Concept of Order* (Seattle: University of Washington Press).

'The Problem of Polarization on the Axis of Color', in Franklin, J. H. (ed.), *Color and Race* (Boston, Mass.: Houghton Mifflin).

'Considerations on the American Academic System', *Minerva*, 6[4], pp. 497–523; co-author with Gerald M. Platt.

'Law and Sociology: A Promising Courtship?', in Sutherland, A.E. (ed.), *The Path of the Law from 1967*, Harvard Law School Sesquicentennial Papers (Cambridge, Mass.: Harvard University Press).

'The Disciplines as a Differentiating Force', in Montgomery, E. B. (ed.), *The Foundations of Access to Knowledge* (Syracuse, N. Y.: Syracuse University Press, Division of Summer Sessions); co-author with Norman Storer.

**1969**

'Research with Human Subjects and the "Professional Complex" ', *Daedalus*, 98[2], pp. 325–60.

*Politics and Social Structure* (New York: Free Press).

Review of *Constructing Social Theories* by Arthur L. Stinchcombe, *Sociological Inquiry* (May).

**1970**

'Some Problems of General Theory in Sociology', in McKinney, J. C. and Tiryakian, E. A. (eds), *Theoretical Sociology: Perspectives and Developments* (New York: Appleton-Century-Crofts).

'Age, Social Structure, and Socialization in Higher Education',

*Sociology of Education*, 43[1], pp. 1–37; co-author with Gerald M. Platt.

'Decision-Making in the Academic System: Influence and Power Exchange', in Kruytbosch, C. E. and Messinger, S. L. (eds), *The State of the University: Authority and Change* (Beverly Hills, Calif.: Sage); co-author with Gerald M. Platt.

'Theory in the Humanities and Sociology', *Daedalus*, 99[2], pp. 495–523.

'The Impact of Technology on Culture and Emerging New Modes of Behaviour', *International Social Science Journal*, 22[4], pp. 607–27.

'Equality and Inequality in Modern Society, or Social Stratification Revisited', *Sociological Inquiry*, 40, pp. 13–72.

'On Building Social System Theory: A Personal History', *Daedalus*, 99[4], reprinted in Holton, G. (ed.), *The 20th Century Sciences: Studies in the Biography of Ideas* (New York: W. W. Norton, 1972).

'Some Considerations on the Comparative Sociology', in Fischer, J. (ed.), *The Social Sciences and the Comparative Study of Educational Systems* (Scranton, Penn.: International Textbook Co.).

**1971**

*The System of Modern Societies* (Englewood Cliffs, N. J.: Prentice-Hall); companion volume of *Societies: Evolutionary and Comparative Perspectives* (1966).

'Kinship and the Associational Aspects of Social Structure', in Hsu, F. L. K. (ed.), *Kinship and Culture* (Chicago, Ill.: Aldine).

'Comparative Studies and Evolutionary Change', in Vallier, I. (ed.), *Comparative Methods in Sociology* (Berkeley, Calif.: University of California Press) pp. 97–139.

'Evolutionary Universals in Society', in Desai, A. R. (ed.), *Essays on Modernization of Underdeveloped Societies* (Bombay: Thacker Spink) pp. 560–88.

'The Normal American Family', in Adams, B. N. and Weirath, T. (eds), *Readings on the Sociology of the Family* (Chicago, Ill.: Markham, 1971) pp. 53–66; reprinted from Farber, Mustacchi and Wilson (eds), *Man and Civilization: The Family's Search for Survival* (New York: McGraw-Hill, 1965).

'Belief, Unbelief and Disbelief', in Caporale, R. and Grumelli, A. (eds), *The Culture of Unbelief: Studies and Proceedings from the*

*First International Symposium on Belief, Held in Rome, March 22–7, 1969* (Berkeley, Calif.: University of California Press) ch. 12, pp. 207–45.

**1972**

'Higher Education as a Theoretical Focus', in Simpson, R. and Turk, H. (eds), *Institutions and Social Exchange: The Sociologies of Talcott Parsons and George C. Homans* (Indianapolis, Ind.: Bobbs-Merrill).

'Higher Education, Changing Socialization, and Contemporary Student Dissent', in Riley, M. W., Johnson, M. E., Foner, A. *et al.* (eds), *Ageing and Society*, vol. 3: *A Sociology of Age Stratification* (New York: Russel Sage Foundation); co-author with Gerald M. Platt.

*Readings on Pre-Modern Societies* (Englewood Cliffs, N. J.: Prentice-Hall); co-author with Victor Lidz.

'Field Theory and Systems Theory: with Special Reference to the Relations between Psychological and Social Systems', in Offer, D. and Freedman, D. X. (eds), *Modern Psychiatry and Clinical Research: Essays in Honor of Roy R. Grinker, Sr* (New York: Basic Books).

'The School Class as a Social System', *Socialization and Schools*, Reprint Series 1, compiled from *The Harvard Educational Review*, pp. 69–90.

'The Action Frame of Reference and the General Theory of Action Systems', in Hollander, E. P. and Hunt, R. G. (eds), *Classic Contributions to Social Psychology: Readings with Commentary* (New York: Oxford University Press) pp. 168–76; slightly abridged from chapter 1 of *The Social System* (Glencoe, Ill.: Free Press, 1951) pp. 3–11, 15–19.

'The "Gift of Life" and its Reciprocation', *Social Research*, 39[3] pp. 367–415; co-author with Renee C. Fox and Victor Lidz; reprinted in *Death in American Experience*, edited by Arien Mack (New York: Schocken Books, 1973) pp. 1–49.

Review of Reinhard Bendix and Guenther Roth's *Scholarship and Partisanship, Contemporary Sociology*, 1[3], pp. 200–3.

'Culture and Social System Revisited', *Social Science Quarterly*, 53[2], pp. 253–66; reprinted in Schneider, L. and Bonjean, C. (eds), *The Idea of Culture in the Social Sciences* (Cambridge: Cambridge University Press, 1973) pp. 33–46.

'Commentary on Clark' (Talcott Parsons' comment on Terry N.

Clark, 'Structural–Functionalism, Exchange Theory, and the New Political Economy: Institutionalization as a Theoretical Linkage', pp. 275–98), *Sociological Inquiry*, 42[3–4], pp. 299–308.

**1973**

'Durkheim on Religion Revisited: Another Look at the Elementary Forms of the Religious Life', in Glock, C. Y. and Hammond, P. E. (eds), *Beyond the Classics? Essays in the Scientific Study of Religion* (New York: Harper & Row [Harper Torchbooks]) pp. 156–80.

*The American University* (Cambridge, Mass.: Harvard University Press); co-author with Gerald M. Platt and in collaboration with Neil J. Smelser.

'Clyde Kluckhohn and the Integration of Social Science', in Taylor, W. W., Fischer, J. L. and Vogt, E. Z. (eds), *Culture and Life: Essays in Memory of Clyde Kluckhohn* (Carbondale, Ill.: Southern Illinois University Press) pp. 30–57.

Review of W. G. Runciman's *A Critique of Max Weber's Philosophy of social science*, *Political Science Quarterly*, 88[2], pp. 345–6.

'The Bellah Case, Man and God in Princeton, New Jersey', *Commonweal*, 98[11], pp. 256–9.

'Religious Symbolization and Death', in Eister, A. (ed.), *Changing Perspectives in the Scientific Study of Religion* (New York: Wiley-Interscience).

'Some Reflections on Post-Industrial Society', *Japanese Sociological Review*, 24[2], pp. 109–13; lecture given to the Japan Sociological Association, 25 November 1972.

'The Problem of Balancing Rational Efficiency with Communal Solidarity in Modern Society', *International Symposium: 'New Problems of Advanced Societies'* (Tokyo: Japan Economic Research Institute) pp. 9–14; memorial lecture at International Symposium on 'New Problems of Advanced Societies' held from 20–4 November 1972, at Keidanren Kaikan Tokyo under the sponsorship of Japan Economic Research Institute with the support of the Ministry of Foreign Affairs.

'The Social Concept of the Present Civilization', *Tribuna Medica* (25 September) pp. 19–20.

**1974**

'Religion in Post-Industrial America: The Problem of Secularisation', *Social Research*, 41[2].

**1977**

*Social Systems and the Evolution of Action Theory* (New York: Free Press)

GENERAL BIBLIOGRAPHY

Althusser, L., *For Marx* (London: Allen Lane, Penguin, 1969).
——, *Politics and History: Montesquieu, Rousseau, Hegel and Marx* (London: New Left Books, 1972).
——, *Lenin and Philosophy and Other Essays* (London: New Left Books, 1971).
Althusser, L. and Balibar, E.,*Reading Capital* (London: New Left Books, 1970).
Aron, R.,*Main Currents in Sociological Thought* (London: Weidenfeld & Nicolson, 1965).
Bellah, R. N., 'Religious Evolution', *American Sociological Review*, 29[3] pp. 358–74.
Berghe, P. van den, 'Dialectic and Functionalism: Toward a Synthesis', *American Sociological Review*, 28 (Oct. 1973).
Bershady, H., *Ideology and Social Knowledge* (Oxford: Blackwell, 1973).
Bertalanffy, L. von, 'General Systems Theory', *Main Currents of Modern Thought*, 71 (1955).
——, *General Systems Theory* (Harmondsworth: Penguin, 1974).
Black, M. (ed.), *The Sociological Theories of Talcott Parsons* (Englewood Cliffs, N. J.: Prentice-Hall, 1961).
Blumer, H., *Symbolic Interactionism* (Englewood Cliffs, N. J.: Prentice-Hall, 1969).
Bottomore, T. B., *Sociology as Social Criticism* (London: Allen & Unwin, 1975).
Box, S., *Deviance, Reality and Society* (London: Holt, Rinehart & Winston, 1971).
Bredemeier, H. C., 'The Methodology of Functionalism',*American Sociological Review*, 20 (Apr. 1955).
Buckley, W., *Sociology and Modern Systems Theory* (Englewood Cliffs, N. J.: Prentice-Hall, 1967).
Carnap, R., 'The Methodological Character of Theoretical Concepts', *Minnesota Studies in the Philosophy of Science*, I (1956) pp. 38–78.
Cicourel, A. V., *The Social Organisation of Juvenile Justice* (New York & London: John Wiley, 1968).

Cohen, J., Hazelrigg, L. E. and Pope, W., 'DeParsonising Weber', *American Sociological Review*, 40[2] (1975) pp. 229–410.

Coser, L., *The Functions of Conflict* (New York: Free Press, 1964).

Dahl, R., *Who Governs? Democracy and Power in an American City* (New Haven, Conn.: Yale University Press, 1961).

Dahrendorf, R., 'Out of Utopia', *American Journal of Sociology*, 64[2] (1958) pp. 115–27.

Darwin, C., *The Origin of Species* (London: Dent, 1971).

Davis, K., 'The Myth of a Functional Analysis', in Demerath and Peterson (eds), *System Change and Conflict*.

Dawe, A., 'The Two Sociologies', *British Journal of Sociology*, 21 (1970) pp. 207–18.

Demerath, N. J., III, and Peterson, R. A. (eds), *System Change and Conflict* (New York: Free Press, 1967).

Dobzhansky, T., 'Mendelian Populations and Their Evolution' in Dunn, L. C. (ed.), *Genetics in the Twentieth Century*.

Domhoff, G. W., *Who Rules America?* (Englewood Cliffs, N. J.: Prentice-Hall, 1967).

Dore, R. P., 'Function and Course', in Demerath and Peterson (eds), *System Change and Conflict*.

Douglas, J., *The Social Meanings of Suicide* (Princeton, N. J.: Princeton University Press, 1967).

Duhem, P., *To Save the Phenomena* (Chicago, Ill.: University of Chicago Press, 1969).

Durkheim, E., *The Rules of Sociological Method* (New York: Free Press, 1964).

Eisenstadt, S. N., 'Social Change, Differentiation and Evolution', *American Sociological Review*, 29 (June 1964).

Foss, D., 'The World View of Talcott Parsons', in Stein, M. R. and Vidich, A. (eds), *Sociology on Trial* (Englewood Cliffs, N. J.: Prentice-Hall, 1963).

Frank, A. G., *The Sociology of Development and Underdevelopment* (London: Pluto Press, 1971).

Galbraith, J. K., *The New Industrial State* (London: André Deutsch, 1975).

Garfinkel, H., *Studies in Ethnomethodology* (Englewood Cliffs, N. J.: Prentice-Hall, 1967).

Gellner, E., 'Concepts and Society', in Wilson, B. (ed.), *Rationality* (Oxford: Blackwell, 1970).

Gerth, H. H. and Mills C. W. (eds), *From Max Weber: Essays in Sociology* (London: Routledge & Kegan Paul, 1970).

Giddens, A. H., '"Power" in the Recent Writings of Talcott Parsons', *Sociology*, 2[3] (1968) pp. 257–72.

Gouldner, Alvin W., *The Coming Crisis of Western Sociology* (New York: Basic Books, 1970).

——, 'Reciprocity and Autonomy in Functional Theory', in Gross, L. (ed.), *Symposium on Sociological Theory: Inquiries & Paradigms* (New York: Harper & Row and John Weatherhill, 1967).

——, *For Sociology* (London: Heinemann, 1973).

Hass, E. B., 'Functionalism and International Systems' in Demerath and Peterson (eds), *System Change and Conflict*.

Hield, W., 'The Study of Change in Social Sciences', *British Journal of Sociology* (Mar 1964).

Hindess, B., 'Transcendentalism and History: the Problem of the History of Philosophy and the Sciences in the Later Philosophy of Husserl', *Economy and Science*, 2 (Aug 1973) pp. 309–42.

——, *Philosophy and Methodology in the Social Sciences* (Brighton: Harvester Press, 1977).

——, 'Humanism and Teleology in Sociological Theory', in Hindess, B. (ed.), *Sociological Theories of the Economy*.

——, *The Use of Official Statistics in Sociology* (London: Macmillan, 1973).

Hindess, B. and Hirst, P. Q., *Pre-Capitalist Modes of Production* (London: Routledge & Kegan Paul,1975).

Hindess, B. and Savage, S. P., 'Talcott Parsons and the Three Systems of Action' in Martins H. (ed.), *Parsons Revisited* (forthcoming).

Hindess, B. (ed.), *Sociological Theories of the Economy* (London: Macmillan, 1977).

Hirst, P. Q., *Durkheim, Bernard and Epistemology* (London: Routledge & Kegan Paul, 1975).

Hirst, P. Q. and Savage, S. P., 'Parsons, Weber and Historicism', *Luften für Kritiska Studier,* 4 (1976).

Homans, G., 'Bringing Men Back In' and 'Commentary' in Turk and Simpson (eds), *Institutions and Social Exchange*.

Horowitz, I. L., 'Consensus, Conflict and Cooperation' in Demerath and Peterson (eds), *System Change and Conflict*.

Hume, D., *An Enquiry Concerning Human Understanding* (London: C. A. Watts, 1906).

Isajiw, W. W., *Causation and Functionalism in Sociology* (London: Routledge & Kegan Paul, 1968).

Jenkins, A., '"Substantivism" as a Comparative Theory of Economic Forms' in Hindess (ed.), *Sociological Theories of the Economy*.

Kant, E., *Foundations of the Metaphysics of Morals* (Indianapolis, Ind.: Bobbs-Merrill, 1948).

Keynes, J. M., *The General Theory of Employment, Interest and Money* (London: Macmillan, 1936).

Kolko, G., 'A Critique of Max Weber's Philosophy of History', *Ethics*, LXX (1959) pp. 21–36.

Kolokowski, L., *Positivist Philosophy* (Harmondsworth: Penguin, 1972).

Koyré, A., *Newtonian Studies* (London: Chapman & Hall, 1965).

———, 'The Origins of Modern Science', *Diogenes*, no. 16 (Winter 1956) pp. 1–22.

———, *Metaphysics and Measurement* (Cambridge, Mass.: Harvard University Press, 1968).

Kuhn, T. S., *The Structure of Scientific Revolutions* (Chicago, Ill.: University of Chicago Press, 1962).

LeCourt, D., *Marxism and Epistemology* (London: New Left Books, 1975).

Lessnoff, M. H., 'Parsons' System Problems', *Sociological Review*, 16[2] (July 1968) pp. 185–215.

Lévi-Strauss, C., *The Savage Mind* (London: Weidenfeld & Nicolson, 1966).

Lévi-Strauss, C., *Structural Anthropology* (London: Allen Lane and Penguin, 1968).

Lockwood, D., 'Some Remarks on "The Social System" ', *British Journal of Sociology*, 7[2] (1956).

———, 'Social Integration and System Integration', in Zollschan, G. K. and Hirsch, W. (eds), *Explorations in Social Change* (London: Routledge & Kegan Paul, 1964).

Lukács, G., *History and Class Consciousness* (London: Merlin Press, 1971).

Lukes, S., *Power: a Radical View* (London: Macmillan, 1974).

Mach, E., *The Analysis of Sensations* (New York: Dover, 1959).

Marshall, A., *The Principles of Economics* (London: Macmillan, 1925).

Martindale, D., *The Nature and Types of Sociological Theory* (London: Routledge & Kegan Paul, 1961).

Marx, K., *A Contribution to the Critique of Political Economy* (London: Lawrence & Wishart, 1971).

Matza, D., *Becoming Deviant* (Englewood Cliffs, N. J.: Prentice-Hall, 1969).

Mead, G. H., *Mind, Self and Society* (Chicago, Ill.: University of Chicago Press, 1967).

Menzies, K., *Talcott Parsons and the Social Imagery of Man* (London: Routledge & Kegan Paul, 1976).

Merton, R., *Social Theory and Social Structure* (New York: Free Press, 1968).

——, *On Theoretical Sociology* (New York: Free Press, 1967).

——, 'Discussion', *American Sociological Review*, 13 (1948) p. 72.

Mill, J. S., *A System of Logic* (London: Longmans, 1967).

Mills, C. Wright, *The Sociological Imagination* (New York: Oxford University Press, 1959).

——, *The Power Elite* (New York: Oxford University Press, 1956).

Moore, Barrington, Jr, 'The New Scholasticism and the Study of Politics', *World Politics* (1953).

Morse, C., 'The Functional Prerequisites' in Black, M. (ed.), *The Sociological Theories of Talcott Parsons.*

Nisbet, R. (ed.), *Social Change* (Oxford: Blackwell, 1972).

Peel, J. D. Y., *Herbert Spencer: The Evolution of a Sociologist* (New York: Basic Books, 1971).

Polanyi, K., Arensberg, C. and Pearson, H. W. (eds), *Trade and Markets in the Early Empires* (Glencoe, Ill.: Free Press, 1957).

Popper, K. R., *The Logic of Scientific Discovery* (London: Hutchinson, 1959).

Poulantzas, N., *Political Power and Social Classes* (London: Sheed &Ward and New Left Books, 1973).

Ranciere, J., 'The Concept of Critique and the Critique of Political Economy', in *Theoretical Practice*, nos 1, 2, 5.

Riesman, D., *The Lonely Crowd* (New Haven, Conn.: Yale University Press, 1969).

Rex, J., *Key Problems in Sociological Theory* (London: Routledge and Kegan Paul, 1969).

Rhoades, J. K., 'On Gouldner's *Coming Crisis*', in *Varieties of Political Expression in Sociology* (*American Sociological Review* publication) (Chicago, Ill.: University of Chicago Press, 1972).

Rocher, G., *Talcott Parsons and American Sociology* (London: Nelson, 1974).

Schutz, A., *The Phenomenology of the Social World* (London: Heinemann, 1972).

Schwanenberg, E., 'The Two Problems of Order in Parsons' Theory: an Analysis from Within', *Social Forces*, 49 (1971) pp. 569–80.

Scott, J. F., 'The Changing Foundations of the Parsonian Action Schema', *American Sociological Review*, 28 (1963).

——, 'The Impossible Theory of Action', *Berkeley Journal of Sociology*.

Smelser, N. J., *The Sociology of Economic Life* (Englewood Cliffs, N. J.: Prentice-Hall, 1963).

—— (ed.), *Readings in Economic Sociology* (Englewood Cliffs, N. J.: Prentice-Hall, 1965).

——, *Social Change in the Industrial Revolution* (Chicago, Ill.: University of Chicago Press, 1959).

Smith, A. D., *The Concept of Social Change: a Critique of the Functionalist Theory of Change* (London: Routledge & Kegan Paul, 1973).

Stein, M. R. and Vidich, A. (eds), *Sociology on Trial* (Englewood Cliffs, N. J.: Prentice-Hall, 1963).

Thompson, K. and Tunstall, J. (eds), *Sociological Perspectives* (Harmondsworth: Penguin, 1972).

Touraine, A., 'Toward a Sociology of Action', in Giddens, A. (ed.), *Positivism and Sociology* (London: Heinemann, 1974).

Turk, H. and Simpson, R. L. (eds), *Institutions and Social Exchange: the Theories of George Homans and Talcott Parsons* (Indianapolis: Bobbs-Merrill, 1972).

Turner, J. H., *The Structure of Sociological Theory* (New York: Free Press, 1973).

Turner, J. H. and Beeghley, 'Current Folklore in the Criticism of Parsonian Action Theory', *Sociological Inquiry*, 43 (1974).

Weber, M., *The Protestant Ethic and the Spirit of Capitalism* (London: Allen & Unwin, 1930).

——, *Methodology of The Social Sciences* (New York: Free Press, 1949).

——, *The Theory of Social and Economic Organisation* (New York: Free Press, 1964).

——, *The Sociology of Religion* (Boston, Mass.: Beacon Press, 1963).

Whitehead, A. F., *Science and the Modern World* (New York: Macmillan, 1925).

Willer, D. and Willer, J., *Systematic Empiricism: a Critique of Pseudo-Science* (Englewood Cliffs, N. J.: Prentice-Hall, 1973).

Williams, K., 'Unproblematic Archaeology', *Economy and Society*, 3 (1974).

Wrong, D., 'The Oversocialised Conception of Man in Modern Sociology', *American Sociological Review*, XXVI (1961) pp. 184–93.

# Index